A Time of Awakening

Values and Ethics Series, Volume 2

A Time of Awakening
The Young Christian Worker Story in the United States, 1938 to 1970

Mary Irene Zotti

Loyola University Press
Chicago

Loyola University Press
3441 North Ashland Avenue
Chicago, Illinois 60657

Library of Congress Cataloging-in-Publication Data

Zotti, Mary Irene.
    A time of awakening: the Young Christian Worker story in the
United States, 1938 to 1970/Mary Irene Zotti.
        p.   cm.   — (Values and ethics series: v.2)
    Includes bibliographical references and index.
    ISBN 0-8294-0716-2
    1.Young Christian Workers. 2. Church and labor—United
States—History—20th century. 3. Catholic Church—United
States—History—20th century. I. Title. II. Series.
BX809.Y67Z67 1991
267'.62273—dc20   90-24689
                                                            CIP

Table of Contents

Foreword

Mary Irene Zotti's interesting account of the Young Christian Workers (YCW) helps fill an important gap in our knowledge of American Catholic history. Blending personal experience with extensive reading of source materials and interviews with former members, Zotti provides a lively account of one important segment of post-World War II activism. Her work will join recent studies of the Grail movement, lay Catholic evangelism, and Dorothy Day's Catholic Worker movement on a shelf dealing with the American Catholic laity that has been too long empty.

When Canon Cardijn launched the Jocist movement, he was responding to one of the major problems of modern Catholicism: how to enlist the energies of the laity in the pursuit of the Church's apostolic mission. The marginalization of the laity ("mere externs," a disgruntled priest called them) was a distinctly modern phenomenon. A century earlier, lay Catholics played important roles in defining the Church's position regarding the waves of reform unleashed by the French revolution. In France, for example, Louis Veuillot spearheaded the ultramontane drive to reject modernity root and branch while centralizing ecclesiastical authority in an infallible Papacy. Charles de Montalembert, in contrast, searched for a common ground with liberalism and called for a free church in a free state. The saintly Frederic Ozanam, less interested in the controversies stirring political life, launched the St. Vincent de Paul Society to draw young men to serve the poor, winning men and women to Christ by the power of Christian love.

Unfortunately, the triumph of an ultramontanism only slightly less extreme than Veuillot's in the Syllabus of Errors (1863) and at the first Vatican Council (1869-1870) all but eliminated the independent lay voices. A defensive church, faced with challenges of liberty and pluralism, created a radically separatist subculture in which unity, loyalty, and conformity mattered above all. Obedience was the major lay virtue; those who questioned or acted independently were automatically suspect. How were such lay people to be motivated to pursue the Church's apostolic mission in the world?

This question seemed less pressing when the priority was not to reconquer the world, but simply to survive. In nineteenth century Europe, science and reason, capitalism and liberalism, reigned supreme. But that era died in the trenches of World War I. Political republicanism, economic liberalism, and the intellectual values of the Enlightment were never the same again. Instead, people turned to new absolutes, communism and fascism among them, each promising to overcome the fragmentation and chaos of modernity. In that setting, one could dream that Catholicism might receive a hearing, that all things might indeed be restored in Christ.

What was needed was an apostolic vision, provided by social teaching of the Church, and new forms of organization to mobilize the laity, under careful episcopal direction, for a counterattack upon modernity, protecting the Church against totalitarianism while restoring a Christian social order. This is what Cardijn, among others, offered, attracting Catholic men and women anxious to make a better world while remaining loyal to their Church.

In the United States, Catholic conservatism never reached Syllabus of Errors proportions. While preachers could wax eloquent about modern hedonism and materialism, they knew that America offered what the more ambitious immigrants who filled the pews wanted: personal and cultural freedom, economic opportunity and political participation. Some Catholic leaders looked forward to the day when a prosperous, educated laity would emerge from the ghettos to bring prestige and influence to the Church and win a hearing for the argument that Catholic Christianity alone could insure the success of the American experiment. In this vision, lay people would become major evangelizers of American culture.

That dream was destroyed in the 1890s, partly by the triumph of ultramontanism in Europe, partly by direct assault. In 1895, Pope Leo

XIII warned American Catholics to associate as much as possible with other Catholics and to develop a docile and submissive attitude toward ecclesiastical authorities. Four years later, the condemnation of Americanism included condemnation of lay liberty within the Church and independence without. The Americanist vision was replaced by a more defensive preoccupation with group solidarity and institutional strength. Revival of intergroup conflict in the 1920s strengthened this defensiveness, which in turn limited discontent with lay subordination.

The depression changed all that. Pastoral and educational work alone would not solve the problems of poverty and insecurity which now hit Catholic working class and lower middle class parishioners. Catholics supported the New Deal and joined the new industrial unions; if they were to be protected against radicalism, and if they were to remain faithful to their church, it would be well for their pastors to back them up. Bishops, priests, and nuns now discovered Catholic social teaching; indeed they joined Pope Pius XI in calling for a Christian reconstruction of the entire social order.

To the extent that attention was truly centered on the needs of the community and the world, to that degree was the need felt for a more active and energetic laity. When the sense of crisis created by the depression eased, so did interest in Catholic Action. But, for some, the contrast between the Gospel message of love and the realities of industrial America were too sharp to allow a return to the complacency of ordinary parish life. They were awakened to a sense of responsibility for the world around them and they believed that they were called, by God and by the Church, to give themselves to winning others to Christ and building a more just and peaceful world. It was this apostolic consciousness, with its resulting discontent with the internal preoccupations of most Catholics and its desire to integrate faith with other areas of life, that marked many of the lay movements which began in the thirties and forties.

YCW appeared on the American scene in this context. The late thirties were serious times. The depression had not really been resolved, but the New Deal was under attack. John L. Lewis's CIO unions, after some heady successes, were reeling under employer counterattacks and a flood of red-baiting, in Congress and the press. The Spanish Civil War, in which Catholicism appeared to be united with fascism, was over, and a confident Hitler seemed poised for war.

Young students and workers could hardly ignore the political and trade union controversies around them. If they were Catholics, they had every right to be puzzled, for their church offered everything from Dorothy Day's dramatic appeal for voluntary poverty to Fr. Charles E. Coughlin's anti-Semitism. The bishops still spoke progressively on domestic economic issues, but few parishes or dioceses had translated the pope's appeal for socially constructive Catholic Action into practice. Young men and women anxious to respond to the needs of the time might therefore be attracted to apostolic movements like the Catholic Worker or the Young Christian Workers.

• • •

The Observe, Judge, Act methodology seems so appropriate, and the combination of Gospel reflection and social inquiry so needed, that one can only wonder why the Jocist movement did not survive in the United States. Ms. Zotti offers some answers centered on the peculiar circumstances of the sixties. Today, while American Catholicism has a stronger sense of social responsibility than ever before, there remains a tremendous need for a theology, spirituality, and strategy of lay action. There are movements which draw the laity to service, and there are multiplying opportunities for lay ministry within the church, but there are few projects that inspire lay persons to see their work, their community involvement, their unions and professional groups, their families, their web of lay life, as the setting of their vocation. Even the much-discussed economic pastoral of the American bishops, "Economic Justice for All," moderated an early Jocist-like emphasis on reaching holiness by implementing human dignity in working life in favor of a more countercultural condemnation of modern materialism.

Yet, if the call of the pastoral letter, and of papal teaching, for social transformation is to be heard in the United States, at least three things associated with the movements described in this text are needed. First, formation of lay leadership rather than futile efforts to bring about a radical change of heart among everyone is needed. Like the pioneers described here, the Church would do well to concentrate on the formation of those it has, rather than complain endlessly about those it does not have. Second, priests, religious—the new breed of church professionals, and the new lay ministers should be trained in the Observe, Judge, Act method, for it is a superb way of bringing Christian meaning into the ordinary circumstances of life. Third, these movements sought a constructive balance between independence and accountability. In the sixties, the pendulum swung in the direction of independence; today it swings in the other direction. Experience, including that recorded here, shows that there is peril in both directions. A reformed Church capable of combining freedom and mutual respect with authority and accountability remains a great need; YCW and the other Jocist groups showed a way that need might be met.

For all these reasons, this text is needed, and will be read with profit by contemporary Christians. Mary Irene Zotti is to be congratulated and thanked for bringing it to us.

David J. O'Brien
College of the Holy Cross
Worcester, Massachusetts
July 15, 1989

Preface

I was born Mary Irene Caplice in Chicago. I spent almost ten years as a leader in the Specialized Catholic Action Movement, six of them as a Young Christian Worker, beginning in 1939. I was inspired and motivated by three outstanding Chicago priests who were pioneers in recognizing the importance of lay people in the Church and, indeed, the role of lay persons in the secular world: Msgrs. John Hayes, John J. Egan, and Reynold Hillenbrand. When I left the movement in 1949, the Young Christian Workers was an established organization reaching out to young workers and inviting them to recognize their dignity as human beings with a mission to make the world a more just and peaceful place.

My husband Ray and I raised six children, four boys and two girls. To assist in paying their high school and college tuition, I returned to work as a grade school teacher and then as a guidance counselor in the Chicago Public Schools. In 1984, when the children were grown, my friend and former co-worker in the movement, Regina Bess Finney, suggested that I write the story of the Young Christian Workers, which had played such an important part in our lives and in the lives of many other young workers in the middle years of this century. At first I was reluctant, but Reggie convinced me that the YCW story in the United States was an important part of American Church history that deserved to be better known. Reggie said she would help, but the Lord had other plans for her. Before her death from cancer in 1985, I promised her to give it a try. This book is the result.

The first five chapters tell the story of the time when I was personally involved. The later chapters are based on research in the archives of the University of Notre Dame Library where the movement records are stored, materials sent to me by former members, and countless hours of recorded interviews with former chaplains and lay leaders.

I owe many thanks to the wonderful priests and lay people who have encouraged and assisted me, not the least being my son Ed, who read and reread my manuscript, pointing out sections that needed clarification to make the YCW story more meaningful to the young people of his generation.

My thanks to the Cushwa Center for the Study of American Catholicism at the University of Notre Dame for a travel research grant which helped to support some of my research. Gisella Csenar Probst and Dorothy Dyer Kroll, former Young Christian Workers in South Bend, generously invited me to stay in their homes on my numerous visits to the university.

Many others were my hosts when I visited their cities to talk with former members: Russ and Ellie Tershy in San Jose, Dave and Rita Joseph O'Shea in southern California, Winifred Neville and Caroline Pezzullo in New York, Margaret Fitzgerald in Brooklyn, Martin and Patty Oliver McLaughlin in Washington, D.C., Bill and Jo Jeske Cosby in Massachusetts, John and Marie Powers Braun in Minneapolis, Msgr. Philip Kenney and Lorraine Noel Provencher in New Hampshire, Frank Ardito, Millard Hughes, and Lloyd St. James in Chicago, and Kay Williams Cox in Detroit. To them and all the wonderful people I met on those trips, I am most grateful.

My most special thanks to my husband Ray who never complained when I left home to travel around the country, in spite of the fact that he had to survive for days at a time on TV dinners, which he detests.

And last but not least, I want to thank the 610 former members who took the time to fill out a two-page questionnaire to tell me if and how the YCW experience influenced them in later years. Many wrote long and interesting letters, some of which I have quoted throughout the book.

Writing the YCW story has been a source of great joy and spiritual rejuvenation for me personally. For that, too, I am very grateful.

Introduction

This is the story of the Young Christian Workers, a movement of lay Catholics in the United States who were awakened to the need to become apostolic Christians before Vatican II legitimized the role of the laity in the Church. It is the story of tens of thousands of men and women who devoted a good part of their young adulthood to building a world based on the teachings of the Gospels and the social teachings of the Church. It is not a definitive history nor a sociological analysis; rather, it is a story of people: young people with generosity and a vision, young people who learned to See, to Judge, and to Act in order to Christianize the world in which they lived and worked.

How the YCW movement began in this country, its struggles, its accomplishments, and the reasons for its eventual demise is important in the still developing story of lay action in the United States. It is a story that deserves to be told.

Many of the Young Christian Workers, especially in the early days, were my friends. We had been born and raised in a church that taught us "to know God, to love Him, and to serve Him in this life, and be happy with Him forever in the next." It gave us a rigid code of behavior and a promise of immortality. It did not encourage us as lay persons to take initiative as apostolic Christians because that was the prerogative of the clergy. Women who wanted to do something out of the ordinary for Jesus were invited to "leave the world" and become subservient members of a religious sisterhood.

That is why we were somewhat surprised when we were asked to get involved in a lay movement called Catholic Action. We soon found out that there was more to being a Catholic than going to mass on Sundays. Gradually we began to understand that Baptism made us sharers of divine life and members of Christ's Mystical Body in the world. This meant that in everyday life we must bring Christ and his teachings to others, that we were lay apostles. We also learned that every person has a God-given human dignity and the right to live in a world based on social justice as well as charity. We accepted the challenge to change the world to bring this about, and we fully expected to do it.

First as a student, then as a Young Christian Worker, I became part of what came to be known as Specialized Catholic Action, an apostolic movement in which people were grouped according to their occupational role. Young workers were to be concerned with the needs and problems of other young workers, students with students, businessmen with other businessmen, and so on. Through the action of men and women in all levels of society, committed to social justice and loving service, the world would ultimately be reformed.

The Young Christian Worker movement, known in the French-speaking world as Jeunesse Ouvriere Chretienne and popularly called "Jocism," was founded by Canon Joseph Cardijn, a young Belgian priest, to meet the needs of young workers who were leaving the Church in large numbers. At the deathbed of his father who died from overwork in 1903 at the age of forty-three, the young Cardijn vowed to devote his life to improve the quality of life among working families so they could live in dignity as Christians. He knew the place to start was with those who were young. After studying various organizations among young people, ranging from the Boy Scouts in England to the Kolping Association in Germany which focused on the Christian formation in work life, Cardijn evolved a method to give young men and women a realistic view of their surroundings and motivate them to take a leadership role in improving the conditions of their lives. Beginning in 1913, he reached out to young workers between the ages of fourteen and twenty-five and convinced them that they had a special importance—they were human beings created by God with a divine mission to serve others. Meeting in small groups and using the method which became known as the social inquiry, Observe, Judge,

Act, his young workers developed self-respect, a social conscience, and the courage to plan and carry out action for change. What began in Cardijn's mind as a kind of junior trade union movement gradually evolved into an organized apostolic movement led by young workers themselves.

In order to form young workers as Christian leaders able to build a just society, the Jocists stressed that theirs must be an autonomous movement by young workers, among young workers, and for young workers. It was a movement of *education* in order that all young workers could discover and realize their divine destiny in the surroundings of their daily life. It must develop among its members a spirit of *service* to meet the real needs of all young workers. Finally, it must *represent* young workers before public bodies and private social institutions which in any way affected their welfare.

Conservative Belgian Catholics viewed this growing new movement of working class youth as revolutionary and very dangerous. Complaints poured in to Cardinal Mercier, the archbishop of Brussels, and in 1924 he felt obliged to condemn it.

Stunned at hearing this after so many years of struggle to help working class youth, Cardijn asked permission to go to Rome to appeal his cause to the Holy Father. To the surprise of many, Pius XI not only approved of what Cardijn was doing, but he encouraged it. "Here at last," he exclaimed, "is someone who comes to talk to me of saving the masses!"

On April 19, 1925, after Cardijn's return from Rome, the Young Christian Workers held their first national congress in Brussels. By 1937 the dynamic spread of Jocism beyond Belgium was demonstrated when eighty-five thousand young workers representing members in twenty-four countries gathered in Paris to celebrate their accomplishments.

When the story of Jocism was first brought to the United States, American Catholics were suffering from widespread unemployment and economic hardship as a result of the Great Depression of the thirties. Socialists and Communists were aggressively attempting to infiltrate the growing union movement. A few socially-activated priests were looking for Christian solutions to the problems of workers. Though many of their contemporaries considered Jocism a European movement that would never work in the democratic, pluralistic society of the United States, some thought it had possibilities. They recognized that an action-oriented movement of Catholic workers was needed and its best chance for success was among the young. They were determined to give it a try.

Starting in 1938, small groups of young workers using the inquiry method of Observe, Judge, Act began to form. After nine years of trial and error and seriously hampered by the absence of young men in World War II, the movement that became the Young Christian Workers began in earnest in 1947. It made many necessary adaptations to the realities of American life as it grew in numbers and strength. Though it never fulfilled the optimistic expectations of its founders in this country, its effects are still being felt.

Over two hundred bishops who attended the Vatican II Council in Rome were former chaplains of the movement in some of the more than eighty countries where the Young Christian Workers spread. It has been acknowledged that their experience working with lay leaders, as well as the writings of Canon, later Cardinal, Cardijn, which circulated widely among the Council members, played an important role in the thinking that resulted in the decrees of the Council on the role of the laity and the place of the Church in the modern world.

Using the YCW method, I decided to get the facts about this apostolic movement of young workers during its thirty-year life in the United States. The next step was to attempt a judgment: Did it accomplish its goal to form active Christian leaders working in the world?

I taped conversations with scores of former leaders in cities around the country and I examined the records of the YCW now stored in the archives at the University of Notre Dame. I also sent questionnaires to as many former members as I could locate to find out if the YCW experience made a lasting difference in their lives.

They were young, idealistic, and sometimes naive but, for most of them, the YCW years were indeed a time of awakening.

1

The Call to Catholic Action

"You must be a new youth for a new world! If the faith is to survive, it must be preached by lay people like you who are living and working among the people in the factories and the stores and the offices where the priests cannot go."

Paul McGuire, an Australian writer and Christian activist, stood before a crowd of several hundred young men and women at a meeting in Chicago in May 1939. His urgent words stirred us to our depths. This was a challenge we could not ignore. He told us we were the ones who must restore the world to Christ—we must get involved in Catholic Action.

How did I happen to be in that audience? I had grown up in a safe and happy Catholic home. We didn't have cars and we didn't have television, so my sense of the wider world was very limited. The world I occasionally saw in movies was a fantasy outside my everyday life.

Dorothy Day, the renowned Catholic activist who with Peter Maurin began the Catholic Worker movement in New York, came to our high school in 1938 and told us about the work she was doing with the poor and homeless in her House of Hospitality in New York. We paid a penny to subscribe to her paper, *The Catholic Worker*, and read about life in the slums on Mott Street. Though the stories were interesting and sometimes moving, that too was a world we did not know.

We were poor but not homeless like the people Dorothy Day wrote about. We really didn't know real poverty because we were loved. Some fathers were unemployed and some of my friends lived in houses with potbelly stoves. My own father was gone, so my mother worked as a schoolteacher to take care of my brother and me. It was her decision that I go to the Chicago Normal School after high school so I could get a job as a teacher after three years. "It's a good job for a woman," she said. "You never know what the future holds."

And indeed I didn't. Little did I know that I would get involved there in something that would change my whole life.

One day in March, while I was still a freshman, Marie Hallinan, my psychology teacher, stopped me after class and asked me to attend a meeting the following Sunday with a priest friend of hers who wanted to talk to a few Catholic students about something important. The main reason I went was because I had been having arguments with a fallen-away Catholic in my class who was now a Socialist. He railed against the Church and talked about the terrible things done by the Catholics in Spain that had brought about a civil war. I was incensed because he was talking about the Church I held dear and I didn't know how to answer him. I felt so dumb. My faith had never before been challenged.

I dragged my friend Margaret Dagenais along for moral support, and we went to the meeting held in a Catholic library and bookshop in downtown Chicago. There we sat down with six fellow students and a soft-spoken priest, Fr. John Hayes. He was a teacher at Quigley Preparatory Seminary who we knew was interested in the labor movement because he had given a talk on the Chicago Teachers' Union which Miss Hallinan had urged all of her students to attend. But he did not talk to us about unions. He talked to us about something called Catholic Action, which he said was a new way of being Catholic.

Fr. Hayes started out by reminding us of the many problems in the world like unemployment and hunger that needed to be solved, problems which the Communists said could be solved if we followed the teachings of Karl Marx. He told us the Church had better answers, based on the teachings of Jesus Christ in the New Testament. Recently, he said, the Holy Father had asked that all Catholics wherever they were should become active in bringing the social and religious teachings of Christ to others, so that the problems of the world could be solved in a Christian way. You started where you were. Pius XI said that workers should reach out as apostles to influence other workers, and students should do the same among other students. Fr. Hayes said that meant us. We should be concerned about the problems facing young people we knew and become active Catholic leaders in our school. We would start by reading the New Testament to find out what Jesus taught and figure out ways to apply what we learned to our everyday lives.

Then, we must observe others around us, get the facts about what was going on, and decide if things could be done in a more Christian way. The next step was to do something about what we observed. Christ wanted us to make our school a better place. That was my first understanding of Catholic Action. It sounded important, and I was flattered that I was asked to be part of it.

Father then told us to look around at our fellow students and see what they were doing, where they hung out, what they talked about. Next week we would come back to talk about what we had observed. In retrospect, I didn't really know how this was going to work, but I had nothing to lose. Besides, one of the fellows in our group worked at the library where we met. He said we could take out books without paying the usual rental fee. I spotted *Communism and Man* by Frank Sheed and decided this was my chance to learn something that would give me the answers I was looking for. That was March 1939, and I was seventeen years old.

We continued to meet every Sunday afternoon for several months. We talked about what was going on at school and whether things were as they should be. If not, we were supposed to figure out what to do about it. Mostly, as I recall, we became more conscious of our fellow students and tried to get to know them better. We also read selections from the New Testament. For several meetings we read the eight Beatitudes and looked for ways to apply them in our lives. What did it mean to be poor in spirit? How were we to suffer persecution for justice's sake? Put up with Virgil, my Socialist friend, perhaps?

At one meeting Father showed us a small leaflet he had received from the Young Christian Workers in England. They were young people doing what we were supposed to be doing. We learned that the method they used was called the social inquiry. It was the recommended way: Observe, Judge, Act as Christians. We went through the motions, but it was still pretty vague to me. I continued to attend the meetings, but mostly I was interested in the books we were taking home that were giving me new ideas about religion, *Mr. Blue, Map of Life, The Woman Who was Poor.*

A School of Catholic Action

Then we heard that a man named Paul McGuire was coming to Chicago in May to conduct a "School of Catholic Action" at Our Lady of Sorrows parish. Fr. James Keane, O.S.M., director of the popular novena to Our Mother of Sorrows, had invited McGuire to bring the idea of Catholic Action to the many young men and women who worked as volunteers at the forty novena services held each Friday at his church. Fr. Hayes suggested that we go to find out what McGuire had to say.

We crowded into the large parish hall with several hundred young novena workers. A dapper, forty-year-old gentleman with an attractive Australian accent began to speak. He told us about Catholic Action and its goal to transform society by the application of Christian charity and justice. The methods which served the Church in earlier days, he said, could no longer serve the needs of the world in which we now lived, a world of huge cities, great wealth, and great poverty.

He stressed that Catholic Action was not concerned with negative things like opposing Communism. Rather, it was a positive revolution to restore Christian values to daily life. The "restoration of all things in Christ" meant that Christ must be at the center of our lives and our behavior should be based on the Gospels. He excited us with the vision of a world in great need of restoration which could only be changed by young people everywhere who would unite under the banner of Christ.

Then he told us the story of Canon Joseph Cardijn, the Belgian priest who was so dismayed by the demoralization of young people when they became workers that he spent many years developing a way to bring them back to Christ. McGuire carefully outlined the Observe, Judge, Act method developed by Cardijn which taught young workers to observe the facts of everyday life, to judge those facts in the light of Christ's teachings in the Gospels, and to take appropriate action.

Jocism, the popular name given to Cardijn's movement, *Jeunesse Ouvriere Chretienne*, was the first of the movements of "Specialized Catholic Action." Pius XI had spoken of the like-to-like apostolate when he said that "workers must be the apostles to workers, farmers the apostles to farmers, students the apostles to students." McGuire then described in detail the five great organizations of Specialized Catholic Action: the Young Christian Farmers (JAC), the Young Christian Students (JEC), the Young Christian Independents (JIC, workers in management and the professions), the Young Christian Workers (JOC, mostly workers in industry), and the Young Christian University students (JUC).

McGuire, using the Young Christian Workers as the model of Specialized Catholic Action, described it as an organization of unmarried workers under the age of twenty-five, based in the parish, and centered around a small group of militant leaders. They looked at the environment in which they lived: their neighborhoods, the places where they worked, and where they and their fellow workers spent their leisure time. They asked questions like: Were the young people happy in their jobs? Did they change jobs often? Why? Did they go to church regularly? What were they looking for in their future, or did they even think about it?

Through such examples, McGuire showed how the young Jocists began to *observe* and to *judge*. Was so-and-so unhappy because he was in a job that did not suit him? Could they help him? If working conditions were unhealthy, could changes be made? If a fellow worker was sick, would it be a good idea to visit him? Was it good for young workers to spend all their time hanging around the bars?

These questions made the Jocists think and helped them develop a Christian conscience. But there was more to it than that. At the end of each meeting, the Jocist was expected to plan some kind of *action* to influence others at work, on the street, in the dance halls, everywhere. The social aspect was always stressed. Talk to someone, get a group together, do what you can for a person, speak up for someone— if necessary to the boss, be active in the union, help organize a local union or a ball team, whatever was needed.

McGuire stressed that young leaders must understand the real needs and interests of their fellow workers and take a leadership role in bringing about necessary change. This was the real essence of

Catholic Action: to be a Christian and to act accordingly, to love others and show it in service, to change the institutions in society that were making it difficult to live a Christian life.

In the established organizations that McGuire described, large services such as employment agencies, training schools for young workers, handbooks, libraries, networks for servicemen, and so on had been developed, but he cautioned us to begin with small actions. It takes time to develop a sound corps of militant leaders, leaders who can "penetrate the milieu" and make a difference. Above all, though, the movement is an apostolate because it reaches out to others, it is an intensely personal apostolate. It requires the sanctification of each member.

McGuire echoed Fr. Robert Kothen, Cardijn's assistant national chaplain in Belgium, "The social problem will not be solved by a simple redistribution of goods. What is necessary, profoundly necessary, is to socialize souls, so that hearts and minds may unite in the Mystical Body of Christ, in that vast association in which one is able to forget oneself, to go beyond one's personal interest in order to seek the general good, the common good. . . ."[1]

After a week of meetings which built up great interest, McGuire left Chicago saying he would return in ten days. Before he left, he promised to help form parish groups among those of us in the audience who were interested. However, he said, "I do not expect you all to become involved, and even if you do, many of you will not continue." Experience in Australia showed, he said, that it was not possible to start a large organization all at once. In his country, he said, an attempt to begin with a large group had petered out, and then a solid movement began with the small number of leaders who had persisted.

There was no noticeable drop off in attendance when Paul McGuire returned with his wife on May 20. We were divided into small groups according to our home parishes. Each group found a spot where they put their chairs in a circle and introduced themselves. From then on, after a session by the McGuires on how to run a meeting, individuals gathered in the small groups to discuss what they had learned.

From the beginning, McGuire compared the group to a "cell" in the Mystical Body of Christ. Just as a cell in the human body divides in two when it increases in size, so too did a Jocist cell divide when it grew too large. Twelve members were considered maximum. The choice of terms was a happy one. *Circle d'etude* was the French term used by Cardijn to describe the small group of militants but in English the translation "study circle" sounded like "study club" which implied something altogether different. Because the doctrine of the Mystical Body of Christ was so basic to the ideology of Catholic Action, those who heard McGuire picked up quickly on the idea of the cell. Specialized Catholic Action in the United States at that time gradually became known as "the cell movement."[2]

The parts of a meeting were gone over, one by one:

(1) *The Gospel Inquiry* consisted of taking a reading from the New Testament, discussing it, and applying its lesson to one's life. For example, we might take Chapter 10, v. 25–37, in the Gospel of St. Luke which tells the story of the Samaritan who helped the man who was beaten by thieves. Discussion might center on who one's neighbors are and lead the participants to think of some unlikely person they could help in the following week.

(2) *The Report* described action that had been planned the previous week and what resulted, acts of service, and new contacts.

(3) *The Social Inquiry.* This was the most important part of the meeting and was allotted the most time. Questions would be developed ahead of time to direct the observations of the members. If the use of leisure was the subject of inquiry, for example, questions might be: How do your fellow workers spend their free time? Movies? Dates? Hanging around? Where? At the meeting, the group would report their findings, then "judge," decide if leisure time was being used in a Christian way. If not, an action was to be planned to try to improve the use of leisure.

McGuire's explanations and exhortations had a tremendous effect on our little group of neophytes from Chicago Normal School. When we saw the big picture, we began to realize what was expected of us. We began to understand what Observe, Judge, and Act meant. We knew we were onto something important for Christ, and we accepted the responsibility of getting involved in action for change. We agreed with the words of Pius XI that this was a time when we could not be content to be mediocre Christians.[3]

At the end of the month when the school was concluded, the cells picked temporary leaders and agreed to continue meeting weekly. A leadership council, composed of the leader of each cell, would meet regularly to pick the topic of inquiry and prepare observation and judgment questions to be used at the cell meetings. McGuire insisted on this to insure unity among the individual cells. Also, the meetings of the individual cells were to be planned ahead with a chaplain.

Over the course of the summer, some of the parish groups, preferring to meet closer to home, found priests in their local parishes to serve as chaplains. Some of these were recently ordained priests who had heard about the Catholic Action in the seminary from Msgr. Reynold Hillenbrand, their forward-looking rector and, I learned later, a friend of our chaplain, Fr. John Hayes. Because our student cell had broken up for the summer, some of us continued for a while with groups in our parishes, but our primary *milieu* (the French word meaning the surroundings in which we lived) was the public school we attended.

In September, our group split into two groups, one for fellows, the other for girls. This was the right way, we learned. Eventually, we had eight cells actively reaching out to our fellow students, helping individuals with personal problems, becoming active in school activities, holding days of recollection and study days on Christian values for our members. Years later, at our twenty-fifth class reunion, Fred Weck, our class president, in his speech to those present said that the most important thing he got from his years at the college was the deepening of his religious faith. In his second year, he had joined a Catholic Action cell.

McGuire on the Road

Our experience in Chicago was only one result of Paul McGuire's speaking tour in the United States and it was not the first. Several years earlier, McGuire had gone to Europe to write about the Spanish Civil War. He made a living as a writer of detective fiction, but as a concerned Catholic he also wrote articles about social issues related to Catholic life. In Europe, he had encountered the apostolic movement of young workers known as Jocists. He was greatly impressed by the gathering of eighty-five thousand members he witnessed in Paris in 1937. He recognized that the movement had a vitality that was reaching out to the ordinary workingman with what he saw as "a revolution in values, . . . the Christian revolution, the restoration of all things in Christ." He saw Catholic Action as instrumental in a broad reorganization of society in which all levels of society—the farmer, the worker, the intellectual, and the middle-class manager— would work together, each in his own position in society, to establish what he described in his writings as a Christian commonwealth.[4]

In his vision of a new world, McGuire made a clear distinction between Catholic Action and what he called Catholic social action.[5] He saw Catholic Action as dealing with personal and religious issues, rather than social problems. We learned later that this was a much more restrictive view of the movement than the Jocists themselves took. But McGuire felt that political, social, and economic reform could not be enacted without moral reform. "In the restoration and strengthening of spiritual life, and in that alone, will men realize their unity one with another, their membership in Christ. But when they have realized it, social reform is inevitable."[6]

Because he was convinced that Catholic Action should begin in America, he came to the States in 1938 and began to seek out ways to reach the American Catholic public. He wrote articles on Catholic Action that appeared in *The Sign* magazine and *Columbia*, the Knights of Columbus magazine. In those days, lectures on subjects of interest to Catholics were sponsored by many Catholic organizations, so this presented another outlet for McGuire's message. With the help of a Dr. O'Donovan in Springfield, Illinois, who ran a speakers' bureau known as Te Deum International, he joined the lecture circuit and spoke in cities from New York to San Francisco. In his early lectures, he spoke about Communism and the civil war in Spain, a real attention-getter in those days. Then he began to give talks about the Catholic Action movement he had observed in Europe.

Paul McGuire spoke with a vigor and enthusiasm that quickly captured the attention of his American audiences. In vivid terms, he spelled out the great things that were happening in other parts of the Catholic world. Many young people who heard him were inspired to join in this great Christian campaign. They were aware of many problems in their own country stemming from economic insecurity and moral weakness. They wanted to know more. After the lectures, young men and women would corner McGuire and bombard him with questions.

First American Beginnings in Brooklyn[7]

In late spring 1938, the Knights of Columbus sponsored a lecture by Paul McGuire at the Waldorf-Astoria in New York where he spoke about Catholic Action and the Jocists. In the audience, at the insistence of his mother, was John Berkery of Brooklyn, a recent college graduate, who attended because his uncle, a K.C. member, happened to have an extra ticket. Berkery was so taken with the idea of Catholic Action that he spoke about it in a talk at his mother's Rosary Society. In the audience was a neighbor who reported that her daughter Betty had been at the McGuire lecture and was equally excited. Through Betty Enoch, Berkery met Gerald Fitzgerald, another young man who had heard McGuire.

Shortly thereafter, Gerry met with three friends who had recently graduated from Bishop Loughlin High School in Brooklyn to talk about Catholic Action. On July 9, 1938, they had their first meeting. They asked Fr. Paul Ward, a Paulist connected with the *Catholic World* magazine, for his help in finding out more about Jocism and an appropriate way to do Catholic Action. After an extensive search of available literature from the United States, Belgium, and Canada, they formed two groups, one in Brooklyn, the other in Queens. Fr. James A. Green became their chaplain. They called themselves the American Jocists.

John Berkery started a group in 1939 which he called the Catholic Action Guild of Flatbush. When he decided to become a priest and left to attend the seminary at Niagara Falls, he continued to meet with the group on his visits home.

Little information about Catholic Action was available in America at that time, other than the articles written by Paul McGuire and a few others such as one by Louis Van Houche in *The Sign*, March 1937, entitled "Jocism: A Christian Challenge." The articles gave general information, but no specific help for getting started. So the early Brooklyn groups translated inquiries they found in Jocist publications from Quebec, Canada, where the JOC also existed. Though they soon realized that the inquiries must be adapted to American conditions, they did learn the method: to Observe facts, to Judge, and to Act.

Inquiries were made on the working environment, dancing, dress, dates and preparation for marriage, movies, family life, the indifference of Catholics regarding their religion, the practice of charity. These were specific areas where religious and moral values could easily be observed. They were the kinds of things that McGuire indicated as the place to start. At each meeting, members were expected to bring in facts about a specific topic chosen ahead of time. The group would make a judgment. Did the facts indicate a problem? Should something be done? What? Early actions included a campaign for better observance of Christmas (cribs placed in stores and places of business and encouraging the use of Christian Christmas cards), campaigns for decent movies, and getting fellow workers to return to the sacraments.

By 1942, sixteen groups with a total of 150 active members were meeting weekly. Four were male, six were young women, and the others were mixed. Each member was expected to recruit a team of co-workers with whom they met informally to share ideas and action at work. All team members were invited to regular general meetings held at their headquarters. This was first a room obtained in 1941 at the Knights of Columbus Club on Prospect Park West. Later a storefront was rented at 229 Flatbush Avenue and the rent was paid by a variety of fund-raising activities.

Almost from the beginning, the "American Jocists" published a monthly bulletin called *The Crusader* containing inquiry outlines, meeting notices, and comments from the chaplain. This was just the first of several publications, including an official handbook in 1939, and a *Bibliography of Periodical Jocist Literature* first published in September 1941.

One early leader described those formative days.

> At first, the American Jocists appealed only to "good" Catholics. As it developed, through the teams, its appeal spread to others. After our leaders had visited Europe and Canada to see successful groups in action, we learned it was important to shy away from holy Joes and Marys and to get red-blooded American Catholics—the kind who so easily become indifferent to their religion, and to go after fallen-away Catholics. We sought the leaders in our offices, no matter how good they were as Catholics. Cell members were no longer made to perform spiritual works, but were made to *want* to pray. . . .

It's hard to count up the successful "actions" of the Jocist inquiries, because it's not just a matter of marriages "fixed," baptisms arranged, Easter duties encouraged, etc., though of course all these resulted. The Jocist action was to change the environment and it was a constant action in the places of business of the militants, in the changed attitudes of their fellow workers.

On the members themselves, there was a profound influence. Their talents for leadership were directed for good. Their spiritual life was strengthened. Their knowledge of the teachings of the Church, of the doctrines of their religion, was increased. They learned how to apply the Church's teachings. As a group, they learned how to work in unison, how group activity was more forceful than individual when applied to the solution of a social problem. Religion came to mean more than going to Mass, singing a hymn, attending devotions. It became not just a part of their live, but life itself. They found out that there was a Christian way of doing everything.[8]

The Brooklyn Jocists also had their problems: the loss of the young men to the draft in World War II plus the difficulty of getting priests who understood that lay leaders must be encouraged to develop responsibility and initiative led eventually to the dissolution of most of the original cells. A new chaplain who took over when Fr. Green went into the service did not understand the worker orientation of the groups and usurped the authority of the lay leaders, bringing in high school and college students and altering the apostolic focus of the original leaders.

Meanwhile, John Berkery, still in the seminary, continued spreading the Catholic Action idea. Because he had permission to leave the seminary to teach CCD classes in local parishes, he made contacts with young workers and started groups in Niagara Falls and Rochester, New York. When he wrote to Cardijn for information and it came back in French, he had a problem. He turned for help to a freshman at Niagara Seminary, also from Brooklyn, who knew French. That was how young Ed Hogan learned about the JOC. He became a convert to Jocism and read and talked about it throughout his days in the seminary.

When Hogan transferred to the Brooklyn diocesan seminary on Long Island, his interest in Catholic Action continued. One day, while recuperating from an illness, he was reading a book about Catholic Action by a Belgian Jesuit, Fr. Fernand Lelotte[9] when Fr. Francis Donnelly, his moral theology teacher, came in to check on his health. Donnelly took one look at the book and asked to borrow it when Ed was finished. Before long, they began a study group on Catholic Action at the seminary. All three, Berkery, Hogan, and Donnelly, became leading YCW chaplains in the Brooklyn diocese in later years. All this from the seed that was planted by Paul McGuire at the Waldorf in 1938.

Toledo and O'Toole[10]

When Paul McGuire lectured at the Catholic Forum in Toledo in the spring of 1938, the Rev. James J. O'Toole, then a professor at DeSales College, was immediately interested. Since the defeat of Al Smith in 1928, he had been concerned that so few Catholics were able to exert an effective influence in American political, economic, and social life. He began to give talks pointing up the need for articulate Catholic lay leadership. After hearing McGuire, Dr. O'Toole gave a series of sermons at Our Lady of Perpetual Help Church developing the ideas promoted by McGuire.

Some weeks later, five young men—some, seniors at DeSales, and the others, workers— came to see Dr. O'Toole at his home. They told him they had been thinking over what he had said and had come to ask what they could do for Christ. In the following days, several young college women also expressed interest, but it was the five men who got started first. They began meeting in November 1938 and within a short time were joined by four others. Within a few months, five cells were in existence, two of workers, one of college girls, and two of high school groups. In the manner that came to be typical of other early groups, they began to publish a bulletin called *The Cells*. The first two copies are undated, but Vol. 1, No. 3, is dated August 1, 1939.

The first issue of *The Cells* begins with the question, "Why?" and answers, "Christ is the solution for any problem the world could ever produce. But, how can we apply this solution to our practical problems and everyday needs? There is a way, a simple way, a way that is open to every man, no matter what his station in life. This way has been outlined by Paul McGuire, the outstanding layman operating in the cause of Christ, who has made a comprehensive study of the action taken in this regard in France, Belgium, and other foreign countries. The way of applying Christ to our lives is through Catholic Action. . . . The main idea of Catholic Action is the Christianization of all man's dealings with his fellow men."

The editor, Jim Kitzmiller, then developed the idea that a person is by nature social, depending on and influencing others. "This natural law can be stated in terms of the Mystical Body of Christ, for anything which is of human value is of Christian value, for Christ redeemed all that is human."[11]

Meeting outlines in the early Toledo bulletins stressed preparation for Catholic Action through prayer and study. Action was primarily concentrated on recruiting new members. They certainly did that. One year later, Dr. O'Toole, in a memorandum to Bishop Karl Alter of the Toledo diocese, listed 225 individuals in twenty-five cells "preparing for Catholic Action." Nine cells were composed of workers, about forty women and twenty-eight men. There were five college groups and thirteen groups of high schoolers. As in some of the other cities in the early days, there was close cooperation among the cells of students and working persons, although each worked on separate programs.

> In regard to the Toledo movement we are, of course, still very much in our infancy. As a matter of fact I am surprised that we have not already collapsed as I had expected a drop in interest and a falling off of followers by this time. From what I can gather, a three year novitiate is the only satisfactory test that the roots have grown deep. . . .
>
> If your Excellency considered it opportune, a letter of encouragement would be the most helpful thing the groups could have.[12]

The memorandum quoted above brings out two ideas that were "givens" in the thinking about Catholic Action at that time:

(1) Before Catholic Action becomes official, there is a preparatory stage which consists of the formation of its members for the apostolate.

"If we are going to convert the world, the first people we ought to convert are ourselves." And, quoting Pius XI, "The profoundly Christian formation of the members of Catholic Action is pre-supposed: fruitfulness comes second."

(2) Catholic Action in the strict and official sense was an organized apostolate, "carried out at the special behest, not merely with the approbation, of the Bishop."[13]

In promoting Catholic Action, McGuire had continually stressed the need for formation of leaders and cautioned that instant growth was not desirable, much less to be expected.

> Catholic Action is not a mass movement. It is a movement of an elite, of the salt and the leaven. . . .We do not mean by a movement of an elite that any Catholics are excluded from it, but that every Catholic who shares in it must be screwed to new intensity of life. Now it is reasonably obvious that we cannot expect from the general mass of Catholics an immediate response to the demand for an intensified Christian life as a necessary preliminary to the apostolate. But, we can expect that a few in each of our organizations, in all our parishes, will respond. It is these who will gradually draw up the others. And it is these with whom Catholic Action is first concerned and who will become the militants, the leaders of Catholic Action.[14]

YCW on the West Coast

John J. Mitty, archbishop of San Francisco, trying to implement Catholic Action, cited by Pius XI in his 1937 encyclical *Divini Redemptoris* as a way to combat Communism, met with Cardinal Pizzardo of the Catholic Action office in Rome, looking for ideas. The story is told that on his return home, he asked three businessmen to set up a Catholic Action program.[15] A search in the archdiocesan archives does not reveal anything specific that resulted.

Then Paul McGuire spoke about the Jocists at the 1938 lecture series sponsored at St. Boniface, a Franciscan parish in downtown San Francisco. At the completion of the lecture series, a group of young men approached one of the parish priests, Fr. Paul Meinecke, O.F.M., and asked what they could do. He arranged two meetings for the group, one with McGuire and another with Aileen O'Brien, a young journalist who also was impressed by the Jocists she had met on her travels in Europe. With the help of McGuire and O'Brien, the group decided that the YCW technique could be effective in the United States and should be tried.

They had no available material in English. All they knew of Jocist technique was Observe, Judge, and Act. But they did have a grasp of the spirit of the movement. They called themselves Young Christian Workers, the name used in England. They formed small groups to use the inquiry method and to study the New Testament, but they never used the cell terminology common in other parts of the country.

According to Fr. Simon Scanlon, O.F.M., one of the original members who later became a Franciscan, the first members were not "downtrodden workers." Most were middle class, even upper middle class in a few cases. They were white-collar employees, a few junior partners in small businesses, and some young professionals. St. Boniface was a downtown city parish in the commercial center of the city and these were the young people who worked nearby or came downtown. The original group at St. Boniface included some remarkable young men: Jack Shelly, who became a congressman and later mayor of the city; Jack Henning, executive secretary of the AFL-CIO of California and later Deputy Secretary of Labor in the sixties; and Jack McGuire, Jack Boyer, and Larry Vail who organized the Retail Clerks Union.

Fr. Simon reminisces:

> People came from all over the city because there was something going on here (at St. Boniface). They had this lecture series which attracted people. So gradually we got into the method which I think was most important, which made it a great thing for the world, the Church. We began to have meetings with See, Judge, and Act. We got involved! Bishop Donahue who was bishop then was interested and we began to get involved in ACTU, the Association of Christian Trade Unionists. Some of them, the four Jacks, got so involved with that, they didn't come much to the YCW anymore.
>
> We had dances, started folk dances. People who had positions in business began to become socially conscious.

Many left their positions and became social workers or teachers or priests and nuns. The method had the effect of getting people involved and seeing the issues.

One of the first things that happened was the draft. There were hordes of young enlisted men in San Francisco who had nowhere to go and were sitting ducks for all kinds of scams. One night, the president of the group saw a young soldier being thrown out of a honky-tonk in downtown San Francisco. He thought the same thing would happen many times in the years to come. So he brought it up at the next meeting.

We decided we should do something about that and so before there was anything like the USO, we started our Friday night dances for servicemen in the basement of St. Boniface Church. Through that, we made contact with a lot of young men.

We also got involved in civil rights and the housing situation, the discrimination policy. There was a Communist operation down the street which was very well organized and getting influential and what do you do, just sit by? So, we organized a labor school. We had good people giving talks on labor law and labor history, public speaking and parliamentary law.

That was in the early forties, before most of us had to go to war. But it thrived during the war. New people came in, many of them servicemen who learned of the YCW for the first time and joined the section. When the YCW boys had to go into service, the young men stationed there kept the YCW in action, and we always had the girls. The basic thing was to See, Judge, Act. It wasn't the organization, it was the method which was important.[16]

In 1938 the Knights of Columbus were nearing the end of a campaign to make Americans aware of the dangers of Communism in their response to Pius XI's call to the laity to fight atheistic Communism. In an attempt to find answers to the moral and economic problems which gave rise to Communism, they prepared to follow in 1939 with a program called "The Campaign for Christian Social Justice." The appearance of McGuire at that time seemed providential for he was suggesting positive ways to combat injustice and bring Christian values into ordinary life. He was what their campaign needed.

In November 1938, the following announcement appeared alongside McGuire's article in *Columbia*:

> Beginning early in 1939, Paul McGuire, author of this and other notable Columbia articles, will deliver under sponsorship of the Supreme Council, Knights of Columbus, a series of lectures on the plan, the objective and the achieved types of Catholic Action. Mr. McGuire is a leader in Catholic Action in his own country, Australia, and will bring to American audiences the fruit of his extensive study and close personal observation of the "participation of the laity in the apostolate of the hierarchy" in France, Italy, Belgium, Ireland, England, Holland and other countries. Those who heard Mr. McGuire during a brief visit to the United States last spring require no testimonial as to his qualifications to discuss the force that transcends all others in the world today—Catholic Action.[17]

In January 1939, shortly before the tour to more than fifty cities began, *Restoring All Things: A Guide to Catholic Action* by Paul McGuire and Rev. John Fitzsimons, then a YCW chaplain in Liverpool and later an English national chaplain, was published and became a Catholic Book-of-the-Month. Ruth Darby, a young Texan school teacher, picked up the book in a local San Antonio bookstore and started talking about Catholic Action with the salesgirl. Within three weeks, they interested a few more and then approached a Redemptorist priest, Fred Mann. With Fr. Mann's help, they began to plan action. Their first action was "Better Life Clubs" for public schoolchildren, hardly a like-to-like apostolate, but it was a beginning awareness of the need to get involved in action.

On February 20, they heard that Paul McGuire was going to speak for the Knights of Columbus, so they arranged to have lunch with him. Thus began another group which called itself "The Fulton Sheen Guild preparing for Catholic Action." They even contacted their archbishop and on May 30, 1939, received a letter from him giving approval for their work and appointing, "con mucho gusto," Frs. Lamm and Mann as spiritual directors.[18]

The San Antonio group continued to meet with McGuire whenever he came into town, and by May 1940 they were publishing *The*

Cells of Restoration, a mimeograph paper with formative articles, news, and program materials. It was at this time they finally began to use the inquiry technique Observe, Judge, and Act, though the problems they observed were mainly limited to religious behavior. A letter published in their newsletter from a member who was in the army in 1943 illustrates this: "I had a chance to practice Jocism today, when I took four fellows who haven't gone to church since they came into the Army with me last month to Mass with me."[19]

In New York City, a group was started by Mary Jo Madden who heard about Catholic Action when she visited in Chicago shortly after McGuire was there. She met Margaret Dagenais from our group who bubbled with enthusiasm about the things that McGuire had told us. On her return to New York, Mary Jo interested a group of friends in the Gaelic Society and went looking for a chaplain. She eventually prevailed upon Fr. Francis Wendell, a Dominican at St. Vincent Ferrer Church on Lexington Avenue, to take them on. Before the year was out, the group was underway.

In Cleveland, when Frs. Reginald McCormick, Vincent Haas, and Charles Hogan heard about the Jocists, they went to Montreal to see for themselves. They were so impressed by Archbishop Charbonneau's pastoral letter on the aims and accomplishments of the movement in Canada that they organized several groups on their return. One group was started at St. Ann parish and included students from John Carroll University. Fr. Hogan started with a group from Ursuline College. In 1942, graduates from the Ursuline group formed a cell of working girls which met at the cathedral parish. That was the core of what eventually became the Young Christian Workers in Cleveland.

Many of the priests who became interested in Catholic lay action in the early days were interested in social issues—Haas later formed the Catholic Interracial Council in Cleveland and Hogan was an active "labor priest"—but they had little direct contact with ordinary young working adults. In their search for prospective leaders, they often turned to students in the high schools and colleges.

Fr. Hayes, who met with us in Chicago on those Sundays in the early spring of 1939, had had the same problem. He and his friend Msgr. Reynold Hillenbrand had long been concerned with the social and economic problems that had afflicted Catholic workers during the depression. When they heard about the Jocist movement, they were intrigued by the idea that lay workingmen and women could be formed as Christian leaders in the workplace. Unfortunately, they worked in the diocesan seminaries and had little pastoral contact with lay people. But Fr. Hayes wanted to try it. Though our school seemed an unlikely place to find workers, he did have two contacts there—a young man who had transferred from the preparatory seminary and a union-minded teacher. Our student cell was the result. We were fortunate to be in that first group and to hear the call to Catholic Action first expressed *publicly* in the United States by Paul McGuire.

Notes

1 Quoted by Paul McGuire, "Apostolate of the Workers," *Columbia*, January 1938, p. 24.
2 Coincidentally, the word *cell* was also used by the Communists to describe their small covert base units in the forties, according to "A Short Glossary of Communist Terms," in Herbert A. Philbrick's book on his undercover experience among the Communists, *I Led Three Lives* (Capitol Hill Press, 1972). Descriptions of the Communist organization in the twenties identify the base group as a "nucleus," according to Harvey Kuehn, *The Heyday of American Communism* (Basic Books, 1984). When the name of the base group evolved into "cell" cannot be precisely determined, but it was not common knowledge when McGuire used the word to describe the Catholic Action group in 1939.
3 Words of Pius XI on a holy card carried by the author in those early days, exact source unknown.
4 McGuire, "Approach to the Christian Commonwealth," *Columbia*, November 1938, pp. 3, 17.
5 Pius X first used the term Catholic Action shortly after the turn of the century. Catholic Action is a literal translation from the Italian *Azione Cattolica*, an organization of lay people established around 1900 to overcome open hostility to the Church, to establish better relations between the Church and the government, and to revive Catholic practice among those who were negligent.

   Pius XI gave Catholic Action its classical definition, "participation of the laity in the apostolate of the Church's hierarchy" (*Ubi Arcano*, 1922). He restricted it to work that was (1) action of the laity, (2) organized, (3) apostolic, and (4) done under the mandate (i.e., the specific command) of the bishop.

   Cardinal Saliege, Archbishop of Toulouse, in 1945, added to this definition when he described Catholic Action in terms of institutional change, having for its task "to modify social pressure, to direct it, to make it favorable to the spread of the Christian life, to let the Christian life create an atmosphere in which men can develop their human qualities and lead a really human life, an atmosphere in which the Christian can breathe easily and stay a Christian" (*Documentation Catholique* 42, 1945).

   McGuire, in 1939, felt Catholic Action was limited to religious and moral reform, rather than social activism. Louis Putz, C.S.C., who was a Jocist chaplain in France during the thirties, has said since that McGuire was wrong on this point, as least as far as Jocism was concerned.
6 McGuire, *op. cit.*, p. 17.
7 Facts of the Brooklyn beginnings are culled from taped conversations with Margaret Fitzgerald and John Berkery, March 8, 1987, and materials from their personal records which they shared with the author. Also, the author has notes of a conversation with Edward Hogan, March 7, 1986.

8 Margaret K. Fitzgerald, "American Jocism, July 1938 to September 1943 (translation)," an unpublished report prepared for Msgr. Francis Donnelly, 1966. Zotti papers.

9 Fernand Lelotte, S.J., *Fundamental Principles of Catholic Action* (Melbourne, Victoria, Australia: National Secretariat of Catholic Action), n.d.

10 Facts for the Toledo beginnings from "History of the Toledo YCS Movement" by Sr. Mary Herman Carey, S.N.D., and materials gathered by her and Patricia O'Dwyer Danford, former YCW leader now on the staff of *The Catholic Chronicle*, Toledo diocesan paper. Zotti papers.

11 James Kitzmiller, in *The Cells*, n.d.

12 Memorandum: To the Most Rev. Bishop of Toledo from (Rev.) James J. O'Toole, November 11, 1939.

13 James J. O'Toole, *What is Catholic Action?* (New York: Paulist Press, 1940), p. 20. This is the first booklet on Catholic Action by an American author.

14 McGuire, "Doing it the Hard Way," *Columbia*, March 1940, p. 221.

15 Louis Putz, C.S.C., to author, July 1963.

16 Simon Scanlon, O.F.M., taped conversation with author, October 4, 1985.

17 Announcement in *Columbia*, November 1938, p. 3.

18 "Red Letter Days," *Cells of Restoration*, Vol. 1, No. 1, May 1940, p. 14.

19 Letter from a private in Sacramento, *Cells of Restoration*, Vol. 1, No. 4, January 1943.

2

A Trio of Pioneering Priests:
Hillenbrand, Kanaly, and Putz

Though our activities in the early Catholic Action cells were small and seemingly inconsequential, they marked a new departure for the American church. They represented a positive first step in the development of a thinking, acting laity. Key to this development was the involvement of priests who would take the work of lay people seriously and encourage their action. It meant that they would have to give of themselves, their energy, and their time, to help young people develop not only a sound Christian conscience but the leadership skills necessary to influence the world in which they lived.

The traditional role of the clergy had been to help Catholics achieve their eternal destiny with God through prayer and the sacraments and a code of behavior based on the Ten Commandments. Papal encyclicals, dating back to Leo XIII's *Rerum Novarum* in 1891, and updated by Pius XI, "On the Reconstruction of the Social Order" (*Quadragesimo Anno*), had sought to change this emphasis. But their significance had not been fully grasped by the clergy nor communicated to the common person in the pew. The need for social action by church members was not easily accepted by many priests. Yet without supportive priests, a lay movement of far-reaching influence could never have started. Lay people did not understand that they had a special role in the redemptive mission of the Church. In the tradition of the time, the laity waited for leadership from the clergy. That is why the leadership of Msgr. Reynold Hillenbrand, rector of the archdiocesan seminary of Chicago, was so critical.

Msgr. Reynold Hillenbrand

One of a handful of forward-looking priests in the thirties, Reynold Hillenbrand combined his natural talents, his love of the Church, and his sensitivity to human need to become a leading figure in the development of new answers to an old question, how to spread the teachings of Christ in the world. He recognized that the world itself was the creation of God and the proper setting in which Christians should work out their eternal destiny.

Reynold Hillenbrand was raised in a family of God-fearing German-Americans with high standards of discipline and personal achievement. After ordination in 1929, he did postgraduate work at Mundelein and then spent a year in Rome before beginning a year teaching English at the Preparatory Seminary. He was then appointed to the newly formed Mission Band, a group of priests specially trained to conduct two- or three-week sessions in parishes throughout the archdiocese exhorting the faithful to know and practice their religion. In his three years traveling through the city, he saw firsthand the problems Catholics were having as a result of the Depression. When he was appointed as rector of St. Mary of the Lake Seminary in 1936, Cardinal George Mundelein introduced him to the seminarians with the words, "I've brought you a man with imagination."[1]

Poet and preacher and lover of God, a man of deep insight and strong will, Hillenbrand put his visionary stamp on the seminary during eight exciting years. The seminarians were exposed to new understandings about liturgical worship and social action. Hillenbrand saw active participation of the laity in the liturgical worship of the Church and the advocacy of labor unions and a living wage as two sides of the same coin: human beings must be fed in soul and body. Though he never interfered with the standard curriculum of philosophy and theology directed by the Jesuit faculty, he managed to squeeze in classes and discussions on social problems on Saturday evenings and during summer vacations. He encouraged seminarians to help out at the Catholic Worker House of Hospitality in the city when they were on vacation, and he invited guest speakers to the seminary to further expose the men to the problems of the real world.

Fr. Gerard Weber, one of his former students, describing the sense of excitement in those days, recalls Hillenbrand saying, "We live in the greatest age of the Church, the most exciting years that the Church has ever seen."

"He convinced us we could do something," says Weber. "He made us sensitive to the liturgy. He gave us a vision. Anything we wanted to do, we could do."[2]

Another former student, Fr. Martin Farrell, said, "Hillenbrand was a great appointment for the seminary. . . . That's why we are in this work. We're following our leader. We really envisioned converting the whole world."[3]

The strength and fortitude of this devoted man is probably the prime reason that Chicago became a national center of the Catholic Action movement. From his first days as rector, Hillenbrand looked to the papal encyclicals for his directives. In 1935 Pius XI had issued directives on the education of seminarians in which he called for intense training in the social teaching of the Church and a firm foundation in the liturgy. This is what Hillenbrand proceeded to implement from his first days at the seminary, in spite of the fact that many conservatives among the clergy saw this as an indication that the young monsignor was a flaming radical.

Strict interpretation of the papal encyclicals was to be his hallmark. It led him to an early appreciation of the importance of lay people in the work of the church. Throughout the years, he interpreted the messages of the Holy Father as the voice of Christ in the world and made those words meaningful to lay leaders in the specialized movements, of which the closest to his heart was the Young Christian Workers.

From the early days of his priesthood, Hillenbrand was concerned about the working man who had to support a family. He and his friend John Hayes were strong supporters of union causes and programs like the Catholic Worker, which sought to alleviate the basic needs of workers suffering the effects of social injustice. Weber recalls Fr. Hayes handing out copies of Dorothy Day's *Catholic Worker* in his algebra class at Quigley Prep Seminary in 1933.

After his appointment to the major seminary, Hillenbrand taught the social principles of *Quadragesimo Anno* and the other papal encyclicals to the deacons while continuing to be involved in a personal program of action. With Hayes, he conducted a series of Lenten sermons on labor questions at Holy Name Cathedral. The two then organized a monthly discussion group for priests interested in the labor problem. He started a labor school at Our Mother of God parish in Waukegan, Illinois, and encouraged other parishes to do likewise. He offered to supply young priests as teachers of the parish labor schools. Donald Runkle, an early Catholic Action chaplain, recalls taking the streetcar with Fr. Austin Graff from their North Side parishes to conduct weekly labor classes on the South Side, often to find apathy among union members they encountered instead of a warm welcome.[4]

From the onset of the depression, Catholics concerned with economic, social, and political questions had been unable to agree upon how to translate the Church's social principles into a concrete program. That is why Pius XI's 1937 encyclical *Divini Redemptoris* was significant. In it the pope stressed that "the most urgent need of the present day" was the "energetic and timely application of remedies" which would ward off the catastrophe of atheistic Communism. Pius appealed for a unity which would encompass "every religious and lay organization in the Church." As he had done previously, the pope stressed the need for lay action. Study circles, lecture courses, conferences and other activities should be undertaken to promote the Christian solution to the social problem. He urged that the doctrines of the Church be translated into practice in everyday life.

In a 1937 conference on Catholic Action called by Samuel A. Stritch, then archbishop of Milwaukee, the need for widespread action of some kind was stressed. A common thread in the many speakers' remarks, however, was the need for lay submission to ecclesiastical authority. Mrs. George Fell of the Toledo Council of Catholic Women, speaking at the closing banquet, affirmed that "a devoted hierarchy and clergy" were "thinking, planning and ever ready to act." Laity could serve as "soldiers of Christ" and fight for the preservation of Christian values, but they should allow the priests to develop the program of action and "follow the opportunities for service" outlined by the Church.[5] Her statement reflected the position of the average lay person of the times: priests were the educated ones, the leaders; lay persons were to be devoted followers.

The National Catholic Welfare Conference had been established by the American hierarchy in 1919 to act as a unified voice of the bishops for the promotion of unity in Catholic Work. Its Social Action Department became highly visible due to the dynamic leadership of its director, Msgr. John A. Ryan, who was responsible for the "Bishops' Program of Social Reconstruction."[6] In 1936, the Social Action Department approved a plan to establish "Priests' Schools of Social Action," week-long sessions for priests in local dioceses to ensure that those engaged in social action would be in full conformity with papal teachings. The first National Catholic Social Action Conference, organized under the direction of Raymond McGowan, Ryan's assistant, was held May 1 to 4, 1937, at St. Francis Seminary in Milwaukee. It provided a platform for the listing of Catholic social concerns. After a statement by Bishop McNicholas of Cincinnati about current social problems such as poverty, hunger, and unemployment, Msgr. Francis Haas explained that justice and the common good would be served by the establishment of a social order based on "the obligations of social charity in Jesus Christ."[7]

After many speeches and discussions, the solution recommended was a cooperative effort towards the social education of priests and the development of conferences explaining social action to the members of lay organizations. Despite the urgent call for fundamental social reconstruction, no one at the conference saw a need to identify the distinct role the laity should play in working out solutions. The lack of trust in the laity was revealed in the concern expressed by many who said that the clergy should train laymen who would safeguard Church doctrine and not go off on tangents.

The Milwaukee conference, which Hillenbrand attended, inspired him to develop a team of priests interested in liturgy, social action, and the lay apostolate to work out some kind of program combining all three elements. He was fascinated by the pope's insistence that there must be a specialized apostolate of workers to workers, students to students, farmers to farmers, and so on.[8] While in graduate school in Rome, he had heard of the Jocists, but he had no firsthand knowledge. On a summer vacation in 1936, he had visited the Jociste Centrale in Montreal to inquire about the theory and operation of their movement. He also spent time on that trip talking to Dorothy Day in New York at the Catholic Worker House.

After the conference in Milwaukee, he asked McGowan for his help in bringing knowledgeable speakers to his seminary to spell out the connection between the gospel and the problems of the workingman. He also spoke to Msgr. Francis Haas asking for more study sessions the following summer. McGowan then asked him to organize a "school" in Chicago. With the permission of Cardinal Mundelein who perceived it as a local diocesan effort, plans were made for a Summer School of Social Action for priests to be held at Mundelein Seminary in July 1938.

The school began on a challenging note. Rev. John Hayes, in his speech on the priests' work, spoke out against the devotionalism so popular in many parishes—novenas and processions—as well as social conservatism. Moreover, he stated that merely academic interest in social questions would leave the clergy "subject to the accusation of hypocrisy or stupidity or both." He challenged them further. "Any priest who is not hopelessly inert should feel himself goaded to some sort of action. The question is, what?"[9]

To this central question, Bishop Edwin O'Hara gave the common episcopal answer. He reaffirmed that priests could not be content with a "purely passive" laity, but must form study clubs among parishioners to spread the social teachings of the Church in hopes that this would inspire them to get involved in social action. He acknowledged that reaching the laity was no small problem.[10]

After three weeks talking social theory, participants began to look at the need for social "action." Bernard Burns, a local Chicago priest, urged the priests to recognize the real meaning of the Mystical Body of Christ and involve laymen in a fellowship of action resulting from their participation in liturgical worship. He took issue with the prevailing drift of the NCWC proposals to educate the laity in the social teachings. He suggested the need for personal action such as the work being done by Dorothy Day and Peter Maurin in their Houses of Hospitality.

A New Voice: Fr. Don Kanaly

Then, a new voice was heard. Fr. Donald Kanaly, a recently ordained priest from Oklahoma who had spent six years in the seminary at Louvain in Belgium, got up to speak about the formation of young lay apostles he had observed among the workers of Belgium. In a stirring speech, he took issue with the study club as a means of social action. "Only action will make apostles," he said. In study groups workers might learn to "think beautifully," but they did not know "how to act" when they got among Communists, "because they are led." He told them about Canon Cardijn's work and how the Jocists applied the papal teachings in real life. The "JOC could save America from Communism," he said, because it would get young workers involved in action. Then he explained in detail the inquiry method of Observe, Judge, and Act, which he had seen in use during his years in Europe.

This was the first time a significant number of priests learned of the Jocists. Kanaly stressed that this was an organization which could treat the total life of the young worker through the efforts of the young workers themselves. Action will "not come from the top; it must grow up from the bottom." He urged the priests to promote its growth by developing small groups of workers capable of leadership and influence. They should encourage them to take action to Christianize their environment. "The whole drive," he explained, "is to prepare them to go into the trade unions to be apostles." European experience suggested that from the JOC would come leaders capable of pointing the unions toward Christian ideals.[11]

Following the summer school, Hillenbrand continued to promote labor schools and study groups among priests, but he wanted to know more about the establishment of youth groups. He wrote to Kanaly asking his help in translating Jocist literature from French into English. He indicated that Chicago would be a good place to start an American version of the JOC since it was the second largest industrial city in the country.[12]

On his return to Ponca City, Oklahoma, that summer of 1938, Kanaly started his first cell of young workers. In reply to Hillenbrand's request, he noted that starting by spreading literature would be difficult, because few American priests saw lay action as a priest's work. He thought it better for interested priests to start small groups in their parish. This would show what could be done better than literature describing the method.[13]

Hillenbrand was not too interested when McGuire appeared and began his school of Catholic Action at Our Lady of Sorrows in the spring of 1939. He viewed the results of the program at Our Lady of Sorrows as a "hodgepodge of groups" with overly enthusiastic priests, bound to make mistakes. "You can't produce Jocism in mass production," he told Hayes.[14] It is very likely that he perceived McGuire at that time as a popular speaker without depth, particularly since the setting for the school was the scene of the highly popular Sorrowful Mother novena. Such a devotion was the antithesis of his views on true liturgical prayer which entailed full participation by lay people in the Mass rather than in novenas. He did later get to know McGuire and found him to be a useful source of information about Jocist methods.

When informed of McGuire's work in Chicago, Kanaly wrote to interested priests across the country, insisting that they keep in contact with one another. "Here," he said, "we have been working for the past eight months and have a state federation in Oklahoma officially recognized by the bishop with a hundred militants and regular cell meetings in about ten cities throughout the state." He was certain that within another year, groups would be established all over America.[15]

In late May 1939, Kanaly reported to Hillenbrand that Cardijn and his assistant, Fr. Robert Kothen, were watching the developments in the United States very closely and had advised him to strive for unity so that there would only be one organization of Young Christian Workers. He quoted them as saying, "You shall never have the YCW in America until you have one spirit, one name, one program, one organism."[16]

To insure this unity, Kanaly announced that the first national meeting of priests to work out a unified direction would be held during or immediately following the second National Catholic Social Action Congress, scheduled to meet in Cleveland in June 1939. At the behest of Bishop Kelly of Oklahoma City, who was on the bishops' committee for youth work, Kanaly had been asked to speak about the Jocist movement in a forum on youth. He urged Hillenbrand to come.

Hillenbrand agreed to come to Cleveland and reported that he had persuaded Fr. Burns, now assigned to the cathedral, that the JOC was a more comprehensive means for Catholics to take action to change the social order than the personalist approach of Dorothy Day. What's more, Burns had agreed to take over some of the groups started by Paul McGuire.[17] A few diocesan priests and several Franciscans at the downtown parish of St. Peter's were also beginning groups among young working people. Some of them had attended the series of priests' meetings held by McGuire during the course of his Catholic Action School on the west side of Chicago. Locally, as well as nationally, Hillenbrand saw the need for unified direction and he felt it was good to have a chaplain in place at the cathedral.

While the various speakers at the Cleveland meeting described their organizations and their plans to promote Christian democracy— the theme of the Social Action Congress—Kanaly and Hillenbrand

Msgr. Donald Kanaly and Msgr. Reynold Hillenbrand.
Date unknown (probably around 1960).

met for dinner to discuss the training of lay apostles. Hillenbrand had been studying literature he had received from the YCW in England but he still had questions. When he asked Kanaly what areas of need should be addressed by lay leaders, the Oklahoma priest wrote the following words on a holy card from his breviary: "domestic, economic, political, international."[18] Thus was the point made that the specialized movements should cover all problems of lay life.

The two then secured Bishop O'Hara's consent to preside at a dinner meeting the following evening for priests interested in Jocism. Thirty priests showed up, including Dr. O'Toole from Toledo who had been invited by Fr. Kanaly beforehand. When the question of adapting foreign procedures to American settings came up, those present agreed to call student cells Catholic Action Students and other groups Catholic Action Cells. The cells would adopt the methods of the European Jocists but the French terms would not be used. Kanaly concluded the meeting by urging the priests to join him in promoting American participation in the international JOC pilgrimage to Rome scheduled for September, just two months away.

Back home in Chicago, Hillenbrand encouraged Frs. Hayes and Burns in assisting the cells formed at Our Lady of Sorrows and suggested that this would ultimately lead to the centralization of all Chicago cells at the cathedral where, he said, Msgr. Joseph Morrison was "most enthusiastic about the JOC."[19] Then he urged Kanaly to conduct classes on Jocism at the two-week summer school for priests he was arranging at the seminary. In his letter to Kanaly, he said the newly ordained priests were "rarin' to go and need your talk."[20]

Meanwhile, Kanaly was getting little response to his plea for American participation in the Rome pilgrimage. He then sent out a circular in which he quoted Canon Cardijn's appeal for an American presence at the Rome meeting. "Come, in God's name," Cardijn had written. "We all await America. The Holy Father expects America. There can be no world pilgrimage, no world YCW without America."[21]

But Hillenbrand was reluctant. Though he agreed that the priests and lay leaders needed a widened vision, he thought the cells were too new to consider sending members to Rome. Also, in Chicago the largest number of cells were still centered at the West Side Servite parish, Our Lady of Sorrows, where McGuire had conducted his Catholic Action School. He did not think it advisable that those groups should take diocesan leadership.

Kanaly disregarded Hillenbrand's words of caution and continued to urge the newly formed groups to send representatives to Rome. He was convinced that the pilgrimage would "make the YCW in America." He spoke about the Young Christian Workers at meetings everywhere and talked up the Rome trip. Actually, in his enthusiasm to carry out Cardijn's wish for the presence of Americans in Rome, he was ignoring his original advice that the movement should start slowly.

Following his thirty-thousand-mile tour of the United States, Paul McGuire was convinced that groups were forming all through the country, but he too urged caution. He was concerned that scattered individual groups would do more harm than good. "Study that does not fulfill itself in action is sterile, but action not directed by study is chaos," he reminded Catholic Action leaders.[22] He urged an organized, unified apostolate that would build slowly as leaders were developed. He felt that a sound movement needed time.

Kanaly's appeals did not go unheeded everywhere, however, and in late August, he took off for Europe with twelve young workers. I attended a farewell party for Elsie Broucek and Bill Blakely who represented the cells formed in Chicago at Our Lady of Sorrows.

Richard Bourret, president of the St. Boniface YCW, went from San Francisco, and Vince Ferrari and Charles Bruderle represented the Brooklyn cells. No one from Toledo was able to go, but several went from Kansas City and Oklahoma.

On September 1, the day they arrived in Paris, the international pilgrimage was canceled due to the declaration of war. Poland had been invaded, and France and Britain had a treaty to come to her rescue. The girls immediately went to England where they waited two months for a boat home. Kanaly told the fellows they could go on to Rome if they wished. Several of the men made a side trip to the Jociste Centrale in Brussels before returning home while Kanaly and two young men opted for Rome. They weren't sure if they would get through France. General mobilization was underway and the country was blacked out. Eventually they did get to Rome where they were received by Msgr. Montini and had an audience with the Holy Father. To this day Kanaly remembers the eerie feeling of walking with the two young American cell members through the empty streets of Rome now bereft of tourists. In any event, the pilgrimage was a bust![23]

Pilgrimage or not, Kanaly was determined to build a strong YCW in America. When he had been a student, Cardijn started coming to the American College at Louvain to talk to the seminarians there. Kanaly recalls those visits:

> He knew if he got something going with us, he had a chance to get something started in America. He used to say, as this thing develops, the future of this will depend to a large part on America as the coming influential nation in the Church and in the world. If it doesn't get roots in America, it hasn't got the future. . . . I was practically the only one in the seminary that was interested. We were all so brainwashed by the bourgeois spirit. We want to associate with the rich, the people with the money, who are the big ones. We see our dignity tied up with money and stylish clothes. His thing (Cardijn's) was dignity because you're a human being, whether you're in rags or in the soup line, or whoever you are.
>
> We had part of a summer off and we traveled around. Cardijn was having a terrific influence. It was a great thing that he came along. The church was rapidly going down the

drain. All over Europe, except maybe Ireland. The Communists were having a field day, I mean they were literally taking over by popular vote. . . .

Labor unions? The Church developed and had its own. To our view, it wasn't very effective. It was a stooge of the Church and the workers weren't going to Church, certainly not in great numbers. . . .

You were born in the working class and you stayed in the working class. There were no aspirations. A worker wasn't supposed to get out of the mine or the mill. He was reconciled to be what he was. That's why the worker thing, geared to the young workers, was so important. Cardijn started with the idea of bringing them out of the Middle Ages and his principal drive was to convince them that they had dignity, and dignity didn't come with money or class. It came because God created you as a human being, and you were equal to the bishop or the pope or the king or anybody. They'd had no idea of their worth as a human being.[24]

Impressed by the tremendous Christian spirit which he observed among the Jocists he visited, Kanaly had become an ardent supporter of Cardijn and an almost evangelistic salesman for the movement after his ordination. His great desire to spread the Jocist idea was undiminished by the failure of the pilgrimage. In December 1939, Louise Hicksman, a member of his first cell in Ponca City, informed priests on their mailing list that the Oklahoma group was planning a national constitution, gave instructions on how to start a cell, and printed a series of social inquiries to be used by all the cells in the United States. They were preparing a national publication, and, because Kanaly was stationed there, Oklahoma for the present was to be the national headquarters. They apparently had the conviction that the movement was off to a running start.

In his column which appeared in *Our Sunday Visitor*, Vincent Mooney, director of the Youth Bureau of NCWC, noted that Kanaly had developed YCW groups in the Oklahoma area and was making contact with other groups. "Considerable experimentation is being done in order to adapt the JOC idea to the American scene. Those interested in the Young Christian Workers' movement are warned lest their enthusiasm run away with their better judgment." Mooney explained that the YCW could not be developed overnight and without a trained leadership capable of directing parochial units, it would be impossible to accomplish anything worthwhile.[25]

Most of the cities, like Toledo where numbers were growing, discouraged Kanaly's suggestion for a national study week, citing their need to feel their way in adapting the Jocist technique to American society. They appreciated Kanaly's energy in promoting the Young Christian Workers but felt he was moving too fast. His firsthand experience did much to recruit converts among the priests and he was of great help to Hillenbrand and others in clarifying the broad ideas. By this time, however, they needed practical help in getting started and training leaders.

A Real Jocist Chaplain, Louis Putz, C.S.C.

Fortunately for the Americans another priest arrived on the scene about this time who had experience with the European movement, and in fact had been a Jocist chaplain in France for six years. Louis Putz, just returned to the University of Notre Dame from Europe, was as enthusiastic about the movement as Kanaly, said Fr. Charles Marhoefer, a Chicago priest who met him while studying on the Notre Dame campus, but was "much more definite in his details and therefore, easier to understand."[26]

Louis Putz had come from Bavaria as a teenager in 1923 to study for the priesthood in the preparatory seminary at Notre Dame because he had an aunt there in the Holy Cross order. After graduation from the university in 1932, he was sent to Paris to study theology. While still a seminarian, he organized Jocist groups in a Communist section of the city where he was living. After ordination in 1936, Louis remained in France, teaching at the seminary in Le Mans and still working with the JOC in his free time. Then war broke out. Louis, a German citizen, was interned in a prisoner of war camp for three months, but with the help of a sympathetic French army commander and later an American immigration office (who queried him about Notre Dame football to establish his credibility), he finagled his way back to the United States. He was still recovering from his ordeal when Paul McGuire reached South Bend on his lecture tour. Motivated by

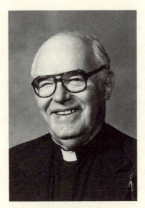

Rev. Louis J. Putz, C.S.C.

McGuire's talk, he decided to start a cell of Catholic Action Students among graduate students.[27]

By March 1940, Fr. Putz had his first cell underway. Within a year, the cells at Notre Dame, by then numbering fifty-five members, were publishing a bulletin which circulated widely through Catholic Action circles. Our groups at Chicago Normal School were on its mailing list and we had several visits from Notre Dame leaders who came to Chicago. In June 1941, Eugene Geissler, first president of the cells at Notre Dame, wrote a manual on the training of lay leaders based on Catholic Action theory as well as the actual experience of the militant leaders at Notre Dame. The apostolic experience described in those writings and the study weeks at Notre Dame attended by students from other schools exerted a tremendous influence on the developing Catholic Action Student movement.

Putz initiated many important ideas which served the specialized movements long and well. Not the least of these was Fides Publishers, which became an important small book publisher specializing in bringing to the United States the works of great Catholic thinkers in Europe that were previously untranslated and unavailable here. Putz proved to be an effective, knowledgeable resource for the new cells and their chaplains. As one commentator said, "Chicago was starving for such a man."[28] By this time, some of the priests who had been attending the priests' meetings in Chicago were becoming discouraged. The movement seemed to be getting nowhere and they had begun to lose interest.

Marhoefer invited Putz to the priests' meetings in Chicago and he first came in late May 1940. Several weeks later, he spoke to a large group of us from the established cells who crowded into a large parlor at the cathedral rectory. He called the JOC a "miracle of the twentieth century" and stressed that it was an apostolate of faith through service. In his meetings with the priests a few weeks earlier, Putz had characterized Catholic Action as "service to others. They already know enough about their religion. . . . We will not convert others by preaching or telling others of our religion, but we will do it by our service."[29]

From that time on, Putz provided material for the monthly priests' meetings and worked with Hillenbrand to strengthen the established cells. It was a liaison that boded well for the future of the movement.

Hillenbrand then arranged a national convention of priests interested in Jocism to meet in Chicago at the end of September 1940. The meeting, held at Holy Name Cathedral, was the first public conference specifically devoted to long-range planning. It drew McGuire, Kanaly, Vincent Mooney, and Henri Roy, O.M.I., from the French-speaking JOC in Manchester, New Hampshire. Participants discussed with McGuire a manual he planned to publish and advance copies were to be distributed to priests who had cells in various parts of the country. For reasons unknown, the manual was never published.

The Chicago chaplains felt a need for more training and Fr. Martin Farrell was chosen to plan the priests' meetings and to develop an instructional program. Many priests were ignorant of basic principles and lacked experience in working with the cells. On January 16, 1941, the first issue of a new publication appeared, the *Catholic Action Priests' Bulletin* written largely by Farrell, but under the direction of Msgr. Hillenbrand.[30] From its first appearance, the *Bulletin* set forth a synthesis of the Catholic Action cell movement: the work of the cells, the formation of leaders, the priests' role in the lay apostolate, the necessity of Catholic Action as outlined by Pius XI and the importance of the Jocist methods. Throughout, the cell movement was shown to be the embodiment of the specific wishes of the Holy Father. The *Priests' Bulletin* soon spread among priests and seminarians nationwide. Its success in establishing a sound intellectual basis for the movement had much to do with the gradual acceptance of Msgr. Reynold Hillenbrand as a national leader of priests in Catholic Action.

Notes

1   Martin Farrell in a recorded conversation with the author, June 6, 1986.
2   Gerard Weber, recorded conversation with author, October 2, 1985. Fr. Weber was a leading chaplain with the Christian Family Movement and pioneered a series of catechetical books for adults.
3   Farrell to the author, *op. cit.*
4   Donald Runkle, recorded conversation with author, October 24, 1985.
5   Mrs. George Fell, quoted by Dennis Robb, *Specialized Catholic Action, 1936–1949*, unpublished doctoral dissertation submitted to University of Minnesota, 1972, p. 30.
6   John A. Ryan formulated the "Bishops' Program of Social Reconstruction" in 1919. It was very radical in its day because of the proposals it advanced, like the minimum wage, limits on child labor, and old-age insurance for workers. Eleven of its twelve proposals were eventually passed into law, though with no particular help from individual Catholics.
7   See Dennis Robb, *op. cit.*, pp. 55–68, for a full treatment of this important conference.
8   Pius XI in *Quadragesimo Anno*, 1941.
9   John Hayes, quoted by Robb, *op. cit.*, pp. 70–71.
10 Bishop Edwin O'Hara, quoted by Robb, *op. cit.*, p. 71.
11 Msgr. Donald Kanaly, Summer School of Catholic Action for Priests, St. Mary of the Lake Seminary, Mundelein, Illinois. Mimeograph, 1938.
12 Msgr. Reynold Hillenbrand to Kanaly, November 17, 1938. Hillenbrand papers in University of Notre Dame archives (hereafter cited as UND archives).
13 Reply of Kanaly to Hillenbrand, n.d. UND archives.
14 Hillenbrand to Hayes, May 3, 1939. Hillenbrand papers, UND archives.
15 Mimeographed letter from Kanaly to "Dear Father," May 1939.
16 *Ibid.*
17 Hillenbrand to Kanaly, June 30, 1939. Hillenbrand papers, UND archives.
18 Conversation between Hillenbrand and Kanaly cited by Robb, from interview with Hillenbrand, June 10, 1970, *op. cit.*, pp. 93–94.
19 Hillenbrand to Kanaly, June 30, 1939. Hillenbrand papers, UND archives.
20 Hillenbrand to Kanaly, *op. cit.* UND archives.
21 Mimeographed letter of Kanaly to "Dear Father," July 5, 1939. Hillenbrand papers, UND archives.
22 Paul McGuire, "The Catholic Opportunity in Modern America," *Columbia*, August 1939, p. 17.
23 Kanaly to author, recorded conversation, November 30, 1985.
24 *Ibid.*
25 Vincent Mooney, "Leads for Leaders," *Our Sunday Visitor*, February 18, 1940, p. 7.
26 Charles J. Marhoefer to Hillenbrand, February 1940. Hillenbrand papers, UND archives.
27 Vincent Geise, "Chaplain to the Working Apostolate," *Today*, November 1954, p. 3.

[28] Robb, *op. cit.*, p. 105.
[29] Martha Stoeck, handwritten notebook, June 1940. UND archives.
[30] Farrell to author, taped conversation, June 6, 1986.

3

Observe, Judge, and Act

The easiest part of this new lay movement for people to understand was the small group base. The graphic picture of the Church as the Mystical Body of Christ made the concept of the cell very clear. Moreover, the support of the small group was invaluable when members attempted to influence others.

In cities where Paul McGuire had spoken, those who responded to the call for action immediately divided into "cells." In the early days, most of the persons involved met in central locations because they came from different parts of town. Only gradually did cells spread into outlying parishes. In San Francisco, members met at the downtown parish of St. Boniface for many years, but they broke into small groups in various parts of a large hall to study the New Testament and conduct their social inquiry. In other cities, cells spread to other locations as they found additional priests to be chaplains. The presence of a chaplain was considered essential.

It was more difficult to understand and learn the inquiry method: See, Judge, and Act. All of us who became cell members in the late thirties were intrigued by the idea that we should make the world more Christian, but our notion of problems usually centered on matters of religious observance and moral behavior. This is apparent from reports of action from some of the early cells. What McGuire described as a simple technique was not so simple when we were not used to looking clearly at the world and had no idea where to start.

A large loose-leaf binder of minutes kept by the secretary of one Chicago working girls' cell from July 1939 to December 1940[1] reveals a fairly typical story. At their first meeting, the girls decided to read from Frank Sheed's *Map of Life* at each meeting "to get to know our religion." Then came the inquiry. This turned out to be a reporting of problems noted or questions that came up in conversation about religion which the girls couldn't answer. For action, it was decided to write a letter to *Look* magazine, objecting to an article on birth control by Margaret Sanger. Two girls were assigned to look up answers to questions they had been asked about the Catholic religion.

Each week the group used the Sunday Gospel for their New Testament discussion and drew a conclusion applied to the work of Catholic Action. For example, when the Gospel of St. Matthew, 22, v. 35–46, cited Christ's answer to the Pharisees about the great commandment of love of God and its corollary about love of neighbor, the conclusion drawn was, "As Christ was able to answer the Pharisees in such a way that they could find no fault or reason for contention, so we should try to grow in knowledge and faith so we too could find satisfactory answers."[2] This conclusion reveals the mindset of the members. A group supposedly involved in apostolic action apparently missed the key idea in the passage about love of one's neighbor.

Gradually, bits of "social" action appeared in the minutes. It was reported that there were cliques in the local parish sodality, and the girls agreed to spread around and help break them up. On another occasion, M.J. Mooney talked to a young man at work, "in the interest of Catholic Action, of course," and after she gave him a copy of the sodality magazine, *Queen's Work*, he called on her twice! Lucky M.J.

By the time the group had been meeting a year, several new members had been added and the girls had learned a lot of answers to what today might be called trivia questions. Details about religious belief and observance were of primary concern. The group by now consisted of a department store cashier, two telephone operators, a bank page girl, one general office worker, and one girl who was unemployed.

On June 28, 1940, members of the group attended the meeting of lay leaders at Holy Name Cathedral where Fr. Putz stressed the idea of service as a way of influencing others. It evidently sank in, for in the minutes of August 21, 1940, acts of service were reported for the first time. A few weeks later, moreover, one member went out of her way to sit next to a black person on a bus, even though there were plenty of empty seats. This incident indicated the beginning of a new awareness toward minorities. In the inquiry section of the meetings, members began to report on "doing Catholic Action," and "influencing people with whom we come in contact." In October 1940, one member came to the conclusion that "we are influenced by others around us more than we realize."

In the fall of 1940, the Chicago chaplains met with chaplains from throughout the country and agreed to a common meeting plan. They had been reading through reports from the cells and were appalled to find that many groups were not using the inquiry method at all. Cell members did not know what to look for and did not ask probing questions that would bring out facts. It was only after a year that the girls in the group just described began to look at what people were doing instead of answering their questions about religion.

Federations of Like Cells

After the national priests' meeting, the chaplains decided Chicago had so many assorted groups that the time was ripe to divide the cells into federations with a common background. Seven federations were established: high school girls, high school boys, teachers' college girls, college boys, working men, working women, and teachers. After the federations were formed, we elected officers and had monthly federation meetings attended by representatives from each cell. Three persons were chosen to put out a joint leaders' bulletin with sample inquiries for all the federations.

The first issue of the *Catholic Action Leaders' Bulletin* appeared in Chicago on November 27, 1940. The topic chosen for the first inquiry for workers was on the attitude of workers towards their employer and co-workers and looked at the matter of pride in one's work. Judgment questions asked how would Christ act if he worked in your place. What should the Christian attitude be towards work and one's fellow workers? It was suggested that actions should relate to ways to improve efficiency on the job and to foster better relations among fellow workers, including ways to be patient with those who are difficult to get along with, perhaps "offering it up" for them.

We at Chicago Normal, which by now had become Chicago Teachers' College, were already putting out our own leaders' bulletin. By the spring of 1941, we had had a Day of Recollection for over twenty girls and a Study Day at a local Catholic college. We had the advantage of a strong model, the Catholic Action Students at Notre Dame.

A major highlight in Chicago in June 1941 was the Summer School of Catholic Action held at the parish hall of Holy Name Cathedral. More than two hundred of us listened to Msgr. Hillenbrand and Fr. James Kilgallon, a local chaplain, talk about the meaning of the Mystical Body of Christ and how it related to the call to the lay apostolate. Monsignor's explanation of the dogma of supernatural life and the living reality of Christ's Mystical Body as the extension of Christ in time and in space was truly awesome. Ideas that were mere words before came alive. "The divine life which man has must penetrate human action. When this is done in an organized way, it is Catholic Action."[3]

Hillenbrand and Kilgallon spelled out an all-embracing conception of the specialized cells as a response to the call of the pope for lay action which encompassed spiritual life and apostolic action. Religion was more than a string of external practices, they explained. Lay action depended on a "profound Catholicity" which in turn rested upon a divine plan which assigned to each man his proper function. Although the cell movement was in its very early stages, they suggested that it was the instrument for social regeneration in the world.

This was the first time most of our local cell members had seen the Monsignor and in his quiet way he gave us a profound understanding of the truths behind what we were doing and a vision of great possibilities. The event touched all of us deeply, an experience repeated over the years when Monsignor spoke to other members of the specialized movements.

It is interesting to note at this point that, although the cell movement was identified as a "lay" movement, the chaplains were making the organizational decisions. In Chicago, chaplains under the guidance of Msgr. Hillenbrand were determined that the movement develop properly. Although they wanted the leaders to take initiative in the life problems they would see, judge, and act upon, it did not occur to them or to us that the lay leaders should be involved in organizational policy matters. We were still used to following rules set down by higher authority. Lay initiative came about gradually as we matured and met leaders from other places.

Each city evolved in its own way. About this time, the Toledo cells separated the men from the women and the students from the workers. The leader of each cell formed a Central Committee. They made a distinction between "militant" members who met weekly and "ordinary" members and recruits who met monthly with the cell members. All cells used the same inquiry. The first general inquiry printed in *The Cells* was on the subject of "Movies." Listed were five observation questions, but no judgment questions. Apparently the individual cells were expected to make their own judgments. Reports of action were sent to the Central Committee monthly and all the cells met quarterly in a "mass meeting."[4]

In June 1939 the major project of the cells, "preparing for Catholic Action," in San Antonio had been the establishment of a library downtown in a room lent them by St. Mary's University, which was also used as a meeting place. At the suggestion of Fr. Kanaly, who visited in April 1940, they divided their leadership group into a young men's group, a business girls' group, and a student group.[5] In May, they began to write separate inquiries for the men and the women. The first inquiries of the young men were on the existence of God and the young women looked at the effects of grace on personality.[6] It is not clear what the latter meant and one wonders how it could have been observed. Apparently they, too, were having difficulty understanding what it meant to observe facts. Their topics sound more like the subject of a study club than a matter of See, Judge, and Act.

In Brooklyn individual cells made up their own inquiries in the beginning, but gradually felt the need for a unified approach. They organized into a loosely knit federation led by an executive board made up of the original members who wrote the inquiry outlines. Having as a guide the Canadian inquiries, they tended to look at specific areas of concern from the beginning, but they too stressed the idea that action begins with oneself. Each leader was expected to keep a notebook and write down facts observed during the week, so the inquiry could be completed in forty minutes.[7]

In 1941 the Chicago priests were disturbed by the shortage of young men in the cells. Out of forty-two cells in a list circulated by Fr. Farrell at that time, only thirteen were composed of young men and eight of these were student groups. "The movement is top-heavy with girls," fretted a writer in the *Priests' Bulletin*. He went on:

> It is perfectly natural that this state of affairs should present
> itself. Girls are more easily interested in the movement

than boys. Material for girls' cells is readily at hand in every parish. On the other hand, boys have to be sold on the importance of the movement. They have to be talked into it. What is even harder, they have to be sought out first. They are not as much in evidence around the church as the girls. For those very reasons, however, it is much more important to get them into cells, to train leaders among the boy workers, if the movement is ever going to have the strength, the force it must have. It must be a masculine movement. It is the men, not the women, we are in danger of losing. Once we have the men we will have no difficulty in getting the women. But if it becomes a women's movement, we will never reach the men.... The drive this year is definitely to get boy worker cells.[8]

The big push, furthermore, was to get young men under the age of twenty-five who had jobs in factories. Their model was the French-speaking JOC in Canada and Manchester, New Hampshire, visited by some of the chaplains a few months before.

In 1930 Fr. Henri Roy, O.M.I., had started *Jeunesse Ouvriere Chretienne* in Montreal, Canada, among gang leaders in the slums, and from those beginnings a dynamic organization had developed in French-speaking Canada. After his initial success, Père Roy went to Belgium to study with Cardijn. On his return, the movement grew to huge proportions and groups were started among married couples, white-collar workers, and students. Soon after, he was invited by Bishop John B. Peterson of Manchester to develop the movement in the French-speaking parishes of New Hampshire.

Several years before Fr. Roy's arrival in Manchester, a few New Hampshire priests had started Jocist sections among young boys and girls who were dropping out of high school after a year or two and looking for work in the local textile mills. When the Second National Congress of the JOC was held in Montreal in 1939, the twenty-five thousand Canadians were joined by 150 Jocists from New Hampshire. When Fr. Roy arrived on the scene, the Manchester JOC really took off. On December 31, 1939, the diocesan council of the JOC held its first meeting. Immediately, they began to publish *La Jeunesse Ouvriere,* a monthly tabloid with Catholic news and opinion which was sold by young Jocists in the French-speaking parishes of New England. Before long, five thousand copies were being distributed each month.[9]

The spirited organization of Jocists had three thousand members throughout New England by the beginning of World War II. Members participated in major campaigns on family life, indecent movies and magazines, as well as a year-long campaign visiting families and encouraging them to send their children to Catholic schools and encouraging teen-agers to remain in school.

After visiting Manchester in 1944, an observer wrote:

In Manchester, New Hampshire, a group of young workers have taken up the banner of Christ and carry it into their homes and shops. They are most of them still in their teens. They work under great odds but with faith and determination. Their spirit is wonderful to behold. Their inspiration is an energetic priest, and their instrument the technique of the Jocists and the motive force behind their work, the zeal for souls, the true apostolic spirit. For four years they have been going out into the streets, into the pool rooms, down dark alleys, in their search for souls lost to Christ. They have talked in their homes, in their classrooms, and in their shops and mills. But they have talked little and acted much. They have taken things into their own hands. . . .

Their headquarters in an office in the center of Manchester is a busy place, day and night. People drop in at all hours of the day and night to discuss, to ask questions. . . . You are impressed by the tremendous activity that goes on in the office and the streets of the city. And, too, by the gayety and complete unself-consciousness. They are doing God's work and there is no thought of whether it is done according to the books or not. In fact, they are surprised and not a little amused when someone asks what books they have read on the subject. All day and far into the night, the work goes on—the preparing of the monthly magazine, of the monthly plans of action that go out to the leaders, of the three weekly papers for small mill towns which are general newspapers as well as subtle means of propaganda. . . .

You sit there listening to their conversation on what is said and done in their haunts, in the pool rooms, in bars, and on empty lots, and you learn about the facts of life in a mill town. You learn under what conditions they work in the mills. . . . Père Roy in true Jocist fashion remains in the background, but he always is on hand to advise and confess the youth that the workers bring in from the highways and byways.

The leaders are the young men and women who were themselves Father Roy's proteges not so long ago. The canny eye of Father has singled out those with the qualities of leadership, young people who are themselves workers in the mills. . . . It has spread out into the mill cities of New Hampshire and into Massachusetts and Rhode Island. They have made several attempts to bring it into the hands of the English-speaking population, but to no avail. Because of the problems of racial and economic differences peculiar to New England, there has been no success so far.

To the statement that the technique will not work among Americans, the answer is that the work is being done. . . . Are not all these young people Americans? They vehemently resent the inference that they are not Americans.[10]

Not everyone was as optimistic about the movement's chances in the United States. In 1938, Richard L. G. Deverall, editor of the *Christian Front*, on hearing about Jocism, had taken a survey of priests. Their consensus was, "It might work in Europe, but never here."[11] French-speaking New England was perceived as more culturally aligned to Quebec and old-country France. Its success there meant nothing to the average American priest.

Several Chicago priests had visited Manchester in 1940 and were tremendously impressed by the energy and the zeal of the young Jocists. They saw enthusiastic, apostolic teenagers, with little high school education, who worked in the mills. They were convinced that the English-speaking movement would never be a real movement without young factory workers. This, they agreed, was where the YCW emphasis should be.[12]

Several cells of factory workers were started in Chicago, and in December 1941 a mimeographed paper appeared entitled *Chicago's Young Catholic Workers*. It was written by factory workers Bud Chiappe and Ray Nowak from the local Hotpoint plant who were in a cell started by Fr. James Kilgallon. One of their first inquiries, which appeared in the third issue, was on the fellows' ideas of God. The next month's issue had an inquiry about the bias fellows had about priests. One of their suggested actions was to introduce some of the fellows to priests in the movement. "Some of these fellows never met priests like these before, ones who can talk their language, understand them."[13]

The Chicago Headquarters Open

In September 1941 the Chicago Catholic Action federations were given space in an old building next door to Holy Name Cathedral. Msgr. Joseph Morrison, pastor of the cathedral, had been supportive of the movement from the beginning and had generously allowed the priests to meet in his rectory. Portions of an old school building on the church property were used by the Catholic School Board and the office of the Confraternity of Christian Doctrine, which coordinated religious education classes for public school children. A large room on the second floor had sewing machines in it and was used by the women who repaired the robes for the choir boys and altar boys. Monsignor said the federation could use it on days when the women weren't there, for meetings and a place to keep their files. Two years later, they were given larger quarters on the empty third floor. Except for times when it was overrun by boisterous choir boys, that broken-down old building at 3 East Chicago Avenue became "a home away from home" for many of the cell leaders. Centrally located, it was ideal for the members who came from many parts of the city to plan their meetings and write their programs. It also became a favorite stopping-off place for visitors—priests, seminarians, and lay leaders from other cities who happened to be passing through town.

In 1943 Loretta Fenton, a pert, five-foot graduate of the high school movement, became the first lay person in the Midwest to devote herself totally to the specialized apostolate. She decided that the high schoolers needed someone free to help train new leaders after school hours. She was also determined to find leaders in lower-paying, nonwhite-collar jobs where she too was convinced the real future of the young workers' movement lay. She worked part time as a waitress and spent three days a week maintaining the office at 3 East, serving the needs of the various Catholic Action cells in the city. The federations contributed small amounts of money to pay for a phone and office expenses. Later Loretta worked in a factory and organized a team among her fellow workers while continuing her own growth as a leader in a working girls' cell. She traveled to Canada and New England to learn from the established groups there, and she helped to strengthen new groups in visits to cities around the country. Fr. Donald Runkle, federation chaplain of the high school girls, encouraged her efforts and raised money to subsidize her travel expenses. In 1945 she began to work full time at the headquarters.

Stritch Meets with Chicago Chaplains

Late in 1942 Samuel Stritch, who became archbishop of Chicago after Mundelein's death in 1939, met with the Chicago chaplains. The time for merely discussing Catholic Action is past, he said. "The purpose for gathering today is to give unity to the movement and to extend the work. It is good for the priests to meet and exchange their experiences and plan their leadership intelligently."[14]

He cautioned them to be prudent in developing the cell structure, for although it could be a blessing for the Church, it also could be dangerous. The possibility existed that leaders could become too much involved in exterior work without an accompanying spiritual growth. Mere enthusiasm would not insure fitness. He saw the movement as a quiet work behind the scenes and he stressed the necessity for careful direction by the priests so that the leaders would develop a deep and sound spiritual life. The people in the movements should have a great sense of realism, rugged piety, and much common sense. He further stated that the cell movement should work through the parishes, wherever possible. He closed by saying that there should be no publicity. "That would spoil it. It is quiet work, even unknown to the general Catholic public. It must be under the surface to be effective."[15]

The stress on careful training of lay people and the restriction on publicity were the controlling messages. Though the cardinal appeared to support the idea of lay action, he also wanted to allay the concerns of conservative pastors who were disturbed by the activist young priests coming out of the seminary with new ideas about social action and lay initiative.

A Wartime Movement

Just as things were progressing well, the storm clouds broke and the United States officially entered World War II. By the middle of

1942 male leaders were being drafted in every city where the movement had started. By 1943 the movement among young men was virtually shut down. Only San Francisco, where many servicemen were stationed, continued to have men.

For all intents and purposes the movement in the United States became a movement of young women for three years. All was not lost, however, because the chaplains gained experience and significant advances were made in developing the cell technique.

By 1943 the roster of working girls' cells in Chicago numbered fifteen, and many of the members in those cells were nearing the age of thirty. The big concern among the priests was that girls graduating from the student groups and going to work would be turned off by the age difference between themselves and the older girls. As early as 1941 priests had worried about the presence of pious older girls with a "do-good" attitude.

> It is easier to form the spirit of conquest and the vital enthusiasm so necessary . . . in those who are under the age of 25. . . . Older girls won't accept a new idea and many of them have a "do-good" idea about the apostolate. . . . They are definitely frightening away the younger element. We started out to have a real Catholic Action of youth. The younger girls actually feel out of place. . . . In Europe, a leader said they never admitted anyone over 25 because girls over this age are more interested in searching out a husband. . . . I did not say that Catholic Action excludes the older people. I merely make the plea that we should give our time to the younger people. I think we can find more success with them.[16]

To get around this problem, the Chicago priests in late 1942 began a new federation of "Junior Working Girls" for recent graduates from the student groups. By 1943 there were four cells in the federation. I was invited to join one that met at Holy Name Cathedral. Because I was interested in seeing the movement develop among ordinary workers, I had taken a job in a war plant rather than go into teaching. Donald Runkle, the chaplain of the high school girls' federation, took over as chaplain of the new federation. In August 1943 we published the first issue of our leaders' bulletin, entitled *Catholic Action: Young Working Girls,* and I became its editor.

Then another problem. Runkle had strong feelings about the kind of working girls that should be recruited into the movement. Because most of the members were Catholic high school graduates in office jobs, he felt they were too middle-class and should not be confused with the working girls in factories and shops that he felt the movement was really designed for. The result: we were told to change our "Young Working Girls Federation" to "Young Business Girls Federation." Some of us did not agree, but we were overruled by the priests. We changed the title on our *Leaders' Bulletin* to Junior Business Girls, but we continued to talk about working girls in the body of the paper. When we featured an article entitled "Heaven Help the Working Girl," Runkle returned it to me with the word "working" encircled and "Who?" penciled in the margin.[17]

Those of us who had jobs in war plants recruited nonoffice workers as team members, but no cells anywhere in the country at that time, except in French-speaking New England, were predominantly factory workers. Fr. James Kilgallon, the chaplain who did form a cell of male factory workers in Chicago in 1941, told me more than forty years later, "Those were the days when we were trying to reestablish the European class system in the United States!" I felt vindicated for my resistance to the idea that office girls and factory workers could not be mixed, especially if they were from the same neighborhood. When trying to organize a cell among workers in the factory where I worked, I discovered that most of them were middle-aged married women whose daughters were working in offices because they had gone to high school.

I did form a team of four girls in the department where I worked. Among other things, we followed up inquiries on the dignity of women by taking a stand and getting our women co-workers to join us in opposing indecent language and innuendoes about sex which were common among our male co-workers on the assembly lines. We became close friends with several black girls who worked with us and defied tradition by taking them to dinner with us in all-white restaurants and on another occasion going with them to the Regal Theater on the black South Side to hear Billy Eckstein, a prominent black singer. This was a result of our growing awareness of the dignity of all people that we absorbed from our study of the Gospels. We did our best to break down the prejudices against minorities that we had grown up with. After some time observing the apostolic spirit and the friendly warmth of our little group, one of our co-workers decided to return to the Church she had left many years before.

Developing the Inquiry Program

From 1940 to 1944 the leaders of the Senior Business Girls wrote their own inquiries. The content varied from year to year but there was growth in their awareness of problems and their plans for action. In one year, they were concerned with the use of leisure time. Another year was spent on a review of the Ten Commandments, dealing with problems like swearing and stealing.

The Catholic Action Students at the University of Notre Dame, in the meantime, had developed a program of inquiries on problems related to individualism versus the common good. This prompted the Senior Business Girls to look at the problems of individualism in the business world. They soon realized that workers in offices were very self-serving. Observation revealed that workers were often paid different salaries for the same work. One did not even tell her best friend when she got a raise. It was also one of the reasons business girls were not interested in unions.

In 1944, under the strong leadership of their new president, Edwina Hearn, the seniors did a series of inquiries on problems related to the common good. This led to looking at the attitudes of office workers towards unions and strikes. After considerable discussion and study on the teachings of the encyclicals regarding the dignity of the working person, action centered on developing a "union mind" and talking to others about unions.

In the meantime, we juniors were concerned with problems which arose from a lack of respect for women. Our inquiries on "The Dignity of Women" were distributed monthly in a four-page leaflet printed at St. Meinrad Abbey in Indiana. In February 1944 our *Leaders' Bulletin* appeared in a new format with a union label. This was a result of indignation by Ed Marciniak[18] and the Catholic Labor Alliance,[19] our neighbors down the hall at 3 East, who advised us of our responsibility as Christians to support organized labor, even though it cost more. By this time, a growing list of subscribers to our bulletin at one dollar a year helped to pay the printer. We had a lot to learn. Even some of our chaplains at the time did not have a "union mind." It was probably one of the first times we recognized what it meant to have a Christian social conscience. That was progress.

The First Study Weekend to Launch a New Program

In the spring of 1944 the Senior and Junior Business Girls decided to use the same inquiry program. We launched the new program at a study weekend at Childerly, an estate that belonged to an organization of Catholics at the University of Chicago. The house manager, Johanna Doniat, was very interested in Catholic Action and through her good graces, Childerly became a regular meeting place for Catholic Action leaders and priests. It consisted of two large homes on a small farm about twenty-five miles outside Chicago. A small chapel at the end of the apple orchard added to the facilities that made it an ideal place for retreats and weekend gatherings.

We invited leaders we had met or corresponded with from other cities to attend our Study Weekend to be held on the three-day Fourth of July weekend. Leaders came from Toledo, Cleveland, Green Bay, and Appleton, Wisconsin. Priests read about the weekend meeting in the *Priests' Bulletin*. Fr. Smith, an oblate from Toronto, Canada, came down with two leaders from the fledgling YCW in English-speaking Canada. Fr. Frank Donnelly from the seminary in Brooklyn, New York, came to observe. Fr. Putz came from South Bend to give us a Day of Recollection before the study part of the weekend began. The program theme centered on the problems related to the business girl's outlook on work in general and her job in particular.

The meeting of 1944 was significant because it established a degree of unity among the cells in the several cities who sent delegates to Chicago. We prepared a comprehensive report of the talks and discussions of the weekend and, in September, Toledo repeated the study week locally and tailored the program for their own use. Others who were at the Childerly meeting began to use the inquiries we printed in our leaders' bulletin.

In New York that same year, inquiries centered on influencing working girls to develop their womanly talents. One action of the Manhattan cell was a series of four lectures on marriage, Christian dress and dressmaking, recreation, and Gregorian chant.

Developing a Common Terminology

During the mid-forties Catholic Action cells continued as best they could, hampered, of course, by the complications brought on by the war. There was no communication with the Jocist leadership in Europe and though the movement, in theory, knew no barriers of language, race, nationality, or geographical boundaries, there was confusion in organization and in terminology. The Americans depended on the French-Canadians who had developed the Jocist movement extensively, but, ironically, a lack of communication between the French and English in Canada sent English-speaking priests and leaders to the United States looking for help.

Various cities were working independently, trying to adapt the movement to the American condition. Local groups often used terminology that was unique to their own locale. To overcome the resulting confusion, Fr. Charles Marhoefer accepted the task of preparing a glossary of terms for all the specialized movements. It was formally adopted by the chaplains from twelve cities when they met at Childerly in November 1944. French words, such as *militants* for leaders and *milieu* for the local environment, were eliminated. It was also decided to use the names common in England: Young Christian Workers for the cells of young workers in the country, Young Christian Students for the students. The cells of married men and married women did not change until 1947, when the cells of married men and women merged into a couples' movement, first called Christian Family Action, and then the Christian Family Movement.

At the end of 1944 the seniors and juniors in Chicago merged and formed the Business Girls' Federation as a "subdivision" of the Young Christian Workers. This was to placate those who thought that someday there would be groups that were truly "working girls" in blue collar jobs. A year later we changed our name to "office workers." That seemed a little less phony. Chalk one up for the lay leaders. We were beginning to make some organizational decisions.

When the second Chicago Study Week was held in July 1945, it attracted thirty-five representatives from six cities. We thought we had a terrific program theme. As a follow-up to the problems based on individualism among workers, "Family Spirit in the Office" seemed a logical next step. We worked long hours developing a program of inquiries comparing the work community to the family. In our naivete, it seemed a good parallel: The relation of employees to the employer was like that of children to a parent, the relation of employees to one another like those of brothers and sisters.

When we showed the program to Msgr. Hillenbrand the evening before the study week began, he set us back on our heels with a vehement, "No! This is all wrong!" We were about to recommend a program which taught paternalism, a concept that was totally in contradiction to the idea that workers were persons of dignity with rights. They were not to be treated by their employers as "children." We got a quick lesson and spent most of that night rewriting the whole program. Scheduled speakers were called in and with the help of Fr. John Egan,[20] our newly appointed federation chaplain, and the monsignor, they rewrote and corrected their talks. To this day, the leaders involved remember with chagrin their initiation into the realities of the labor movement. Afterwards, Msgr. Hillenbrand suggested that Ed Marciniak of the Catholic Labor Alliance and Ed Hackett, one of the CLA members and head of the telephone workers' union, conduct classes in labor for us before we wrote the inquiries on work life.

Fr. John Egan and the Girls' General Council
at Barat College, 1948.

One positive outcome of the Study Week was the decision to publish a small magazine to spell out the objectives of the Young Christian Workers and to spread among young working girls everywhere the ideas developed in our inquiries. The first issue of *Impact— A Magazine for Working Girls* came out as a bimonthly in November 1945. It later became a monthly and distribution of the magazine became an ongoing action.

The first issue clearly identified the thinking of the girls' YCW at that time. "Adam Fell for Eve" by Edwina Hearn was a sprightly article which stressed the "natural" role of women as collaborators in the plan of God.

> Women typify real beauty in the world—and love. God made us that way. Our job is entirely different from our male counterparts. God would never have entrusted the important job of Motherhood to a bunch of helpless clinging vines, but neither did He picture the mothers and potential mothers of the world as strong, stalwart Amazons. He planned for us to work along with men as helpmates, not as competitors. Women are intended to be the "soul of society." . . . Our task in society is to make men aware of the truth and beauty and goodness of God by reflecting that beauty and goodness in ourselves. . . .
>
> Women doing strictly womanly things is something to strive for, but, unfortunately, we must face the fact that under our present economic setup some of us have to be employed in offices, and that "some of us" make up the vast army of business girls. Can we reflect the beauty and goodness of God, even while working in an office?[21]

An article by June Gardner of the Catholic Labor Alliance reflected on the apathy of many girls to the economic structure and the need to support legislation on full employment, fair employment practices, and a minimum wage.

Joan O'Dwyer of the Toledo YCW followed with an article calling for the recruitment of strong leaders as apostles. "We must convince them that the YCW is not just another organization, but a dynamic movement of lay leaders fighting to bring the world back to Christ. We must convince them that it is a definite responsibility given us by Christ Himself. Above all, we must make them see the need in the world today and make them want to do something about it. This is our challenge."[22]

Differences Arise

As the movement grew among the young women, the leadership of the Chicago cells did not go unchallenged. Several groups on the East Coast, influenced largely by the Ladies of the Grail, began to develop a different point of view about the apostolate among young women. The Ladies of the Grail were members of a quasi-religious order who came to America from Holland in 1941 to develop an apostolic movement among young lay women. They sought out leaders in the developing apostolic movements and offered to assist in their training. Dr. Lydwine Van Kersbergen and Joan Overboss were robust, strong-minded women with definite opinions about the role of women in society. They felt strongly that American women were being masculinized by working in factories and offices. To be truly Christian, a woman should dress modestly, wear little makeup, and do "womanly work," primarily in the home.

The Ladies conducted retreats and training programs at first at Doddridge Farm in the Chicago area and later on a farm in Loveland, Ohio, called Grailville. Cell members from New York, Brooklyn, Toledo, and Chicago were among those who attended. Dr. Van Kersbergen developed innovative methods to form these young women in a spirituality based on participation in the liturgical worship of the Church and a recognition of their unique dignity as women, as nurturers, in society.

Those of us from Chicago developed a keener insight into the richness of the liturgy and a new perspective and appreciation of ourselves as women. The inquiry theme on womanliness we juniors developed in 1944 was a direct outgrowth of the Grail influence. The idea, however, that women should make bread, wear handwoven material, and stop using cosmetics was a little too much. We in Chicago were convinced that we should be "leaven," immersed in the world in which we lived and worked. We felt that the external behavior and dress encouraged by the Grail would have a negative affect on our co-workers. That was not our idea of leadership and "penetration of the masses."

Other persons, however, were very impressed by the Grail approach to Christian life for young women. One of these was Fr. James Coffey, a Catholic Action chaplain in Brooklyn. He became a strong advocate of the Grail and sent many young women to them for training. In New York and Brooklyn, growth of the cells was seriously affected by this difference in understanding of what constituted the Christian ideal. Fr. Coffey and Fr. Donnelly both taught at the seminary in Brooklyn and each competed for the support of other priests. Fr. Coffey pushed the Grail view of "womanly" work, and Donnelly, influenced by Msgr. Hillenbrand and the application of papal social teachings related to work as outlined in the Chicago *Priests' Bulletin*, agreed with the thinking of the Chicago leaders that young women should bring Christ into the world of work.[23]

The New York groups were also influenced by the thinking of Dorothy Day and Carol Jackson, the founding editor of *Integrity* magazine, an outspoken Catholic magazine which bemoaned secularism and commercialism. Carol formed a group called "The Outer Circle" and held discussions on lay theology in her apartment. She was a sometime member of the Manhattan cell in the beginning and many New York cell members attended "The Outer Circle" discussions.

Neither Dorothy Day nor Carol agreed with the Jocist idea of being a "leaven" in modern industrial and commercial society. Like the Ladies of the Grail, they advocated a society in which women could find fulfillment in the traditional role of women as care-givers and homemakers. Though they admitted it might be necessary for some women to work in offices and factories, it was not the ideal Christian way. As a result, some New York cell members did not like the inquiry programs developed in Chicago that focused on problems "in the office."[24]

In New York City, Fr. Francis Wendell, O.P., who in the beginning almost had to be coerced into acting as chaplain by the first eager group of Catholic Actionists in Manhattan, became a devoted chaplain who gave freely of his time to the leaders of the group that set up headquarters at 1335 Second Avenue. He tried to keep an even balance in the dispute. As editor of *The Torch* magazine, he often published articles on the developing movement of Young Christian Workers. Some of his articles on the training of lay leaders were gathered in a book entitled *The Formation of a Lay Apostle*, which was of great value to chaplains in later years. Many of the young women he trained—Mary Tuohy, Caroline Pezzullo, Rita Joseph, Josephine Furnari, Dorothy Curtin, and Marylu Langan—later became organizers and officers on the national YCW staff which came into existence in the late forties.

Reaching Out with Services

As the cells developed more awareness and learned how to reach out to others more effectively, they began to organize group services to meet needs they observed. Such services included parish libraries, homes for girls who needed a place to live and educational programs on social problems, and marriage preparation. In the process, many members developed leadership skills and talents they didn't know they had.

Two Chicago leaders, Mary O'Neill and Catherine O'Connor, had for some time been thinking about setting up a home for working girls who needed a place to live. The Chicago priests discouraged them because they did not think they were ready for such a responsibility. When Mary and Katie spoke to Fr. Louis Putz about their idea at the 1944 Study Week, he invited them to come down to South Bend. He had been wanting to see the YCW start in South Bend, but being committed to his work at the university and the student cells there, he had not been able to do anything about it. Having two experienced leaders was the perfect answer. Mary O'Neill moved to South Bend first, followed by Katie a few months later. Over the years, the YCW house on Taylor Street became a center for Young Christian Workers as well as a home for girls who needed a place to live.

A year later the girls in Chicago rented an apartment about a mile from the 3 East headquarters. Irene Moloney took over as "house mother." For five years, the apartment on North LaSalle Street took in girls in need of a place to stay. Some were working girls sent by priests; others were YCW contacts who moved to Chicago from other cities. It gradually evolved into a home for leaders who worked full time when the national headquarters was established in Chicago in late 1947.

In New York the YCW girls rented an apartment on the fifth floor of the tenement walk-up above the store front that was their meeting place. It was originally intended as a place where members could stay overnight after late meetings. Members who worked in Manhattan but lived in Brooklyn or the Bronx had a long trip home and the rent was cheap. It too eventually became a place for girls who needed a place to live in a healthy, congenial atmosphere. No New York leaders themselves lived there permanently, however, and after about five years, the apartment was given over to the "temporary" occupants.

Major services that developed in several cities were courses in homemaking skills, various crafts, marriage preparation, and social problems. The first of these educational programs was initiated in Cleveland to meet the needs and interests observed among young working girls. The courses were conducted at the cathedral and proved so popular they were later taken over by the archdiocese as a permanent service of adult education. Lectures and discussions on Christian values and social teachings were also a popular service of the Manhattan cell.

After the war the leaders in Toledo started the Toledo Council of Catholic Youth as an organization for out-of-high-school young people. It became part of the Catholic Youth Organization in the diocese. Once the Council was established and began to provide the activities and services needed, the YCW leaders were free to go on to other things.

The Cleveland and Toledo projects, both of which were eventually taken over by others, are examples of the thinking of many cell leaders. It was not their intention to run everything that needed to be set up. They were indeed acting as leaven, as initiators of action, as starters.

In other cases the cells worked through organizations already functioning. The Chicago groups in the forties did not organize marriage preparation courses. Instead they supported and sent young people to the Pre-Cana Conferences for engaged couples which were started by the married women's cells in conjunction with the Cana Conference.

The services of the San Francisco YCW, on the other hand, were definitely flying the YCW banner. In this, they reflected the public stance taken by the French-speaking Jocists in Canada and Manchester, New Hampshire. Situated as they were in a port of embarkation, the Young Christian Workers there offered many kinds of services. In 1944, Bob Anderson, a Navy veteran who had visited many of the Catholic Action groups in Canada and the United States, was hired by the St. Boniface section as a full-time manager for the Catholic

Servicemen's Center established in the parish by the Young Christian Workers.

In a letter to Archbishop Mitty dated February 7, 1945, Fr. Paul Meinecke gave the following report:

> Following our Archbishop's general mandate to get Catholic Action going in every parish, Father Lawrence Mutter, pastor of St. Boniface Church, appointed Father Paul Meinecke to organize Catholic Action at St. Boniface in January 1939. . . .
>
> We were careful to follow the papal directives on Catholic Action while at the same time we wanted to follow Canon Cardijn's advice not to copy European Jocism slavishly. We have worked out an American type of Jocism adapted to the needs of our American working youth. . . .
>
> Our experience and growth of our group here in San Francisco, from a single cell of five to the present membership of over five hundred, have convinced us that American youth can be trained and led to undertake their responsibility in the lay apostolate of Catholic Action.
>
> The aim and purpose of our organization is to group, train, assist, and represent the young workers, so that they may re-Christianize the whole of their own lives, the whole of their environment, and the whole mass of their fellow workers. It is specialized Catholic Action, the participation of the laity in the apostolate of the Hierarchy. Our files bear witness to the Apostolic accomplishments of both our civilian members, as well as our many service members at home and overseas.[25]

The report then lists their activities in various categories: *religious*, weekly cell meetings, classes in apologetics and Christian doctrine, monthly Communion and Holy Hour plus two or three open retreats a year; *cultural and social*, weekly dances, glee club, camera club, picnics, and sports (including a baseball team that competed under the YCW banner in city tournaments); and *economic*, a credit union and occupational and financial counseling.

Jim McLaughlin, general manager of the YCW Center at St. Boniface after Anderson, said years later that he thought the YCW was supposed to meet *all* the social and religious needs of young people.[26] This, of course, was a very different concept from that understood by the leaders in the East and Midwest. Communication over great distances made such differences unavoidable.

The Status at War's End

When World War II ended in August of 1945 there were three major interpretations of the Young Christian Workers: San Francisco, Chicago, and New York. Leaders in the three cities were dedicated to the lay apostolate but differed somewhat in philosophy. San Francisco had the big numbers and popular services to the point where midwestern leaders wondered if they really used the social inquiry. Chicago and the midwestern cities close to them were dedicated to *quietly* influencing the working environment, helping individuals with problems, doing personal acts of service, and improving poor working conditions when they could. Some strong, outspoken leaders in the New York area favored the development of a Christian way of life outside what they saw as the unholy and irredeemable atmosphere of commercialism and industry, though not all the New York members were convinced that this was the best answer.

All of us throughout the country looked forward to the peacetime expansion of the movement when we could better respond to the papal call for Catholic lay action. Such expansion required the recruitment and formation of young workingmen in leadership roles in order to have the right balance. This was just a matter of time.

As the war came to an end there was cause for optimism. We had deepened our awareness of the needs and problems of young workers through the social inquiries. We had learned to take positive action and organize services for young working girls. Chicago had become a center of initiative and planning.

Former Members Look Back

Perhaps I really began as a team member in high school YCS. Then, when I graduated, Fr. Louis Putz approached me with "Are you happy with what you are doing? Do you think working girls have any problems?" Next move: I was attending weekly YCW meetings. Blithely, when Father asked us to come next week with a list of our friends, I came with a list of 70+. How was I to know that he would say, "Now you will use your lists as a contact list, your team. You will help change their lives." 70+? Observe, Judge, and Act. Acts of service. See Christ in others. I got so I couldn't even sit on my way to work on the bus. Crowded buses, and just when I got comfortably seated, there was Christ standing beside me and He needed a seat. (South Bend)

Being a Young Christian Worker was a very important and wonderful time of my life at that time and, as I look back now, exerted a great influence—for the better—on my life. This was during World War II and our group at St. Boniface Church served as a meeting place for many Catholic service personnel as well as for many civilians from the San Francisco Bay area. Many excellent social and recreational activities were offered, which drew us to the real meaning of the center. . . . Being a Young Christian Worker, I was able to bring a more Christian influence to my workplace and with those I associated with outside of the office. Out of that experience I know I grew as a Christian and became involved in activities which gave me many opportunities to put my earlier training into practice. (San Francisco)

I think the inquiry method of "Observe, Judge, Act" cannot be equaled as a method of spiritual formation. By always observing our environment in the light of the gospels and assuming responsibility to act as Christians in that environment, we learned or acquired habits and convictions and a way of life that would not leave us. The inquiry may have been the best part of specialized Catholic Action. It can form individual consciences and those individuals will affect those around them throughout their lives—families, neighbors, co-workers. (Cleveland)

I feel the specialized Catholic Action movements were planting the seeds for involvement of the laity—lay ministries, etc.—since Vatican II. Now we are called all together "The People of God."

During those days, we felt good just to be "auxiliaries of the Church." I still reap its fruits and hopefully share them, too! (Toledo)

I believe the YCW completely changed me. It opened up the idea that one should be a leader, even in a small way; that laymen were important in the Church, not just the hierarchy. . . . The necessity to tell at the meeting what action had been taken forced me to do something between meetings, no matter how small. Otherwise, I would have been tempted to put it off. (Chicago)

Notes

1   Binder of minutes of St. Joan of Arc cell given to author by Donald Runkle, November 1985. Zotti papers.
2   Minutes, St. Joan of Arc cell, meeting of September 22, 1939.
3   Notebook kept by Martha Stoeck. UND archives.
4   *The Cells,* December 27, 1940. UND archives.
5   *Cells of Restoration,* San Antonio, Texas, Vol. 1, No. 1, 1940. UND archives.
6   *Cells of Restoration,* San Antonio, Vol. 1, No. 3, n.d. UND archives.
7   Program for the Session of the American Jocists, Rev. James A. Green, Forest Hills, Long Island, New York, March 10, 1941.
8   *Catholic Action Priests' Bulletin,* Vol. 2, No. 2, October 1941.
9   Facts of early Franco-American history from recorded meeting with former Jocists, Manchester, New Hampshire, March 16, 1986. Bound set of *Jeunesse Ouvriere* in Zotti papers.
10 Leonard Austin, "Miracles in Manchester," *The Torch,* March 1944.
11 Richard Deverall to Paul Hanley Furfey, cited by Robb, *Specialized Catholic Action, 1936–1949,* unpublished doctoral dissertation submitted to University of Minnesota, 1972, p. 79.
12 Runkle to author, November 1985.
13 *Chicago's Young Catholic Workers,* Vol. 1, No. 1, December 1941.
14 "The Archbishop on Catholic Action," *Catholic Action Priests' Bulletin,* Vol. 2, No. 2, October 1941.
15 *Ibid.*
16 Anonymous letter, *Catholic Action Priests' Bulletin,* June 19, 1941.
17 "Heaven Help the Working Girl," *Catholic Action, Business Girls' Federation,* November 1943. Zotti papers.
18 Ed Marciniak, first president of the Catholic Labor Alliance and editor of *WORK—a Paper for All Who Work for a Living,* was a strong supporter of lay Catholic activism in the workplace. He was a generous teacher of the early leaders in the specialized movements whose knowledge of the social teachings of the Church regarding unions, labor legislation, and social justice was limited when they entered the movement.
19 The Catholic Labor Alliance led by Ed Marciniak was organized in 1943 to promote social justice in work and economic affairs among workers and managers alike. It also dealt with fairness to minorities, interracial justice, and related issues.
20 Msgr. John J. Egan was a young priest when he became the chaplain of the girls' branch of the Young Christian Workers. He was later named by Cardinal Stritch as director of the Cana Conference, an organization devoted to the improvement of married life. He devoted many years to the development of urban social ministry in the Church and organized an educational program at Notre Dame University for clergy, religious, and lay persons interested in urban ministry.
21 Edwina Hearn, "Adam Fell for Eve," *Impact,* Vol. 1, No. 1, November 1945, p. 3.

[22] Joan O'Dwyer, "We Need Leaders," *Impact. Vol. 1,* No. 1, November 1945, p. 15.

[23] Comments of John Berkery, et. al., recorded conversation, March 9, 1987.

[24] Former New York YCW members to author, recorded conversation, March 8, 1986. Zotti papers.

[25] Letter from Paul W. Meinecke to Most Reverend Archbishop John J. Mitty, D.D., February 1945, with enclosure, "Summary of the Programs and Progress of the Saint Boniface Section of the Young Christian Workers Movement," Chancery Archives, archidiocese of San Francisco, photostat. Zotti papers.

[26] James McLaughlin to author, recorded conversation, October 2, 1985. Zotti papers.

4

Young Christian Workers at Last

It was a cold Chicago night in early March 1946. A half dozen leaders of the Girl Office Workers' Federation of Young Christian Workers huddled over Cokes at a little table in the drugstore across the street from 3 East after our monthly federation leaders' meeting. The topic of conversation was the invitation that Msgr. Hillenbrand had shared with us that evening. Did we want to send someone to Europe?

Europe? Incredible! But the invitation was real enough. Msgr. Hillenbrand had received a letter from Fr. James Bermingham of the Youth Bureau of the National Catholic Welfare Conference extending an invitation to a representative of the Chicago cells to attend a national congress of the JICF (*Jeunesse Independente Chretienne Feminine*) to be held in Paris from April 23 to 25, celebrating its tenth anniversary. The original invitation had been received by Cardinal Spellman in New York from a visiting French businessman who did not know if or where an American counterpart to the JICF was in existence. He had passed the invitation to the Youth Bureau in Washington where Fr. Vincent Mooney recognized that Msgr. Hillenbrand was the key person to contact.

The idea was exciting, but such a trip was highly unlikely. The details were vague, and furthermore, who had any money? The JICF (Young Christian Independent Girls) was the Specialized Catholic Action organization of the middle-class girls in France, thought by some to be the counterpart of the office workers in this country. It would be a chance to learn what was going on in Europe and to get firsthand ideas that would really help us in America to move ahead.

"Wouldn't it be great?"

"It's crazy. It costs too much. Only the rich go to Europe."

"How much would it cost? I heard that passenger planes are going there. It would take too long on a boat."

"Flying across the ocean? I don't believe it!"

"Maybe we could raise some money to send someone."

"You girls are nuts. There's no way. That's only six weeks from now."

And so it went on. When we parted to take our various streetcars home, no decision had been made. Even the dreamers did not have much confidence that the idea was workable, but we hated to admit it was an impossibility.

The next day Loretta Fenton called Edwina Hearn. She said she had been thinking about it all night. "After all, if we have faith in God, nothing is impossible. I think you should talk to Fr. Egan and see if something can be worked out. You are the federation president. You should go."

In the next few days we discussed the idea with our chaplain, Fr. John Egan, using the inquiry method which had become second nature.

What Are the Facts?

The invitation was a rare opportunity to see specialized Catholic Action in operation in the places where it had attracted hundreds of thousands of young people. We in America had for too long been cut off from direct contact with the Europeans who could give us practical help and renewed vigor in developing our own apostolate.

On the other hand, the war had been over just a few months and conditions were not favorable for travel in Europe. The only persons generally permitted to go there were on government business or reconstruction matters. Passage on the few planes and ships crossing the ocean was not easily obtained. The fare for one round-trip flight was $675, the equivalent of more than four months wages for most working girls. This did not include the cost of housing and food.

There would be only six weeks to make all necessary preparations, to get a passport and the visas required for entrance into each country, airline reservations, and money for expenses. Was it prudent to send a young American girl with no travel experience on such a journey into the unknown?

Judgment:

The lay apostolate is a necessity. Such a visit could be a major boost for the movement in the United States. With God's help, nothing is impossible.

Action:

Let's go for it! We have nothing to lose and everything to gain.

By the end of the week, the decision was made. It was decided to ask everyone to pitch in to raise the necessary money. On March 12, a letter went out to leaders of cells in other cities, sharing the invitation and asking their support.

> It is possible that your group may be in a position to send someone with our representative, but, knowing that it will not be easy to meet the expenses, we imagine that with your smaller numbers, it may be even more difficult for you to do so. If you cannot undertake this on your own, would you lend Chicago your financial assistance? . . .
>
> We know the trip will prove worthwhile because it will be the sacrifice of individuals who will remain at home that will give our representative the grace to accomplish our purpose. Each individual who makes a sacrifice to send someone else will be sending a part of herself, and the Catholic Action movement in this country will benefit greatly.
>
> Since the time is short, may we hear from you within the week?[1]

Support was soon forthcoming from cells across the country. Fund-raising in Chicago began among high schoolers, married men, college students, as well as the girls' cells. Someone donated two pair of nylons, still a much sought-after rarity following the cotton-stocking days of the war years. Almost one thousand dollars were raised in a raffle for the nylons!

The Aim: To See the Movement In Action

Once the decision was made, it was decided to raise enough to send two girls, since one girl traveling alone did not seem wise. Edwina Hearn was chosen to represent the senior girls and, since Betty Hull, the former junior president, was skeptical of the whole idea, I was chosen to represent the juniors. Edwina and I decided that once in Europe we would visit as many other countries as possible where we could see the movement in action. Using the help of everyone we could find with any clout, and considerable shoe-leather-chasing around, we managed in three weeks to get passports and visas for five countries.

During this time we learned that the Canadian JICF leaders were going first to Belgium to attend a Catholic Action meeting being held the week before the Paris Congress. Not wanting to miss anything of importance, we decided to take that in as well. This tightened the time schedule considerably, and on April 9, less than four weeks after the initial decision was made, we took off for New York where we had to contact Fr. Bermingham for further information. He told us to call M. Louis Devaux at Cartier's, the international jewelry firm, when we reached Paris. He was the member of the Catholic Action committee in Paris who had brought the invitation to New York. He would be our host and make necessary arrangements for us in Paris.

A blizzard in Newfoundland caused our plane to be grounded for thirty-six hours, so it was 6:00 A.M. on Palm Sunday when we arrived. Cartier's was closed, of course. What to do? A friendly steward on the plane suggested we go to one of the hotels used by Americans. After finding two such hotels filled, we arrived at the Hotel Crillon, across from the American Embassy which, we found out later, was limited to visitors representing the United States government. When we were asked at the desk what agency in Washington we were from, we nonchalantly replied, "NCWC," and were given a room.

Now, completely on our own and with only a smattering of high school French, we found the JICF headquarters in the phone directory and miraculously the girl who answered spoke English. The local leaders took us to dinner and sent someone to pick up our train tickets to Brussels. After a good night's sleep at the posh Hotel Crillon, we headed for Belgium on a day-long train ride through countryside still showing signs of wartime destruction.

The headquarters of the JOC, surmounted by the huge figure of a workingman, was the first thing we saw as we left the Brussels railway station. We managed to identify ourselves to the Jocists there, and they put us up for the night at the headquarters of the Jocist girls. Then on to Ghent for what turned out to be a meeting of the International Union of Leagues of Catholic Women (UILCF).

Christine de Hemptinne and Her Story of Catholic Action

The meeting was in session, but we were warmly greeted. *"Les Americains sont ici!"* the cry went up. Our surprise at being so readily welcomed was better understood when a few hours later two Americans representing the sodality of Our Lady arrived. They were the expected Americans, and the American "Jocists" had stolen their thunder. After the comedy of errors was finally straightened out, we were taken under the wing of Mlle Christine de Hemptinne, the middle-aged leader of the youth section of the UILCF, and with the help of Carmen Greville, an English delegate to the meeting, we gradually made some sense of what was going on.

Present were representatives, young and old, from Catholic Action organizations in a dozen countries, not limited to the specialized form of Catholic Action with which we were familiar. Wearing Jocist pins which Bob Anderson of the San Francisco YCW had sent us before we left home, we were asked many questions about the "Jocists" in America. Women at the meeting reported on the progress of Catholic Action in their respective countries. In answer to a request, Edwina even gave a brief talk describing the NCWC, the principal American name which the Europeans knew, explaining that it was not an organization of lay apostles, but a coordinating arm of the bishops.

Mlle de Hemptinne spent some time questioning us about our apostolic involvement. When she learned that we had weekly meetings, studied the New Testament, and made inquiries into problems, she said, "That accounts for your formation." She said that most of those who had come to their meetings from the United States in the past were untrained and did not know what was going on. She felt frustrated in trying to communicate with the NCWC and asked our help in this regard. In her view, Catholic Action was a religious apostolate which reached out to others to bring them into active participation in the Church, regardless of the exact methods used. She emphasized that the JOC in Europe was strictly a workers' movement and not the only form of Catholic Action. Given her aristocratic background—her father was a count who we later learned owned a coal mine—this was not a surprising statement, but it took us a while to grasp the full significance of her explanation.

She told us Cardijn had started trade union groups concerned with social and economic problems rather than an apostolic movement to save souls, whereas she had been personally trained by the Holy Father to start Catholic Action among young girls back in the early twenties. Cardijn's movement gradually developed an apostolic thrust while her organization, which she said included all social classes, began to incorporate the idea of social action in addition to religious evangelism. We later learned she was the leader of a lay institute called the Filles de Marie, which was involved in training girls to be concerned with the spiritual needs of others, a different kind of apostolate from the one we understood, more like the apostolic role we thought of as belonging to the nuns and priests. Leaders of many of the Catholic Action groups who belonged to the International Union of the Leagues of Christian Women were members of the *Filles*.

Mlle did not tell us about the conservative Catholics who had complained to their cardinal that Cardijn's organization was revolutionary and smacked of socialism. And she did not tell us about the support Cardijn later received from Pius XI who saw Jocism as a means of restoring religious faith among members of the working class because it dealt with the social conditions that were so demoralizing. She was obviously trying to sell us on her interpretation of Catholic Action. We just listened.

When we later met Pat Keegan, the president of the English YCW, in London, he filled us in on the rest of the story. He told us that as both organizations grew, competition for members had developed in many parishes. Cardijn held out for all young workers and de Hemptinne wanted all the girls. De Hemptinne went to see the cardinal and after some study, he advised specialization according to environment, and Mlle relinquished all her working girl members to the JOCF ("F" for *feminin*, designating the girls' branch of the movement). This was done after 1928. By the mid-thirties, the specialized groups, JAC-JACF (*agricoles*, farmers) JEC-JECF (*étudiants*, students), JIC-JICF (*independentes*, middle class), JOC-JOCF (*ouvrieres*, workers), and JUC (*universitaire*, university students) were organized. That was how the neat "A-E-I-O-U" arrangement of the movements had come about. It gave us a better understanding of what McGuire had explained about the like-to-like organizations which we knew as Specialized Catholic Action. Looking back, I don't think even he knew the full story.

Trying to Get the Picture

On our return to Brussels, we spent the evening at the Jocist headquarters. Over dinner with two Italian Catholic Action leaders, two girls from Prague who were trying to reactivate Catholic Action in their country, and four Belgian leaders, several of whom spoke Flemish, a multilingual conversation ensued. In spite of communication problems, we were thrilled by the sense of spiritual unity and enthusiasm for the apostolate that was so apparent.

The next day was Good Friday and we attended mass at the JOC Centrale celebrated by the renowned Canon Joseph Cardijn of whom we had heard so much. We even had breakfast with him, but, since he knew very little English, our conversation did not amount to much more than "bonjour" and a few smiles.

During the day we visited the headquarters of the other specialized movements and picked up copies of their publications. The social action we observed among the JICF groups we visited often consisted of nonworking middle-class girls helping out in poor families where the mother was ill or having a baby. This was a far cry from the like-to-like apostolate that we had been told was characteristic of the European movement. Our conversation with Marguerite Fievez, Cardijn's secretary, later that evening was pleasant enough, but we had the feeling that she wasn't too sure about us either and where we fitted into the Catholic Action setup. Our language differences undoubtedly added to the problem of mutual understanding. We were really struggling to figure out how things were done in Europe so we could get ideas to bring back home.

The one thing that came through from all those we met was their strong commitment as apostles for Christ expressed in the service of others; but there was more to Specialized Catholic Action than we realized. We thought we had a general idea of what it meant, but we were unprepared for the class differences and how they affected the views of the Europeans and the kind of action they advocated. Gradually, we realized that we didn't quite fit into the bourgeois class that the JICF represented, but neither were we exactly like the Jocists. The Jicistes were what we would call upper middle class. Many of them didn't hold jobs and their fathers had high management positions. Working-class boys and girls went to work at age fourteen, after the equivalent of a grammar school education. We had more education than the Jocists, but we were wage earners, not the daughters of wealthy men. "We have to be careful," we said in a letter home. "They don't understand that we make up a group that doesn't exist as such in Europe."[2]

The congress in Paris a few days later was a grand spectacle. The Mass in Notre Dame Cathedral, attended by ten thousand Jicistes and hundreds of chaplains, was especially impressive. We had never seen so many Catholic Actionists gathered at one time, much less heard ten thousand persons sing the Mass together. Those were the days when most people attended Mass as silent observers.

Getting the YCW Story in England

It turned out that the part of the trip where we got the most help was England, where we had no language problems. After visiting some members of the Young Christian Girls organization, the English counterpart to the JICF led by Carmen Greville, we eventually found the YCW girls in the grimy industrial city of Manchester. When we discussed the YCG with their chaplain, Fr. Yarnitsky, we learned that Carmy was a bit of an autocrat and ran her organization with little input from the members. She too was of the upper class and more concerned with spiritual matters than with social action, in spite of the fact that many members of her organization had jobs. Some YCG members had told us they would rather be in the YCW because it was more realistic.

In London we headed for the Offley Road headquarters of the Young Christian Worker boys. (In England, the headquarters of the girls and that of the boys were not even in the same city.) There we met Pat Keegan. It didn't take Pat long to find out that we were wage earners and not wealthy middle class like the "bourgeoisie." He said we really did belong as Young Christian Workers. When we told him

Canon Joseph Cardijn with Patrick Keegan of England.

of the meeting with Mlle de Hemptinne in Ghent, he explained how the Young Christian Workers differed from her kind of Catholic Action, which was primarily religious and directed by members of the upper classes. The movement fathered by Cardijn was an apostolic movement immersed in the everyday life of the young workers, not apart from it. The secular world must be reordered, he said, so that young workers could achieve their salvation in their daily environment, rather than be demoralized by it.

Pat insisted that we remain in Europe to attend the International Study Week of the JOC to be held in Brussels the last week in June. All the national English and Scottish YCW leaders were going. Pat said Cardijn had been learning to speak English and there would be English-speaking sessions. There we would get a fuller understanding of the spirit and methods that were so important.

Making a Decision

We had originally planned to go to Rome from England and return home on May 27. Edwina was due back on her job the first of June. I had quit my job to make the trip, so I had no deadline. By this time, both of us had been thinking about the need for permanent workers in the movement at home and we mentioned the possibility in our letters home to Fr. Egan. Every place we'd been, people were amazed that we were trying to organize the movement while holding down full-time jobs.

On May 11, Edwina wrote to Fr. Egan:

Have just finished writing several important letters. No. 1 to the firm of S J & H tendering my resignation in favor of being a permanent worker of YCW and the other to Mother telling her that I did it. Goodbye $210 per month and hello hard times. Mary is throwing in her sponge too, although she isn't telling her Mother about it yet. That will make Loretta, Mary and me at 3 East. Won't that be fun? We realize, of course, that there is no money to pay us a wage as yet, but if the treasury can scrape up enough to pay our telephone, light and insurance for a month or so until we dope out a way to earn an income for YCW—Mother's pension will pay the rent at home and she doesn't eat much, so her $10 a week at the orphanage should feed us temporarily. I am sure she will be willing. If she isn't, I will be surprised.

We decided it is about time a few of us in America cashed in on a few of the sacrifices YCW in other countries have been making. It must have been their sacrifices that gave us the grace to see how necessary it is for us. Their sacrifices and Pat Keegan's Irish personality! He is head of YCW here, as you know, and wot a guy! He is a human dynamo and sells a bill of goods, believe me.

He gave us the business for two solid hours and we sat with our mouths open. He told us the great hopes Cardijn has for America, says that we must take the lead in the Movement since we are the most important country politically. . . .

Pat told us of the necessity for permanent workers, and of the necessity of a national organization. Naturally, Mary and I realized we couldn't go home and talk someone else into giving up their job to pioneer as a permanent worker with hardly any income, at least to start—hence the decision.

We asked Pat what the qualifications should be for

headquarters "permanents." He said, first, one who is a real worker, i.e., a wage earner in an employee capacity, one who has known the insecurity of being a wage-earner and the problems of the working world. He may be office or factory—not professional or an employer or one who hasn't worked. Having been an employee since the depression years when I started at 15 dollars a week and didn't get up to 18 for three years, and having worked in at least 10 different offices in every "employee" capacity except that of charwoman, and sometimes during the war years I felt as if I were that too, I felt I could qualify on qualification No. 1.

Next, each headquarters permanent must be a leader, i.e., must be able to run a cell meeting or a general assembly whenever that may be necessary. He must be thoroughly familiar with YCW methods, purpose, techniques, etc., and on that score I guess we both qualify at least as well as any other YCW girl at present. At each H.Q. there must be an organizer and a publications manager. Think we fit in here all right too, at least until some others quit their jobs and join H.Q. forces.[3]

We quickly realized that the Brussels meeting was crucial so we made the necessary arrangements to stay in Europe the extra month. Our money was running low, but Pat said not to worry. He arranged our stay as nonpaying guests of the English Grail who ran a house on Sloane Street in London for girls in the Armed Forces. The head of the Grail in England, Baroness Bosch von Drakestein, was Pat's good friend. She took us under her wing and mothered us during our London stay.

Pat offered us a pound a week for expenses and said we could work it off by typing for the boys at headquarters. What an opportunity! These were the advisers we had been looking for. But first we had to go to Rome to see the Holy Father, a visit strongly desired by Msgr. Hillenbrand. He wanted us to get a special blessing for the Chicago Catholic Action Federations personally signed by Pius XII. Italy at that time was off limits for Americans, so with the help of Msgr. Daniel Cunningham, head of the Catholic School Board who happened to live in my parish and knew me, we got a letter from Cardinal Stritch saying he wanted us to see the pope. Another example of the improbable connections we had made in planning our trip.

The Audience with Pius XII

We had told Maria Colosi, the Italian Catholic Actionist we had met in Belgium, that we were going to Rome. She made the necessary arrangements and, on our arrival in Rome, we received a formal written invitation to meet with the Holy Father in special audience at twelve noon on Thursday, May 24. After two days of visiting an assortment of Catholic Actionists, collecting more publications, and touring the Vatican Museum, we presented ourselves at the Vatican in the prescribed black dresses and black veils loaned by Maria. When we were ushered into the room where we were to await the pope, we were surprised to see Mlle de Hemptinne who was there for a private audience. She really did have close connections with the Holy Father. She said she would tell the pope about us since she was going in first.

When our turn finally came, we were awestruck. Pius XII spoke to us in English for ten minutes and asked about our work in America. When we asked for a special message to those at home, he said, "Tell them they must be loyal to the Church and always attached to Christ. . . . Teach the young workers truth and justice and charity."

Seeing the Holy Father and talking to him was the emotional highlight of our journey. We also appreciated the chance to bask in the warm Italian sunlight and eat ice cream and oranges. After freezing in England and living largely on tea and bread, this was a real treat. Then we headed back to England. Because of the great wartime destruction in Italy, rail travel to and from Rome was impossible. We had managed in Paris to get a ticket to Rome on TWA, but a return trip was out of the question. So we finagled a seat on Air Transport Command, an American military airline. Our return flight was delayed for three days because of mechanical troubles. When we arrived at the Rome airport on the third day, we were unexpectedly offered a flight on a B-26 bomber that was being returned to Paris. No fancy commercial flight would ever compare with that flight, riding in the plexiglass nose cone looking down on the blue Mediterranean. We sat in that choice spot at the invitation of the crew who were delighted to have a couple of American girls on board.

Arriving back in London via the boat-train from Paris, with a bag of oranges for our hostesses at the Grail House, we were whisked off to their country place for a few days of much needed rest. In England, the Grail was doing different work than in the United States. Their aim seemed to be filling unmet needs in England, like the hostel for service women and the publication of attractive and readable translations of the papal encyclicals, done in blank verse. Moreover, they were very supportive of the goals of the YCW. The following weeks we worked at the YCW headquarters a bit, but mostly we observed and talked. We attended general meetings in local sections and were invited to a Study Day for chaplains. In between times, we visited with Frank Sheed and Maisie Ward who operated the prestigious Catholic publishing company, Sheed and Ward, and spent a day sight-seeing with Paul McGuire who was visiting in England at the time.

One weekend, Baroness Bosch took us to a retreat at a Cenacle Convent outside London that was being conducted for Catholic members of the English nobility. While waiting in line for confession on the second day, Edwina spoke to the woman next to her who introduced herself as Lady Hartington. On recognizing Edwina's American accent and learning she was from Chicago, she said, "Oh, my father owns a building there." Edwina, thinking in terms of two-flats like the apartment building where she lived with her mother on the North Side of the city, casually asked, "Where?"

"The Merchandise Mart," came the answer. Kathleen Kennedy, daughter of multimillionaire Joseph P.? Indeed it was. She was the Kennedy who had married an English lord outside the Church but now was apparently back in the fold. We were, without doubt, moving in circles beyond our own level.

The International Study Week of the JOC

Finally came the day for our return to Belgium. On June 24, 1946, the first International Study Week of the JOC began.

Gathered in Brussels were over one hundred leaders from eight European countries, including four delegates from Germany and Austria, young workers who had so recently been the enemy. There were delegates from Australia and several from North Africa and the Belgian Congo. The delegates discussed the problems facing young workers and the need to spread the young workers' organization throughout the world in order to rebuild a Christian society. We sat with the English-speaking group as observers.

Key to the establishment of the movement in other countries was the insistence of the Belgian leaders that it develop in what they regarded as the authentic way. The YCW had unique characteristics as a movement of young workers and they were protective of this identity. This was spelled out in the following statements:

> (1) The problem of working youth is the very basis of the YCW. This problem must be put *in the light of the dignity and the eternal destiny* of each worker. That truth itself and its discovery by the young workers themselves is the great force and inspiration of the YCW spirit.
>
> This movement must have the following characteristics:
>
> An *autonomous movement* by the young workers, among the young workers, for the young workers; *a movement of education* in order that all young workers can discover and realize their vocations, their destiny in their life and in the surroundings of their lives; *a movement of the apostolate* with, as its aim and ambition, the bringing of this education to the whole masses of the workers; *a movement of organized Catholic Action* to which the Hierarchy gives an official mandate: the penetration of the working class and the conquest of the masses of workers to the Church; *a national and international movement* because the problems to be solved are so universal.
>
> (2) Working youth has vital needs. The movement must help them to satisfy these needs. The YCW must develop in all its members and militants a genuine spirit of service which makes them sensitive to all the needs of the masses and which makes them anxious to help the masses and bring relief in difficulties.
>
> The service is (a) a means of penetration into the masses; (b) the means of incarnating the charity of the Gospels; (c) a means of training leaders. To be true and vital, a service must correspond to the *real needs* of the young workers.

(3) A YCW which is not from its very beginnings directed to and centered on the masses is not an authentic YCW.

(4) The uplifting of the working masses is impossible without the working masses themselves. The role of the YCW is to animate and to direct the action of the masses along the line of its full development. In order that this development of the masses be achieved, the program of the services and activities of the YCW must be worked out for the masses of young workers and *not merely for its own members.*

(5) *The YCW must have a great number of genuine worker-leaders,* engaged in those surroundings which are most representative of the workers' lives. They must be militants who are trained and formed for the conquest of these surroundings.[4]

In speaking to the Jocist delegates present, Cardijn spoke of the Christian mystique which transcends national frontiers, based as it is on liberty and responsibility among all the sons of God, even those of goodwill who do not have the gift of faith. He stressed that the International YCW existed not just to save the working masses in a few countries but to solve the world problems they all faced.

Sitting among the Europeans who had just gone through a war, and seeing leaders from so many countries, it was obvious that we had very different backgrounds. Yet Cardijn made us feel that we were all very important and very close. The dignity of being a worker with a God-given destiny was something we all shared.

It was only later that we realized how much American working conditions differed from the facts of European working life. Though young workers in the United States at the turn of the century had had many of the same problems that were still being experienced in Europe, we had had the benefit of many advances that came about after Roosevelt's National Recovery Act in the thirties. The Wagner Act in 1935 and the Fair Labor Standards Act in 1938 raised the status of the labor unions and prohibited certain unfair labor practices. It also regulated child labor, prohibiting full-time work by children below the age of sixteen. Eighteen became the minimum age for hazardous work. Young European workers often went to work at age fourteen. A year after our visit, the school-leaving age in England was raised to fifteen, an age when American teen-agers were required by law to remain in school. This is one reason the Jocists stressed the need for education and career training for young workers.

Canon Cardijn in the United States

Even as the meeting was going on, plans were underway for Cardijn's first visit to the Americas, as part of his desire to make Jocism an international movement. On May 20, 1946, just a few days before we saw the Holy Father, Cardijn had a long visit with him and received a letter giving the YCW his blessing and encouraging its future action and development. Pius authorized Cardijn to go to the Americas to encourage the movement in the western hemisphere.

Immediately after the end of the study week, we headed home, arriving in New York on the Fourth of July. A few days later, Cardijn

Canon Joseph Cardijn.

arrived in Montreal for two days with the Canadian JOC chaplains. His plans were to stop in Boston, New York, and Washington, D.C., on the way to Costa Rica for a Pan-American meeting of Jocist chaplains from Central and South America, accompanied by Fr. Victor Villeneuve, O.M.I., national chaplain of the Canadian Jocist movement, who would be his interpreter.

When the YCW in San Francisco saw a press release that Cardijn was coming to the United States, they immediately invited him to visit their headquarters. When they were told in a letter from Fr. Villeneuve on June 21 that time would not permit such a visit, they wrote again and the canon agreed to come if they could arrange transportation for him to Costa Rica. In spite of considerable difficulty, this was done and the itinerary was changed. The two Jocist chaplains agreed to travel from Washington to San Francisco by way of Chicago.

We knew nothing of this at the time, of course. After a brief stop in New York to report on our trip to the YCW leaders there, we went up to Boston to meet with Archbishop Cushing, head of the Youth Department of NCWC, the official sponsor of our trip, only to learn that Cardijn was scheduled to see the cardinal one half hour later. We were glad we arrived first, because we were able to present the American view of the Jocists Cushing had asked for when he knew we were going to Europe. We also met with Fr. Bermingham and others at the National Catholic Welfare Conference in Washington, D.C., where Cardijn followed us a few days later. In effect, we were functioning as advance agents for the canon. We learned later that Cardijn and Cardinal Cushing did not hit it off personally, with the apparent result that the YCW was never encouraged in Boston, although it did have a strong foothold in Lowell, an ethnic French community in the Boston archdiocese.

We were hardly home in Chicago when, on July 16, Cardijn arrived. After a meeting with the chaplains who had gathered from several nearby states, he met with a group of Young Christian Workers and Young Christian Students. This is what he told them.

> We cannot be strong in our international movement without America. We need the young working boys and girls of America. I am so happy to find everywhere in the United States the same apostolic spirit, that spirit of new Christian-

ity, in the new world as well as in the old. I have been in New York, Brooklyn, Boston, Lowell, and now in Chicago, that great center of the working world. I have found young boys and girls with the same spirit of conquest, ready to form cells, to make local federations, to begin here in America the strongest movement of young working youth in the world. We must unite in a great, a strong international movement to protect the millions of young workers of every country, not only in Belgium, not only in France, not only in England; all the continents of the world united by a new youth who will build a new world. A world with more respect for the young girl, for the young boy, the divine dignity of every worker in the factory, in the mills, in the shops, in the offices. . . .

We will conquer. Our revolution will succeed. Ours is a spiritual revolution, not a political uprising. We will assure a new youth for a new world. We believe in the influence of Christ. We believe in the reign of Christ. We believe in the salvation of Christ, in the happiness of the working masses here and in eternity. In all the shops, offices, and mills of the world, we shall spread the reign of peace, of justice, of charity. . . . Then we will bring glory to God and happiness to all classes all over the world.[5]

Two days later he was met by thirty-five Young Christian Workers at the San Francisco airport and escorted in a cavalcade of cars with a police escort to the YCW headquarters at 109 Golden Gate Avenue. At an afternoon meeting with priests, religious, and seminarians at the headquarters, Cardijn pointed out that the most important period of a young person's life was between school and marriage. It is in these years that he must have the unique formation that the Young Christian Workers can provide, where the social doctrine of the Church is explained, guidance is given, and recreation is provided.

When later he spoke to the large crowd of YCW members and their guests, he prefaced his remarks by saying, "It is the first time I speak English! Before I came to America, I never spoke English. I am 64 years old and I said, 'I will learn to speak a little English.' Okay?"

Then he read the speech he had prepared in which he called on the young workers to build a new youth, a new humanity conscious of its dignity. He said that many of the problems of youth are the result of international economic problems and the YCW should enter the international institutions which can solve them. He told them about the leader of the Belgian YCW who had been chosen the previous year to represent the working youth of the world at the Conference of the International Labor Office in Paris. Before delegates of governments and trade unions, he had presented the charter of the Young Christian Workers stating the need for education and protection of young workers still in their teens. This, he said, was just a beginning. But, to really have a strong influence on the international institutions that could bring about change, the United States must be involved. And he pleaded with them to develop the leaders, the apostles, the "militants" who were necessary to save the working youth of the world.[6]

YCW leaders who heard Cardijn in cities from east to west determined to work harder at building their organization, knowing they were just beginning. New groups starting in many cities were still working as independent groups, striving to develop leaders who would "change the world," at least their small part of it. They did not understand fully the significance of Cardijn's words, but they were impressed by the intensity of his concern for young people.

The Goal: An Authentic YCW in the States

Back in Chicago we began to prepare for our annual Study Week to be held in September. Fired up by our European encounters, Edwina and I, now working full time at 3 East headquarters, were determined to share what we had learned with all the YCW leaders who came to the study week. Although we had no real authority as a national center, we had developed a degree of expertise as a result of our experience and our travels. We invited all the girls' groups we knew of.

Forty-four girls representing groups in fourteen cities arrived at Childerly on the Labor Day weekend. For the first time, there was representation from such widely separated places as Oakland, California; Washington, D.C.; Detroit, Michigan; Cincinnati, Ohio; Richmond, Virginia; and Rochester, New York. Although we never took a count, the leaders at the meeting probably represented several hundred active leaders.

To the assembled group, we reported on our new understandings of the authentic YCW movement. Following the directives of the JOC International Office, we felt justified in stressing that all members of the YCW must be unified in ideals, method, and spirit, and we echoed the words of the European leaders that no groups should use the YCW label "unless they follow the basic ideals of the original movement." We felt that we had the foundations for a unity which transcended the narrow localism of previous ventures, where each group was free to do its own thing.

We had been told in Europe that the social inquiry should be based on a common theme identified by the leaders. This would insure a unified attack on observed problems by leaders in all the sections. It prevented a hit-or-miss approach which could result in splintered actions that would not get at the root of social problems. It also guaranteed that all members would be forced, over a period of time, to review realistically all areas of the young worker's life. Therefore, we prepared a tentative inquiry program which would focus on the various areas of life where the YCW should exert social responsibility: work, the family, the parish, social organizations.

We also described a new feature to be added to the meeting called "The Review of Influence." Leaders would report on specific situations encountered in daily life, outside the observations made as a result of a specific social inquiry. This was a broadening of the report previously made at meetings when leaders reported on acts of service and contact with persons who had specific religious and personal problems. The Review of Influence would give leaders an awareness that they must always be looking for opportunities to make new contacts in their neighborhood and at work and to gather "Facts of the Week." These would include remarks, incidents, and other evidence of attitudes which reflected the life, outlook, or concerns of young workers that might require corrective action. One person lost his job. Another complains about her boss. Several girls spend their whole paycheck for new clothes. Some are depressed because they have no place to go at night. What do these facts say about the lives of young workers? Earlier individual action and reporting had been based on religious convictions and charity towards others. The Review of Influence would stimulate a growing awareness of needs in all areas of the young workers' lives and make members conscious of the totality of their apostolate among young workers.

The attempt to settle definitely the basic characteristics of the Young Christian Workers and plan a common program of inquiries was not entirely successful. Leaders in some cities still wanted to use their own inquiries instead of those prepared in Chicago. Since we had no authority, we suggested, as a step towards unity, that those who did use the inquiries or adapt them, should report on their experience and, after four months, meet to compare notes and suggest ideas for the following year's program.

The characteristics of the organization and method were reprinted in our *Leaders' Bulletin for Cell Members* which by that time had a wide circulation. *The Voice of the YCW* in San Francisco published translations describing the method and form the movement should have and carried on an extensive exchange of correspondence in its columns with leaders in other cities and other countries. *The Priests' Bulletin* published by the Chicago priests spread the idea further and many priests were anxious to get involved now that the war was over. In many cities, seminarians had organized groups to study the Jocist method of Catholic Action and they published their own newsletter, *The Forum*. The sum total of all these publications was that more and more priests were learning about the Young Christian Workers and were becoming interested in getting started. The big aim: Get more young men.

Signs of Progress

As young men returned from the war, interested priests began to seek out leaders and start groups. The emphasis was on getting fellows who worked in factories and blue-collar jobs. It was slow going. Many young men returning from the service were taking advantage of the G.I. Bill and going to college. Their parents, many of them immigrants with little education, encouraged their sons to take advantage of the opportunity. Others, away from home for three or four years, were finding wives. This cut down on the available young, single workingmen in some of the parishes where prospective chaplains were looking. Boys just out of high school were still being drafted. By the end of 1946, however, male sections were underway in Chicago and on the East Coast.

In Chicago the various specialized movements included married men, married women and the Young Christian Students, both high school and college, in addition to the YCW. Each of the movements was growing and active and all showed up at 3 East from time to time. We called ourselves the Catholic Action Federations and by this time we had on the wall the personally signed blessing of the Holy Father addressed to Catholic Action Federations which had arrived from Rome.

Then we had a further sign of progress. The groups of married men and women had developed an extensive action spreading the program of Cana Conferences for married couples. The one-day and weekend meetings designed to improve the quality of Christian living in the family were becoming very popular. Also, Pre-Cana Conferences for engaged couples were spreading like wildfire. In these conferences, held in parishes throughout the archdiocese, a priest, a doctor, and a married couple spoke at consecutive weekly meetings to engaged couples, giving them practical information and suggestions to prepare them for the realities of married life. Running such a large program was becoming overwhelming. The leaders of the married men's groups approached the cardinal with a request for a full time priest-director.

On October 19, 1946, the appointment of *two* full-time chaplains was announced by the Chancery Office. The Rev. John J. Egan was placed in charge of the Cana Conference program and Rev. William Quinn was appointed to "special work in Catholic Action." Fr. Egan was already chaplain for our working girls' federation and Fr. Quinn had made a successful beginning with young workingmen. His job now was to coordinate the work of all the Specialized Catholic Action federations in the archdiocese.[7]

This development was important, because many Chicago priests were being criticized by their pastors or the rectors of the seminaries where they taught for spending so much time with the cells. Msgr. Hillenbrand was no longer rector at the major seminary. He had been transferred to the pastorate of a north suburban parish in 1944. No explanation was ever given for his transfer, but many suspected it was because his views on training priests were not appreciated by the Jesuit faculty and his views on social action and labor were opposed by conservatives in the archdiocese. Thus, the appointment of a priest to serve the specialized movements was seen as a positive sign from the archbishop. This was important because it was hoped that eventually the specialized movements would be mandated by the archbishop as official Catholic Action.

In January that same year, the San Francisco YCW had asked Archbishop Mitty for a full-time chaplain. Their request had been denied, though he was supportive of their programs. He also stated that they should not attend out-of-state meetings for the time being. "We *must* stick to the wishes of the hierarchy if we are to remain Catholic Action," said Arthur Ronz in a letter to the Chicago office. "When we are permitted to do so, we will visit you, we wish to exchange ideas. . . . Canon Cardijn called for unity and we have always pleaded for the same thing. . . . That day is not yet, but we are earnestly waiting, praying and working for it."[8]

By this time, all the specialized movements (young workers, students, and married men and women) were clarifying their role as lay members of the Church. They were no longer willing to sit back as praying, paying church members primarily concerned with personal piety. The message of the so-called social encyclicals on social justice in the world, beginning with *Rerum Novarum*, On Capital and Labor (1891), and continued in *Divini Redemptoris*, On Atheistic Communism (1937), and *Quadragesimo Anno*, On Social Reconstruction (1941), had clearly identified the need for Catholics to be concerned with the problems of industrialism and the resulting injustices and dehumanizing conditions impacting on the lives of twentieth-century men and women.

The doctrine of the Mystical Body of Christ further developed a recognition that Christians must be conscious of Christ's incarnation in human life and take responsibility for improving the conditions of daily life so that all men could live in dignity. This understanding was the underlying theme of the Jocist movement which we brought back from Europe. It greatly expanded our role as lay persons in the Church. Developing a social conscience and taking initiative for constructive action in all areas of life became a hallmark of the developing lay movements, particularly the Young Christian Workers.

Applying these understandings would take time and energy as the movement increased its membership and spread throughout the country. "A new youth for a new world" was the rallying cry of Joseph Cardijn and we were happy to echo him. The Young Christian Workers had high hopes as 1947 began.

Looking Back on the Forties

The YCW had a very important influence on my life. It helped me to overcome thinking about myself and my problems. When we used the inquiry method, it made you go out and act on your observations. I started asking people about themselves, their problems, where they worked, if they had problems at work. Pretty soon, it became easy to talk to people and try to come up with solutions. I even quit one job to find another office with a large group of employees to try to come up with more problems to solve.

[Some years ago] when my youngest son was giving me so much trouble for about five years after his father died, and he was arrested for drunk driving, I found myself one morning driving to a drug center for help. As I walked up those steps and sat talking to one young man about this problem, a whole flood of memories came back and it was as if I was back to those years yearning to help, as he was trying to do, and then realized it was a very happy and rewarding time of my life. (Toledo)

I was attracted to the YCW by the people involved in it and by the potential for revolutionizing the face of the earth and therefore being involved in an important historical event which I anticipated as being almost immediate. (Oh, maybe it would take ten whole years to straighten things out!) YCW was going to democratize the Church (who could fail to see our point of view?) and to bring more humane values to all of society.

I'm sorry that I cannot recall in any detail what our group was so busy about. We did produce a local radio program that interpreted and dramatized "liberal and thoughtful" values. We rented and renovated a downtown flat that was to serve as headquarters for Christianizing all the office workers in Wilmington, Delaware. We faithfully reported what progress in communicating our ideals we had made in our offices each week. We made some attempt to establish interracial communications. And we encouraged each other to seek good Catholic mates, or vocations.

My most vivid memory of YCW days is that we invited the bishop of our diocese to view and bless our new headquarters facility—and I spilled all the spaghetti I was trying to drain into the bathtub. We scooped it up and said what the bishop didn't know probably wouldn't hurt him. Which was true, except that when the bishop praised our pasta, I got so flustered, I blurted out the horrible truth! That was good for lots of laughter later. In *summary, nice young people, hardworking, idealistic, earnest, senses of humor . . . and a bit naive.*

Being involved with the YCW was a lovely way to spend positive thought and energy for someone who was idealistic, not interested in being a "swinger" and not too clued into the realities of politics. On a trip to France in the late forties, I hustled around to contact Jocists in Paris. That was an interesting experience that elucidated the difference between our somewhat romantic, white collar goals in Wilmington, and the nitty-gritty salary-and-working conditions goals of the JOC leaders in Paris. (Wilmington, Delaware)

Notes

[1] Letter from Edwina Hearn and Barbara Marksteiner to leaders of cells in Toledo, Appleton, New York, Cleveland, Youngstown, South Bend, and Dracut, Massachusetts, March 16, 1946. UND archives.

[2] Letter, Mary Irene Caplice to Fr. Egan, April 17, 1946. Zotti papers.

[3] Letter, Edwina Hearn to Fr. John Egan, May 11, 1946. Zotti papers.

[4] Statement of Emilie Arnould, president, Belgian JOCF, at International JOC Semaine d'Etude, June 1946. UND archives.

[5] Cardijn's address quoted by Dorothy McGinley, *Impact*, September-October 1946, pp. 15–20.

[6] "Cardijn Addresses YCW," *The Voice of the YCW*, 109 Golden Gate Avenue, San Francisco, California, August 1, 1946.

[7] "Full Time Chaplains for Catholic Action," *Young Christian Workers, Office Workers' Bulletin*, October 1946.

[8] Arthur Ronz in letter to Caplice, October 24, 1946. UND archives.

5

A National Movement Takes Shape

As we grappled with the task of promoting a strong and unified YCW among young women in the United States and supported the beginning efforts among young men, we were notified that the Canadian JOC was to host an International Study Week of Young Christian Workers in Montreal, June 22 to June 29, 1947, to celebrate its fifteenth anniversary. The strong Canadian JOC had been the chief model for the movement in North and South America during the war years. Canon Cardijn recognized the value of capitalizing on its prestige among pioneering groups on the western side of the Atlantic to insure the proper development of a truly international movement of young workers.

Fr. Villeneuve, at the suggestion of Pat Keegan, asked us in Chicago to organize a representation from the United States to attend the study week as nonvoting delegates. The established and mandated national movements were sending official delegates. We were also asked to prepare a summary of the current status of the movement in the United States. On January 11, 1947, a letter and questionnaire was sent to all known YCW cells in the country. Answers came from twenty-one of the thirty-five cities and towns contacted.[1]

On the basis of the responses, we sent a fact sheet on the status of the movement to all known cells. Forty-nine cells of working girls existed, comprising a total of 1,901 members. Two hundred eighty of these were cell leaders with a total of 311 on their teams. All leaders in the cells were supposed to have teams, but this was obviously not the case. The others were general members who attended monthly meetings and participated in activities of the movement. It was estimated that an additional 6,500 persons had been influenced through campaigns, services, and publications. About half of the groups based their inquiries on material drawn up at the annual study weekends in Chicago. Permanent services, primarily preparation for marriage programs, had been established by almost half the groups. Eleven cities had conducted inquiries on work and working conditions in the last six months. The others were more concerned with spiritual and moral dangers, such as indecent literature and movies and bad language. Only a few cells of young men were reported, and they were all very new.[2]

Plans for the Montreal meeting went forward. San Francisco picked their own representatives, but an interregional meeting was held in New York to decide who would represent the cells of young women in the Midwest and the East. All of the existing cells of young men were asked to send representatives.

A surprising response came from Manchester, New Hampshire, where there had been such a vibrant JOC prior to World War II. Lorraine Noel had written that they were no longer in existence as an organized Catholic Action movement and therefore could not fill out our questionnaire.[3]

Then, on June 10, 1947, just two weeks before the opening of the Montreal International Study Week, all the American delegates received a letter signed by four former leaders of the Manchester JOC expressing grave concern over the progress of the Catholic Action movement among young workers in the United States. They bemoaned the fact that the movement as described in the fact sheet sent out from Chicago was "lacking in the virility of dynamic Christianity" and "although some of the groups have been in existence for five, six, and seven years, its influence in the working world is practically nil."

They went on to say that less than one percent of the membership was truly representative of the mass of workers in shops, factories, and mills who, they stated, were the overwhelming majority of all workers; the male section of the movement was practically non-existent; and finally, that the inquiries were apparently prepared by chaplains, either directly or indirectly, and consequently "over the heads" of the average young worker in both language and subject.[4]

Moreover, they blamed the American deviations from true Catholic Action on the influence of the Canadian movement which they claimed was "no longer reaching the masses" and had lost "the conquering spirit" it had in 1939, the year of its seventh congress. This, they said, was because the Canadian movement was being dominated by the priests with the laity "relegated to the role of leaders by proxy."[5]

Upon receiving the letter, Mary Tuohy in New York wrote to Edwina, "I find it difficult to understand a letter of this kind being sent at a time when unity and strength should be uppermost in everyone's mind. In regard to some of the statements they make of your report, I wonder if they realize that it just covers the girls' movement in this country, and then not entirely."[6]

We were all surprised and confused by the strong criticism of the New Hampshire leaders. Some of what they said was true. We didn't have large numbers, we didn't have enough males, and we did need more workers in factories. On the other hand, the war had made the organization of young men virtually impossible in most parts of the country, whereas they had a five-year head start before the war took its young men. They also had had the full support and a mandate from their bishop and the benefit of an experienced full-time chaplain who had spent time in Belgium learning directly from Cardijn. Chaplains in the rest of the country were working without the support of their bishops and in the little free time they could take from other duties.

Though we agreed that we had a definite need for more workers from the factories and mills, as Edwina Hearn told Mary Tuohy, this was expected to change as the movement grew.[7] Moreover, we had doubts that the overwhelming majority of young women in the cities where the YCW was starting were in the kinds of work predominant in the mill towns of New England.

As to the complaint about the inquiries, we knew that we in Chicago wrote them ourselves, though we did consult with our chaplain, especially on the judgment part, after our fiasco with the inquiry program on the dignity and ensuing rights of workers in 1945. Also, we were high school graduates, not young teenage dropouts like many of the New Hampshire Jocists. That may have made a difference in our writing style.

Years later we learned that the JOC had been disbanded in Manchester when a new bishop was assigned to the diocese and Fr.

Roy was recalled to Canada. Roy was an energetic priest with unlimited zeal and a great ability to inspire and challenge his young
teenagers to heroic action. "These young people [the Jocists] must be
made to see with their own eyes the physical, moral, and religious
distress of their working companions," he wrote in a Jocist publication. "They must put their finger on the needs and realize the pitiful
state of their souls. It is only after discussions [through the inquiry]
that they are inflamed with zeal and aroused to feverish activity. . . ."[8]

His unconventional methods, however, were not always acceptable to more traditional priests. One example was his habit of hearing
the confessions of young workers brought to him for counsel by the
Jocist leaders in a large van parked outside the JOC headquarters. This
was something the conservative new bishop could not tolerate; hence
his decision to disband the movement.

The World Comes to Montreal

When the International Study Week opened on June 23, twenty-
one girls and fourteen fellows from fourteen cities were among the 180
lay leaders present. Nineteen chaplains made the trip as well as
numerous seminarians who were not officially listed. The established
movements in Europe sent key leaders from their national teams.
Delegates came from a dozen countries in Central and South America,
including ten from Costa Rica and five from Brazil. There were even
several leaders representing China and Japan. In all forty-two countries were represented.[9]

Sessions were held each day in language groups. Leaders from
each country present reported on the problems of working youth in
their country and on the status of their national movement. Talks
were then given on the development of an authentic YCW movement. Outside the formal meetings were the even more important
personal contacts made among the leaders from all over the world.

The week left us excited by the tremendous spirit among the
experienced leaders and more determined than ever to build a strong
movement in the United States. At the urging of the international office,
the priests and young men from the States held a caucus and agreed to
meet again in the fall to form a national organization for the men.
Chicago was chosen as the headquarters because it was centrally located
and was the only city with a full-time chaplain. Tony Zivalich and Ed

Dansart, leaders in the first postwar cell started by Fr. William Quinn, accepted the responsibility of planning a study program for the Thanksgiving weekend and, with the help of Pat Keegan, developing a manual to help new young men's groups get started.

Ed Dansart.

Pat and Fr. Edward Mitchinson, the English national chaplain, stayed several weeks in the United States to help American leaders and chaplains lay the groundwork for unification. Pat returned a month later to help Tony and Ed prepare for the fall meeting. In August, Ed became a full-time worker at the Chicago headquarters and began work on the proposed manual for new groups. In October, Tony Zivalich came on the full-time team.

Immediately following the study week in Montreal, fifty leaders representing the YCW women throughout the country met in Syosset, Long Island, for a three-day meeting to make plans for a provisional national organization. We divided the existing sections into four regional areas and chose leaders from each to be responsible for coordinating established sections and organizing new ones according to the guidelines outlined by the international leaders. The area leaders along with the elected national officers would form a governing council. Edwina Hearn was elected president, and Mary Tuohy, the leader of the central section in New York City, was elected secretary. As director of publications, I too was elected to the council. The council agreed to meet twice yearly and be responsible for planning policy, outlining the annual program theme and directing further expansion.[10]

We voted to establish headquarters in Chicago and Mary Tuohy agreed to move there in October. Edwina, Mary, and I would function as a committee to direct day-to-day operations. Fr. John Egan accepted the position of chaplain for our branch of the movement.

The report issued in Syosset said the YCW was "*one* movement composed of boys and girls," and we were the girls' branch.[11] Also, "YCW leaders must be genuine workers in close touch with the daily life of their fellow workers, at home, in the neighborhood, in the factory and the office. . . . In a neighborhood where factory workers predominate, YCW leaders should be factory workers; in a neighborhood of office workers, they should be office workers; in a neighborhood of various occupations, the principal varieties should be represented among the leaders."[12]

The committee was then charged with preparing a beginning manual for the young women and the writing of the yearly program of social inquiries based on input from all the sections. Since this would take time, we decided to use the English edition of *How to Start a Section*, with necessary adaptations, for four months to insure that all members understood the common terminology and method. Dues were also agreed upon and each section was asked to raise fifty dollars by the first of October for the needs of the new headquarters. A new *Leaders' Bulletin for YCW Girls*, to be issued monthly by the general committee, would replace all the bulletins put out previously in local federations.[13]

Planning Committee Established

Back home in Chicago, we knew we had undertaken a big job. Our numbers were small and the country was large. Much planning was necessary. Patrick Keegan, president of the English YCW, played a key role helping us do that. In 1946 he had become the executive secretary of the International YCW Bureau, established in Brussels after the war. Cardijn charged him with the task of fostering the expansion of the movement in the English-speaking countries. During the ten years he remained on the leadership team of the International YCW, Pat made many trips to the United States to assist our American leaders. This was especially critical in the early years.

On July 24, 1947, the full-time leaders and the two full-time chaplains, Egan and Quinn, met with Pat and Msgr. Hillenbrand at the Hillenbrand family home. We decided to form a YCW Planning Committee which would meet at regular intervals to discuss policy, make expansion plans, and report on progress.

Pat started off that first meeting with a report of his meeting with Msgr. Howard Carroll, secretary of the NCWC. Carroll had offered the assistance of the national secretariat in developing the movement. He said the movement should get the approval of the NCWC which represented the bishops, and "any formation of a national committee or council should be made through them." Because the NCWC saw as its purpose the "promotion of unity in Catholic work," they felt it necessary to have a controlling voice. Moreover, "official" Catholic Action was by definition the agency responsible to the bishops who empowered it through their individual mandates.

To protect the integrity and the uniqueness of the movement, Pat made two suggestions. First, we could avoid conflict with the NCWC guidelines if we substituted the word "general" for "national" in describing the new organization of Young Christian Workers. Secondly, we would have more freedom to move forward if we called ourselves simply a movement of young workers rather than Catholic Action. These were important distinctions.

Furthermore, said Keegan, it was good that Chicago would be the center because Cardinal Stritch had supported the groups and Edwina and I were already experienced leaders. "We need to assume this responsibility immediately and be definite about it." He then recommended that Msgr. Hillenbrand, because of his recognized leadership among priests in the movement, sit in on all major meetings in the role of overall chaplain to the Young Christian Workers. Fr. Egan had already agreed to be chaplain to the women's branch. Fr. Quinn would continue to advise the men, though his primary assignment from Cardinal Stritch was to serve as chaplain to *all* the specialized movements in the Chicago archdiocese, which included the Young Christian Students and the Christian Family Movement.[14] The suggestions made good sense and we all agreed.

Another decision was to drop the word "cell" and use the YCW terminology common in other English-speaking countries. This change was made in some of the young women's groups after our 1946 study week, but everyone had not gone along. Now it would be mandatory. The base unit would be the parish section composed of a leaders' group, teams led by individual leaders, and general members not on teams. The leaders would meet weekly with the chaplain present to discuss the gospel and liturgy,[15] report on action accomplished, and make a review of influence. The social inquiry would follow on a topic chosen by the national program committee that related to the young worker's life. Teams would meet informally, usually biweekly, to work on the action of the inquiry with the leader. A monthly general meeting would be held for all team members and other interested persons to generate interest and enthusiasm for the YCW program and to promote the idea that each young worker should be a Christian witness at work and in the community. Finally, it would serve as a social gathering for the young workers in the neighborhood.

The YCW Planning Committee thus began to set policy for the combined movement of young men and women, and it became a clearinghouse for ideas. One of its chief concerns was to make contact with priests and bishops in dioceses where the YCW had not yet started and help to organize new sections.

Shortly after that first meeting, the chaplains arranged to give a private retreat for the new governing team. It served as a reminder that we were doing the Lord's work. The plans and the travels and the organizing would depend on a prayer life centered on the Mass and a high degree of personal discipline.

First Study Weekend for Young Men

In November 1947, the fellows' sections were formally unified. Thirty-seven young men met at Childerly in Wheeling, Illinois. Leaders came from Manhattan, Brooklyn, South Bend, San Francisco, St. Paul, Detroit, Youngstown (Ohio), and Scranton (Pennsylvania). They represented occupations ranging from office workers to mechanics, stock handlers, and a bartender. Tony Zivalich of Chicago was elected general president unanimously, and Ed Dansart of Chicago was elected general secretary and put in charge of publications, including a monthly bulletin for leaders. Details on the organization of sections were carefully outlined, and it was agreed that office workers and factory workers could be mixed in the same section.

In small discussion groups, facts were presented on working conditions which needed changing, like the New York garment factory where twenty-five workers worked in a steamy room with no ventilation, and the Western Union station which was a fire hazard. They talked about the lack of solidarity among workers, i.e., workers who were always out for No. 1, and the fact that many workers did not realize their right to be treated with dignity as human beings at work.[16]

The first study weekend was important because it set a firm pattern of organization and established a factual approach to problems. A general council was set up including Tony and Ed, the full-timers in Chicago, plus a representative from the four cities where sections were firmly established—Manhattan, Brooklyn, South Bend, and Chicago. They made plans to work out a program of inquiries related to working life and the council agreed to meet in the spring.

Life at Headquarters

By this time the third floor at 3 East Chicago Avenue was getting crowded. Loretta Fenton was still coordinator for the high school girls and secretary to the priests. Mary Tuohy had arrived from New York, so there were now five of us working full time for the Young Christian Workers. A few months later, two full-timers arrived to work for the Midwest region of College YCS, and they took over a room. Down the hall was Ed Marciniak and the Catholic Labor Alliance which continued to be a resource for the growing movement, though always an independent organization.

Lunch was at a long table in the hall. Everyone brought a bag lunch. There were no toilet facilities, and in time of need a person would have to go down to the second floor where there was an old-fashioned bathroom with an overhead tin water tank for flushing. The secretary in the Confraternity of Christian Doctrine office next door had long been used to peace and quiet. Annoyed by the steady traffic and the noise of flushing water, she complained one day to Fr. Dan Cantwell, the Labor Alliance chaplain. "Well, Mrs. K.," he answered, "They're good people, but they're not angels!"[17]

Life was rugged and serious but never boring. Besides the steady stream of local leaders arriving for meetings of one kind or another, leaders from other cities stopped by, as well as seminarians and priests passing through town. One especially interesting visitor was Fr. George Kalovic, a priest from Eastern Europe who had been in a prison camp during the war, didn't wear a Roman collar, and carried his breviary wrapped in a newspaper. On one occasion he talked Edwina and Tony into accompanying him on a hair-raising drive to Pennsylvania to organize young workers in the coal-mining towns there. He had no inhibitions about driving through the mountains at breakneck speed, and he was just as undaunted in his approach to potential chaplains. He was one of several priests who conducted study days at headquarters to broaden our vision and perspectives.

Our ongoing work was correspondence with section leaders, visits to sections, and analysis of the reports coming in from sections on their action. On the basis of such input, we wrote and distributed the *Leaders' Bulletin*. Until October 1948 each bulletin contained the social inquiries for the weekly meetings, the gospel inquiries, and the discussion questions on the liturgy, as well as reports of actions. It was also the primary means of sharing news and ideas with members throughout the country. Beginning in 1948, program outlines were put out in booklet form semiannually, later annually, and the monthly bulletins provided background information on the program as well as news of the movement.

How to Start a Section of YCW, an introduction to the movement with a program of beginning meetings, was published by the young men and became a staple for priests and leaders beginning new sections. In 1949 the young women finally put out their own edition of *How to Start.* These booklets were a means of insuring that all new groups would conform to the YCW method and pattern of organization.

For eight months the *Bulletin for YCW Girls* was printed, but money shortages prevailed, and, beginning in June 1948, the publications of both branches were mimeographed. *Impact, A Magazine for Working Girls* continued as a means of reaching out to working girls outside the movement. Circulation averaged over three thousand throughout 1947 and 1948. A special issue on marriage in May 1948, designed to focus on the subject of the year's inquiry program, sold out a printing of 17,500. The appeal of that issue was enhanced by the cover picture of Loretta Fenton and her new husband John Brislen on their wedding day. Loretta was the first to leave the hallowed halls of 3 East to get married.

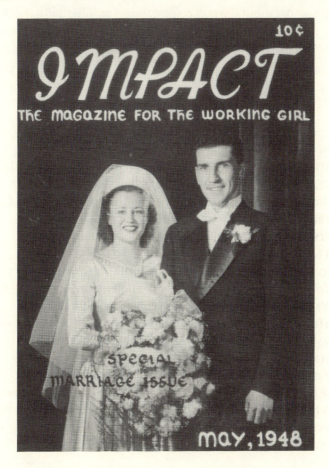

In 1950 everyone else had to leave because the pastor of the cathedral parish decided to tear the old building down to build a high school. The diocesan offices in the building, along with the Chicago YCW Federation, the Cana Conference, and the Catholic Labor Alliance were given quarters in another building in the neighborhood owned by the archdiocese. The national offices of the specialized movement found temporary quarters in two rooms of a parish building on Deming Place. When the parish needed the space in 1954, they once again had to find a place for the national headquarters.

In 1954 an old four-story, forty-five room building at 1700 West Jackson Boulevard was found, and the national headquarters of all the specialized movements moved in. Men on the national team had bedroom space on the third floor. Though they did not have to pay rent, the movements were responsible for all maintenance and upkeep. A house on the far West Side of the city was purchased with an interest-free loan from Catholic Charities to provide living quarters for the girls.

The Problem of Official Recognition

Throughout the late forties the YCW movement struggled with the birth pains of an emerging lay movement. In the words of one observer, the YCW "viewed specialized action as a total apostolate [and] they did not wish to be defined simply as another Catholic organization. Their aim was to bring clergy and laity together as members of an organism, the Body of Christ, and to see that both worked together, each in their own field, so that the Church could go out into the world and change it. Restoration of society, however, called for either a restoration of an ancient understanding of the layman's role or the articulation of a new one."[18]

In following Keegan's advice to drop the label "Catholic Action," we set aside the idea that we were participating "in the apostolate of the hierarchy." The focus of our tactical changes was the issue of priestly authority over lay movements. Each bishop had jurisdiction over the faithful in his own diocese. The differing views of individual bishops toward the YCW complicated the development of a national movement and weakened the authority of its leadership. Several situations illustrate the problem.

At their first council meeting in 1947, the young men had discussed the rules of affiliation and decided that when a diocese had only one section, it could act independently, but when two or more sections were recognized and affiliated by the general committee, a federation should be formed. It would be the duty of the federation officers to affiliate new sections to itself. In Brooklyn, Rev. Francis Donnelly, the unofficial coordinator of the movement there and an early supporter of the Chicago initiatives, took issue with the decision that YCW sections in a diocese must organize in a federation. He felt the need to proceed with caution in dealing with the bishop. "The YCW is a lay movement," he wrote, "but it must fit into the ecclesiastical setup."[19]

Donnelly felt that a federation was a diocesan organization and setting it up without the approval of the bishop would be a tactical mistake. Moreover, he felt that, as the spokesman for the movement in his city before the bishop and among other priests, he should have the right to make such basic and important decisions. He was in a better position to judge the local situation. When the time seemed ripe, he added, "the other chaplains and myself will see to it that we federate with due approval."[20]

Even the most supportive chaplains wanted to make decisions that the lay leaders felt were their prerogative. Fr. John Egan and Edwina Hearn, responding to Donnelly's complaint, stressed the argument that the lay officers had the rightful authority to make decisions on organizational matters.[21] Before the year was out, Bishop Malloy gave his approval to the YCW in the Brooklyn diocese, and the discussion was ended. Brooklyn formed a federation.

Since the Young Christian Workers in San Francisco had been told by Archbishop Mitty that they were not to affiliate with any group outside their own archdiocese, those who attended meetings in Syosset and Chicago were present merely as observers. When they wrote in the spring of 1948 that they were still not ready to affiliate, the women planning a council meeting in Scranton, Pennsylvania, in April told the San Francisco leaders they would have to be excluded because the council was an official policy-making body. They could, however, attend the annual study weekend because it was not a policy-making event. At the council meeting itself, the participants declared that they were the body responsible for interpreting policy set by the International YCW and formulating new policy consistent with it. Pat Keegan and Cardijn himself had affirmed their leadership.[22]

In early May, Joseph E. Scheider, new director of the NCWC Youth Department, visited the Chicago headquarters and proposed that the YCW affiliate with the National Catholic Youth Council. Msgr. Hillenbrand and the lay leaders were tempted by the prospect of official recognition, but an NCWC official friendly to the movement warned that Scheider did not really understand the YCW and wanted it to be just another youth organization under the control of the NCWC's Youth Department. We declined Scheider's offer. We softened our refusal to Scheider by saying that the movement was not yet ready to seek national prominence.[23]

We agreed among ourselves that we were different from other youth organizations which were primarily concerned with the personal and religious behavior of Catholics. Though we emphasized the importance of living a Christian life, we were convinced we must be concerned with the problems of social injustice that affected working people. Since this was not always understood by church authorities, we felt we had nothing to gain from official recognition at that time.

The status of official Catholic Action was further muddied when Pope Pius XII, in September 1948, issued a new statement in which he recognized the sodalities of Our Lady as fulfilling the requirements of Catholic Action. He commended all who possessed "excellent zeal for the apostolate" but warned that those who desire to reduce what was done in the interest of souls "to a single pattern" made an error that was "completely alien to the mind of the Church."[24]

This new statement destroyed Hillenbrand's earlier analysis of the specialized movements, which was based on Pius XI's statement that Jocism was the preeminent expression of Catholic Action. By the end of 1948, he clearly sympathized with Keegan's suggestion that a mandate from the bishops no longer be a priority.

In many cities where chaplains were concerned about the need of a mandate from the local bishop, members were cautioned to move slowly and organize quietly.[25] In several dioceses individual priests who asked permission from their local bishop before starting were not allowed to go ahead, though a few like Bishop Buddy in San Diego strongly encouraged parish priests to start YCW sections.

Public Action vs. Quiet Initiative

In Chicago, Hillenbrand mistrusted large mass meetings and public statements as shallow expressions. He was also mindful of Cardinal Stritch's earlier restriction on publicity. He encouraged the more in-depth formation of an elite corps of leaders who would influence others quietly, the leaven penetrating the masses. This was not the style of the European Jocists, who saw public gatherings as a useful tool. When the International Study Week was held in Montreal, press releases had been sent out to newspapers, and journalists were invited to attend press conferences to learn and report on the movement of Young Christian Workers.

It was this difference in approach that accounted for the confusion some Americans felt when Pat Keegan spoke about the three key elements of the Young Christian Workers: education, service, and representation. Education, of course. Service, absolutely. But representation? For a long time this was understood as the need for individual Young Christian Workers to speak out and represent their fellow workers on the job or in the union.

Gradually we realized that there was more to representative action than that. When the girls' introductory manual was published in 1949, representation was explained this way: "If the YCW is to serve young workers in their needs, it must also represent them before those public and private bodies which control and influence the conditions that effect young workers. In every way possible, the YCW represents young workers through existing organizations and institutions such as unions, civic groups, etc. In the name of working youth, the YCW must initiate action, make demands, influence public opinion, and create the necessary favorable conditions for the integral uplifting of all working youth."[26]

Obviously this kind of representation required building the name recognition of the YCW as a viable force in the public mind, something not possible when we were told to be quiet and unobtrusive. Because the general headquarters was in Chicago, Msgr. Hillenbrand insisted that the instructions of Cardinal Stritch be followed even though we were no longer concerned about an official mandate. This is probably one reason why few people in the forties knew about the Young Christian Workers.

On one occasion when a local newspaperman in Chicago wanted to do a story on the YCW, the answer had to be no. When a Catholic Radio Forum in Pennsylvania requested facts for a program about Canon Cardijn and the Young Christian Workers, we again felt we had to refuse aid. As Tony Zivalich explained, "Our movement is not a secret or underground one.... Information is given freely to interested individuals or groups, ... but not to the general public." At its current stage of development, the YCW found it advantageous "that we do not become too obvious."[27]

Return to the Parish

One major stumbling block for some sections was the decision made at the 1947 planning committee meeting to break up the existing central sections and send leaders back to their parishes to start sections there. Parish sections were the norm in Europe, and it was felt that this was a more natural way to recruit, since members of a section would be from the same neighborhood. Also, it would be easier to get local priests as chaplains. Many leaders did return to their parishes and start sections, but it did not always work out. In some cases there was no priest in the parish willing to serve as chaplain. In others, young women who worked and recreated in the downtown areas of cities like Chicago, New York, and Cleveland no longer had regular contact with young people in their home neighborhoods. It was not the base of their social life.

By the beginning of 1948, all Chicago sections were in parishes and other cities were moving in that direction, though some leaders had serious problems finding local priests to serve as chaplains. Caroline Pezzullo, who came from New York to succeed Edwina Hearn as girls' president in 1948, wrote to one such leader, "Most [prospective leaders] we talk to can't follow through unless we have chaplains lined up in the parish they are in. Almost every way we turn, that seems to be the crux of the problem."[28]

The fellows insisted from the beginning that sections must be parish-based. "Unless the curate in a parish is the chaplain, and unless the young workers in the leaders' group are representative of the parish, unless they hang around and have influence with their natural groupings of friends who will become their teams, and unless they develop a real neighborhood and workers' consciousness and do all in their power to serve, educate, and represent the young workers in their parish, they are not following the YCW pattern. . . . I am sorry," continued Red Sullivan in a letter to a prospective leader, "but this is the way things have got to be. I hope you can do something the way I have outlined."[29]

A key issue for the YCW men was finding new leaders. Few were to be found around the parish church. Once a leader was found, he could find others in the neighborhood. The problem was finding a leader in the first place. Where did the fellows hang out? Often, it was the neighborhood bar. Bar hopping became a common tactic for YCW organizers. Over the years beer drinking became an identifying mark of many a Young Christian Worker. It established him as "one of the boys," while providing a congenial setting to meet and share concerns with others. Some of the girls took up cigarette smoking for a similar reason, and some former members recall "smoke-filled" meeting rooms.

Acting on Real Problems in Work Life

The inquiry program from October 1948 through July 1950, was on the problems of working life, although the monthly breakdown of the inquiries in the two branches differed in specifics. The aim of the movement was clearly described in the introduction to the program on working life in the 1948–49 Girls' Inquiry Booklet, and without the restrictive "girl," it describes both branches.

> Aim: To help a girl worker become aware of the various conditions in her work life which are opposed to her dignity as a human being and which result in the abuse of her rights as a person.
> To help her see how the abuse of these rights affect her whole life and how a better unity among girl workers would help to safeguard them for her.
> As someone said, the above aim is a "large order."
> Actually it is not only the aim of this year's program, but the over-all aim of the YCW. No matter what program the YCW might take, it should always serve to make us aware of our dignity as human beings who are destined, here and

now, to be sons of God. In the same way each program should serve to make us aware of the obstacles standing in the way of achieving this destiny. . . .

At the Cleveland study week one of the most important conclusions was: "we must face the fact that YCW must help to reorganize the social order; and we as workers must be particularly concerned with the changes in the economic structure, the conditions of which affect the whole life of young workers." . . .

The weekly actions which we and our fellow workers carry out will not, of course, bring about a complete solution to the whole problem. They should, however, bring about some sort of change, no matter how small. . . . The change must be either on the condition itself or upon the worker who is being affected by the condition.[30]

Inquiries focused on concern for other workers, the new employee, the person with personal problems, and physical conditions at work such as lunch facilities, cleanliness, lighting, and safety. The following year, the program centered on "the importance of work in the life of the young girl," and how it affected her development as a person. With this in mind, the matter of career choice and using one's talent in the job became a concern as did the need to help new high school graduates in the parish find suitable jobs.

A New York section set up an employment service, and Jo Salerno quit her job to work full time running it. In six months, seventy-seven young women applied to the service for help. In the three years that the service existed, 135 were placed in jobs and uncounted numbers received counseling, advice, and encouragement.[31] It was discontinued when Jo left and no one was available to take her place.

Actions in the men's sections included helping young workers get jobs and spreading information about free job aptitude testing conducted by the U.S. Employment Service. One section found jobs for ten young workers, and they all later became YCW team members. Other YCW members got involved in their unions and brought in new members. One YCW leader who brought in twenty new members to his union was made a union steward. Another became active in his union and helped put out a pamphlet promoting it. As a result, membership in the union tripled. Another leader started a union where he worked. A section in Ohio developed a service for visiting sick workers and raised money for a young worker who spent fifteen months in the hospital after an accidental shooting.[32]

In February of 1949 Caroline Pezzullo and Tony Zivalich, accompanied by Msgr. Hillenbrand and Pat Keegan, took an extended tour of the West Coast. Although their principal objective was San Francisco and Los Angeles where special meetings were planned, they stopped along the way in many cities to talk to priests about the YCW.

Unfortunately, on the return trip, the travelers had a serious car accident. The lay leaders were hurt slightly, but Msgr. Hillenbrand was seriously injured and had to remain in the hospital in Tulsa for eighteen months with a shattered hip that required extensive surgery. Though the national leaders visited him for consultation on several occasions, it was Fr. Egan and Fr. Quinn who replaced him in day-to-day operations.

By 1949 the YCW consisted of forty-five girls' sections in nineteen cities and twelve sections of young men in nine cities.[33] It had survived the first few years of trial and error. Due to a head start during the war years, the young women had grown in organizational skills and many new sections were formed, especially in cities where existing sections provided a model.

Those of us who were the first national leaders in the women's branch began to leave the movement around this time and were replaced by younger leaders. Some former YCS members moved directly into YCW groups, thus providing trained leaders to start new sections and move quickly into positions of greater responsibility. Early in 1949, I left the movement and was replaced by Mary Lou Genova who became director of publications. She had been a high school leader before becoming editor of *Impact* magazine in 1948. Viola Brennan, a college YCS leader, became president of the Chicago Girls' YCW Federation in 1947 and followed Mary Tuohy as general secretary-treasurer in October 1949.

The Need for Full-time Organizers

With the expansion of the movement a major goal, the leaders had to establish priorities. Trained organizers were needed to help start sections in cities where the movement did not yet exist. In January 1949, John Kelly from Brooklyn and George "Red" Sullivan from Chicago were taken on as full-time workers to travel the country, contacting priests, and training leaders. The need to train and support organizers to work in various parts of the country, however, took money, even though full-time workers and organizers never earned more than their board and a few dollars for personal expenses. Dues were collected from all members, but they were never enough to cover expenses. In July Russ Tershy came from San Francisco to oversee fund-raising. Before this, isolated attempts to raise money were tried, and some of the active priests organized "Friends of the YCW," volunteering a month's pay per year to the movement. They also sought donations from individuals who supported the goals of the movement. Often, when the organizers went into a city, they were supported by local priests and leaders.[34]

One fund-raising idea that became a regular part of the program was the St. Theresa's Day offering by each member. St. Theresa of Lisieux had been named as patron of the Young Christian Workers by Pius XII because she was a modern saint with a missionary spirit. Cardijn often spoke of the need for young Christians to be missionaries in the everyday world. Her feast day on October 3rd became a day of celebration for YCWs throughout the world, and the American leaders asked individual leaders to contribute their pay for that day to help support the work of the movement. Over the years many sections had social affairs in October to raise money. St. Theresa's Day gatherings with mass followed by a large dance became common.

Additionally, it was decided to cut costs in day-to-day operations. One such cut was the elimination of *Impact* because it was not self-supporting and expanding it into a more competitive magazine or newspaper would require an expertise and an outlay of capital that the movement simply did not have. More to the point, there was no one to replace Mary Lou Genova as editor when she left to get married. In October 1949, it was announced that the magazine would fold and unused subscriptions would be taken over by *WORK*, the newspaper of the Catholic Labor Alliance. That publication was geared to the social action message of the church and fit in very well with the educational goals of the YCW. Moreover, it was not limited to women readers. It was hoped that at some future date the movement would publish a four-page newspaper. (It finally did, eight years later!)[35]

Caroline Pezzullo and Joseph Cardijn, 1951.

The International Connection

In 1949, when the American YCW was just getting on its feet, the International JOC announced its twenty-fifth anniversary celebration in Brussels to be held the following year. The American leaders were expected to participate, but Tony Zivalich and Caroline Pezzullo felt it was more important to use their limited resources to build a strong national movement at home than spend money chasing off to Europe. Pat Keegan agreed in a letter to Caroline: "I told them in no uncertain terms at the International Bureau that the best move towards the International YCW is a strong YCW in America, and I still hold to that. I am not so sure that the canon would agree with my line . . . because he is building on this International Study Week. . . . Regarding yourselves, my view is that it is doubtful if it would be worth all the effort and cost at this stage, but the next time we have one, you will be in a better position and able to contribute something wonderful to the event."[36]

Cardijn did not agree with this thinking and wrote to Msgr. Hillenbrand, still in the hospital in Tulsa.

> I am very sad to hear that the American YCW hesitates to send a delegation of leaders—boys and girls—to the International Study Week and Jubilee Congress to be held in Brussels from 3rd to 10th September 1950. It seems that the reason of this attitude should be lack of money which does not allow to cover the expenses of that delegation.
>
> This decision—if it should be maintained—would be very harmful for the International YCW. The U.S.A. plays today the most important role in international affairs. At all international meetings they are represented by a strong delegation; at international meetings for Youth also, as for the World Assembly of Youth, World Federation of Democratic Youth, Jamboree of Boy Scouts, etc. . . .
>
> The Holy Father personally insists on the important role the YCW has to play in the actual evolution of the world. . . . The Holy Father worries seriously about the recent Congress and Festival organized at Budapest during three weeks by the Communist countries at which eighty-two countries of the world were represented—and he considers the International YCW as the only movement capable to give a positive answer to such demonstrations and attempts to dechristianize more and more the Working Youth.
>
> I would be personally affected by the absence of a delegation from the States. Pat Keegan, myself, and several other leaders of the movement have done various trips over there in order to help in spreading the movement. Nobody amongst the delegates at the Conference would understand this absence of the most important country in the world.
>
> I would be very grateful to you, dear Monsignor, if you could help the leaders of the Chicago HQ and encourage them strongly, so that they might find the financial assistance necessary for their participation to that Conference. . . .
>
> The latter shall allow to all the YCW delegates to study more seriously the problem of the Young Worker and the method of action and influence among themselves; it shall

also allow them to take contact with the delegates of forty countries, and above all to discover more deeply the urgent necessity of a steady collaboration between all the Young Workers and leaders of the various countries of the world. . . .

I apologize again for such a letter and thank you in advance for your very helpful intervention.

Very devotedly and sincerely yours in Christ,

Canon Jos. Cardijn[37]

Needless to say, this urgent appeal, in spite of its somewhat convoluted language, had the desired effect. Tony and Caroline, accompanied by Fr. Francis Wendell, O.P., representing Msgr. Hillenbrand, made the trip to Brussels. Tony was even prevailed upon to march in a stadium procession during the congress carrying the American flag.

By early 1950 the national leaders were confident that a movement that would profoundly affect young men and women and bring Christian values into the working world was underway. "Right now," said Ed Dansart, "we have sections in twenty-three cities. Four guys working full time and three girls. We also have hopes of increasing the organizers some time during the year."[38]

Expansion of the movement was sure to continue as organizers from headquarters moved around the country, selling the great ideas of the movement to young men and women and to the priests who would be their chaplains. Once sold on the idea, it was assumed that the new leaders would take the ball and run with it. The trick, as the national leaders saw it, was to get enough trained organizers in the field, young men and women thoroughly grounded in the YCW method and fully aware of the problems facing young workers. They must be versed in the social teachings of the Church, able to speak to a group, and to establish rapport with individuals. A demanding job for a young man or woman about twenty-five years old with just a few years in a local section—but those who took on the task were idealistic and undaunted. They were totally convinced of the rightness of their cause. Who could help but agree?

Looking Back on the Late Forties

The YCW awakened and deepened my faith at a time when I was slipping away from the Church. Its fruits were tremendous. (San Francisco)

It helped form my social conscience and gave me an understanding of the Church that I would never have gotten from my parish life. This understanding made it very easy for me to accept the changes that came about with Vatican II, and prepared me to deal with the whole question of personal responsibility, looking for the deeper meaning, considering matter over form. I have the feeling of being part of "The Movement"—and I take that to include the workers' movement, the civil rights movement, the women's movement . . . and this sense certainly started with my experience at 3 East. (Chicago)

Some of us became union workers, even officers. We printed Christmas cards to "put Christ back into Christmas." We brought people back to the Church. We worked in hospitals as volunteers. (New York City)

Much of YCW produced a type of idealism, but overall I think the effect was toward an increase in Christian maturity and awareness that permeated all aspects of life subsequent to YCW. Perhaps a form of Christian "osmosis" took place. (San Francisco)

I think my experience with YCW helped my maturing process and encouraged me to take risks that I ordinarily would not have taken. It exposed me to new ideas, new types of people, sometimes in opposition to my family's wishes. . . . My overall reaction to my experience in the YCW is that it instilled in me a social conscience that I otherwise would not have had. This has overflowed into my personal life ever since. (Brooklyn)

YCW opened my eyes to the concept of human dignity. It raised my consciousness to the social conditions which obstructed human dignity and human growth. That interest and that search has never stopped. (New York City)

YCW (and Friendship House) made Catholic Action come alive. It forced me into continued updating and reading of the Church and its mission. It provided me with a sense of community and blessed me with extraordinary friendship. . . . YCW was like going into a foreign land and becoming aware of beauty, architecture, love, Christ's presence. I still think of myself as a not-so-Young Christian Worker. (Washington, D.C.)

Notes

1. YCW questionnaire, YCW papers, UND archives.
2. Report on Present Status of YCW Girls in the United States. YCW questionnaire, UND archives.
3. Letter of Lorraine Noel, Manchester, New Hampshire, to Edwina Hearn, February 1947. *Ibid.*
4. Letter from Paul E. Demers, Mike Gengren, Frank Lamarre, Lorraine Noel to "Dear Fellow Workers in Christ," June 10, 1947. UND archives.
5. UND archives.
6. Mary Tuohy to Edwina Hearn, June 16, 1947. UND archives.
7. Edwina Hearn to Mary Tuohy, June 17, 1947. UND archives.
8. Henri Roy, O.M.I., *The YCW Movement* (an advertising brochure), Manchester YCW, 1945, p. 10.
9. First List of Participants to the International Study Week. Also Second List. Zotti papers.
10. "Report of Study Week," *Leaders' Bulletin for YCW Girls*, October 6, 1946. Zotti papers.
11. The use of the term "girls" to describe the feminine branch of the movement reflects the terminology used to identify young women in the forties and fifties. Most young women in those days identified themselves as "girls" and applied the term "women" to their mothers' generation. The young men, on the other hand, were more conscious of the derogatory connotation of "boys" as children and preferred to call themselves "guys" or "fellows." Even they reserved the word "men" for those who were older or married. The European Jocists in their early and mid teens were more appropriately called "boys and girls." The persistence of the term "girls" for young women is a possible indication of the low status of women in society at that time.

    The use of the word "girls" persisted until the sexes were mixed in the mid-fifties. After that, the term "young adults" came into use.

    We have tried to identify the feminine gender as young women as much as possible, except where we use direct quotes from the period.
12. Report of study weekend, Syosset, New York, July 4–6, 1947. YCW papers, UND archives.
13. *Ibid.*
14. Minutes of the YCW Planning Committee, 8:00 P.M., July 24, 1947. UND archives.
15. The inclusion of a short discussion on some aspect of the liturgy had been added to the meeting agenda in the Chicago cells, because Msgr. Hillenbrand felt that an understanding and practice of liturgical worship was essential to the development of a proper lay spirituality necessary in the movement. This became part of the agenda for all sections in the country when the sections were unified.
16. Report on Chicago Study Week, 1947. Handwritten notes of Tony Zivalich. Zotti papers.

[17] Story reported by Regina Bess Finney in conversation with the author, June 1984.

[18] Robb, *Specialized Catholic Action*, 1936–1949, unpublished doctoral dissertation submitted to University of Minnesota, 1972, p. 293.

[19] Rev. Francis B. Donnelly to Mary Tuohy, January 10, 1948. YCW papers, UND archives.

[20] *Ibid.*

[21] Robb, *op. cit.*, p. 301.

[22] YCW Girls General Headquarters to Eileen Labrecht, San Francisco, and Josephine LaTorre, Oakland, February 20, 1948.

[23] Tony Zivalich to Pat Keegan, May 7, 1948.

[24] Quoted by Robb, *op. cit.*, p. 315.

[25] Mary Tuohy in letter to Rita Lefevre, North Hollywood, California: "It is not necessary that there be any official approval or mandate." She then recommended that the chaplain of a new group could let the Chancery know of its existence at an appropriate time.

[26] *How to Start a YCW Section for Girls*, Chicago, 1947.

[27] Tony Zivalich and Edwina Hearn to Klara Koepell, secretary, Lebanon Catholic Radio Forum, November 11, 1947. UND archives.

[28] Caroline Pezzullo to Rosemary Smith, Cleveland, April 28, 1949. UND archives.

[29] Red Sullivan to Bill Roberts, Wauwatosa, Wisconsin, March 15, 1949. UND archives.

[30] Introduction to Girls' Program. "Working Girl at Work," October 1948. Zotti papers.

[31] Action reports in YCW papers, UND archives.

[32] *Ibid.*

[33] YCW Girls' General Council Meeting Report, March 26–28, 1949 and YCW Second General Council Meeting Report, March 5–6, 1949. UND archives.

[34] Russ Tershy to author. Recorded October 1, 1985.

[35] *AIM* was a four-page tabloid newspaper first issued in December 1958 with funding from Foundation for Youth and Student Affairs. It lasted two years until funding ran out.

[36] Pat Keegan, letter to Caroline Pezzullo, September 27, 1949.

[37] Joseph Cardijn, letter to Reynold Hillenbrand, 1950.

[38] Ed Dansart to Paul Connelly, St. Louis, January 19, 1950. UND archives.

6

Building a Movement of Young Workers

When the Korean War broke out in 1950, thousands of young men were drafted into the armed forces. This had a disastrous effect on the new sections that the early organizers had started with such optimism. Many sections were left with no leaders. By the Study Week in September 1950, the number of fellows' sections was cut in half.

The interruption of a working career for a minimum of two years caused a heavy turnover in membership. A key problem in every male section was to recruit and train at as fast a rate as the armed forces enlisted and drafted section members. The time required to reach young men after high school graduation and before they entered service was reduced to only a year or so. Several solutions were attempted. One idea was to set up a separate division for young fellows still in school to prepare them for early work life and the draft, called Pre-YCW. This didn't work because the Young Christian Students were already organized in many of the high schools, and their attention was on school problems rather than conscious preparation for work.

Then the national leaders developed a special program for high school seniors and others expecting to be inducted into the services. *Going in the Service?* was a straightforward pamphlet telling pre-inductees what kind of routine to expect and describing social pressures and temptations they would meet, complete with discussion questions for small groups. It was used successfully in some parishes and high schools, particularly those run by the Christian Brothers who in 1951 had gone on record advocating pre-induction training in their schools.

Following Men into Service

The YCW then decided to reach out to men in the services. They published a booklet of sixteen meetings, using the inquiry method on specific problems of military life, entitled *Now That You're in Service—What Next?* which they distributed to former members who had been drafted—and to military chaplains. Although no formal records were kept of its effectiveness, numerous YCW groups were active in various camps. Don Slattery of Chicago had a YCW group for a year on Okinawa, and several of its members started YCW groups in their home parishes afterwards. Veronica Salvado entered the movement as a WAVE in San Diego and later came to headquarters where she worked as secretary to the national chaplain. Tom Laughlin made his first contact with the YCW when he was a soldier at Ft. Hood in Texas. After his release from service, he started sections in his home town of New Orleans.

Priests in parishes were encouraged to give priority to fellows over twenty who were free from the draft. They also were advised to organize on their own, because the headquarters had neither the financial resources nor the personnel to send organizers out into the various cities and dioceses requesting aid. In previous years enthusiastic organizers traveled the country helping priests start sections, and many depended on their help. George Sullivan, who had become YCW president in 1950, stressed in October 1952, that the responsibility and initiative for starting sections must be on the local level, with advice and encouragement from headquarters.

Six months later he complimented the priests who began to rely less on organizers and, indeed, had experimented in presenting the social inquiry to new members and had developed realistic ways to start new sections. As long as the fundamentals of the movement were insured, he said, they were free to mold the YCW to fit local situations, adding "Our movement 'moves' on what is happening to its members and the effect they are having on the lives of others."[1]

The Search for "Genuine" Workers

The constant goal in organizing new sections in the fifties was to seek out prospective leaders who were "genuine workers" and focus attention on working life as the identifying element of the movement. Only young workers themselves could influence other young workers and improve the conditions of working life. Therein was the heart of a continuing difficulty in the development of a young-worker movement in the United States. Who were the young workers?

In Europe it was easy to know. People were born into a social class that determined their adult lives. If they were born into the working class, they were expected to go to work in their early teens, an age when most Americans were attending high school. Young men could become apprentices in the trades, but their aspirations were limited. Because they were so young, they usually took whatever unskilled work was available in local industry, without regard to particular skills or talents they might have—one of the reasons why education and job training became an important service of the European JOC. Young workers were easily dehumanized by the conditions of industrial production. Employers were more concerned with the profitable production of goods for sale than with a good life for their employees. Unschooled and inexperienced, young workers had little voice in determining the conditions of their lives. Moreover, and this is a critical point in the development of a movement of unmarried young workers, they were single for at least ten or twelve years before they had sufficient means to contemplate marriage.

In this country, unlike Europe, there were no strict class lines. Children of laborers could and did take advantage of educational opportunities and get better jobs than their parents. Legislation in most states made it mandatory that young people stay in school until age seventeen. Unemployment in the depression of the thirties encouraged many young men who might otherwise have quit school and followed their fathers into industry to remain in high school until graduation. Competition for jobs in the unionized trades resulted in the requirement of a high school diploma for entry into many apprenticeship programs.

In 1940 *Fortune* magazine published a portrait of the American people which revealed that nearly eighty percent of the population considered itself middle class. This group included industrial workers, white-collar workers, civil servants, technologists, professionals and businessmen, both big and small. Americans simply did not think of themselves as workers in the sense that Europeans did. "According to the survey," said a writer commenting on it, "the category 'middle class' in America reflected no economic realities, no distribution of income, no sociological classifications. . . . 'Middle class' for the American is a broader and more rewarding concept than Marx's bourgeoisie, which own the physical means of production and property, or Marx's proletariat which only owns its labor."[2]

Being middle class in America, continued the author, is a state of mind that any person can make his own. It does not refer to a person's confined position in the social structure, nor is it limited to preferred occupations. "The popular imagination has so closely identified being middle class with pursuing the so-called American dream that 'middle class' has come to be equated with a good chance for advancement, an expanding income, education, good citizenship—indeed with democracy."[3]

Education: An American Priority

Another factor complicating the search for the "genuine" worker was the matter of education. American working people tended to be much better educated than their European counterparts and for that reason tended to be much more upwardly mobile. Immigrant Catholics bought into the American dream, and the education of their children was a high priority. Moreover, in the effort to provide religious training in a pluralistic country, bishops often insisted, under pain of sin, that Catholic parents send their children to parochial schools. The liberal arts curriculum of Catholic high schools was designed to train graduates for white-collar jobs. Indeed the only job-related skills in the curriculum were typing, shorthand, and bookkeeping. It is not surprising, therefore, that many young people who came into the YCW were Catholic high school graduates who worked in offices, particularly those in the large commercial cities where the movement had its early growth. They did not wear the blue collars that defined a genuine worker in the eyes of some of those who envisioned a young-worker movement in the Jocist mold. A recent survey of former YCW members conducted for this book indicates that while a majority of YCW members in the forties and fifties had fathers who worked in blue-collar jobs that did not require formal education, their children generally finished high school and more often than not, took clerical jobs when they graduated.[4]

When the establishment of the G.I. Bill after World War II offered veterans a free college education, the picture changed. High school graduation had been the goal; now it became college. Though a few still did not graduate from high school, others went on for at least a year or two of college, if not a degree. The lines dividing social levels became less distinct. In the fifties it was possible to have factory workers, office workers, and even a rising young professional in the same family.

The increase in college attendance greatly diminished the pool of available young working men who could be recruited as Young Christian Workers, especially in the large cities. One study of graduates from a Catholic boys' high school indicated that only about thirty-one percent of those between age eighteen and twenty-four were unmarried workers. The others were either in school, in service, or married.[5]

In the late forties many YCW leaders were convinced that the movement was primarily intended for young blue-collar workers. Winifred Neville from the Manhattan YCW was among the many so-called professionals who were told they did not belong in the movement. She was employed as a teacher in a Catholic high school, not the kind of worker that the YCW leaders were trying to reach. Her apostolic spirit and desire for social justice had been deeply ingrained in the years before the movement began to restrict its membership to what were perceived to be genuine workers. Frustrated, she formed the Walter Farrell Guild, an organization geared to "doing what needs doing," apostolic action for persons who did not fit the YCW guidelines. Using the O-J-A method, they concentrated on the works of mercy. A major action developed on "burying the dead." They discovered that many Catholics without resources were not being given a Christian burial. They developed a program called "Who Cares?" and from 1962 to 1966, when social security began to pay burial expenses for indigents and Catholic Charities took over, they collected money from interested friends and arranged for hundreds of Christian burials. They found priests in the archdiocese willing to say a mass for each person they buried.

Win led in organizing a teachers' organization which eventually became a union in the New York Catholic schools. She also formed groups of Young Christian Students in the high school where she worked, preparing them for membership in the Young Christian

Workers when they left school. Many of her students became active YCW leaders.[6]

Other persons who joined the Catholic Action cells in the early days were social workers and nurses. They too were perceived to be ineligible for the YCW, even though they came from worker families. Some of them tried to form groups of young "professionals," but they had limited success. The stress was on workers in industry. Office workers and telephone workers, though not blue-collar workers, were perceived to be wage earners and they were acceptable.

Ironically, many of the young workers who joined the YCW in later days developed a sense of social responsibility and a desire to be in a career where they could be involved in human service. They returned to school to get the college education required for certification as teachers, social workers, and nurses.

Stephanie Dalidchik was a waitress in Chicago when she joined the YCW. She later moved up the job ladder to become an office worker. As a YCW organizer she developed managerial skills she didn't know she had. Years after she left the movement, she became the first woman vice-president in her company, a position in which she felt she was able to help workers at lower levels. In 1976 she was named as one of the top corporate women in the country by *Business Week* magazine.[7]

"We always had trouble defining 'worker'," said Joe Kelly, a YCW leader in the fifties. "Some people thought a worker had to have dirty fingernails, and some said that anyone who had to earn a living should be considered a worker."[8]

The YCW and the Unions

One of the most important tenets of the YCW was that work had a positive value in itself. This was often a new idea to those who grew up thinking a job was just a way to make money. Fr. Edward Mitchinson, national chaplain of the English YCW, wrote an article on the Christian idea of work for a 1951 inquiry program in England. It became a standard treatise on the subject for the English-speaking movements. Reprinted in pamphlet form, *The Doctrine of Working* was widely read and studied by members of the YCW throughout the fifties.

An essential part of the education in the YCW is to give back to the young workers and to build up a belief in work—a new spirit, a sense of the grandeur of work, and of respect for work itself, however humble. . . . We must give them the meaning of the words of the [YCW] song, "Your work, your dignity, your pride." We must use this doctrine as our standard of judgment of others to work, the attitude of management to work; as a standard for judgment of certain types of work, so that we see the contradiction between the production of shoddy work or of pornographic literature or other harmful goods, and the idea of work as a cooperation with God in his creation. . . .

The social character and the ideal of work follows, too, from this first doctrine. Work can never be a private individual affair. It is always social—for society, for the service of others. It is social in the sense of the human society which it serves. Work binds and links the worker with his fellow men whom he serves by the product of his work. It is social in a cosmic sense in that it binds and links the worker with created nature which he refashions. . . .

Work has a personal value, too. When a man works, he works as a man—intellect, heart, will, soul, and body. If the whole man really works, the whole man is developed, and because he is a man, he has a right and a duty to wholly human work. He has the fundamental right to find in his work, the duty of going to his work, the means of developing his whole human personality, and still more of safeguarding, expressing, and developing his divine dignity as a son of God, a brother of Christ.

This is the standard for our judgment on any form of work which, instead of developing a man, diminishes, dehumanizes, and degrades him. This is the standard and ideal for our part in the whole long and difficult task of humanizing and Christianizing conditions of work. . . .

The other more obvious and pressing aim of work will follow—support for oneself and one's dependents. . . .

Christ was a worker before He died on the Cross. It was by the whole of His life, not only His passion and death, that He redeemed us and the world. . . . Because you are one with Christ, because you share His life as the Son, you are his instruments for the redemption of working youth. Joined with His daily work, with His sacrifice, every moment, every bit of daily work is a means of redemption for young workers. This is the point of offering your work, of joining it to Christ each morning in the YCW prayer.

In the YCW, we are vitally concerned not only with the redemption of persons but with the redemption of things, of surroundings, of institutions. We have the mission of "restoring all things in Christ." We know that the young workers will be saved or damned eternally in and through the environment in which they live. You know so well that your mission is not just with rod and line, not just with the net, but that it is of changing the water in which the fish must live. We must realize that the world of matter must be transformed and Christianized, not only as a means of aiding the redemption of men but in order that created nature may present a true pattern of glory to God. In Christ "all things came into being, and without Him came nothing that has come to be." (1 John:3) Through sin came disorder into the world. Through redemption continued in the apostolate, all things, the whole order of nature, must be restored in Christ.[9]

Msgr. Hillenbrand emphasized the latter idea at the 1953 Study Week: "We are dedicated to an institutional apostolate. We are not out just to change people, we're out to change things, the things which endure when the people change, when people move on, when people die. We want laws which will help people who come after. We want labor unions to stay in a plant after we are gone. . . .

"On the other side, we also have to change people and give them the idea of justice. You have to give them the idea of charity, but charity without justice is a complete fraud . . . I don't want your charity. You are not giving me justice. That is a Christian attitude. I want the basic things due me as a human being."[10]

Involvement in unions was seen as the primary means of improving working conditions and was strongly advocated in the YCW programs on work and economic life. Strong, open, and honest unions were perceived as the embodiment of the Christian spirit in the workplace. Indeed, the training of young people to get involved and be a Christian influence in the unions was a major goal of the movement in the fifties.

Dorothy Curtin, the girls' secretary in 1952, wrote to an inquirer that the movement itself did not have a direct involvement in unions, but "we do encourage our members to understand and participate in unions. In fact, some of our members are working directly with unions independently at the present time."[11]

Over the years YCW sections organized meetings and training sessions to educate young workers about unions with the help of organizations such as the Council on Working Life in Chicago and the Catholic Labor Conference in Detroit. One of the first Catholic labor schools in the country was started by the YCW in San Francisco in the early forties. Many YCW members started unions in their place of work or became very active in unions. Some of the girls joined unions dominated in the fifties by Communists and tried to make their voices heard, but they were usually unsuccessful because they did not have the expertise to combat the tightly controlled ruling clique.

The story is told of one YCW member who attended several meetings of a white-collar union in Chicago that was Communist-controlled. She was stopped one day by a gentleman who identified himself as an FBI agent and asked to talk to her. He wanted her to join the union and gather intelligence information for him about what was going on at the meetings. The young woman was frightened and refused to get involved. It was only some weeks later that she had the courage to tell a fellow YCW member about the incident.[12]

100 Percent Union

Some persons who had developed organizing skills in the YCW took employment as union organizers when they left the movement. Tony Zivalich, the first YCW president, became an organizer for the Teamsters in the South. Upon his retirement as an organizer in 1984, he was asked by Mayor Andrew Young in Atlanta to serve as a liaison between the unions and the city government. Jack Dunne became an organizer for the Hatters' Union in Chicago when he left his job as a YCW officer in 1960. In that job he recruited other ex-YCW organizers to work for the union. Later he became president of the Union of

Technical Engineers, a white-collar union. Ted Zelewsky, one of the organizers recruited by Jack, stayed in his job with the Hatters' Union for thirteen years until hats went out of style and the industry collapsed. Others went into unions with a better future!

The Building Service Employees Union in New York had the organizing services of Roger Alvarez and Vincent Mase from the Brooklyn YCW, Pat McDonough in Oakland, and Pete Sheehan in Washington, D.C. Ross Williams of Oklahoma became president of the Oklahoma State AFL-CIO. Maria Gallego Quesada, who was an electronic assembly worker when she joined the movement in San Jose, went back to school for more education and twenty years later became a deputy labor commissioner for the state of California. Tom Doyle from the San Diego YCW became a labor lawyer after service as a union organizer and state labor commissioner. Plumbers, carpenters, communication workers, teachers, machinists, municipal and state employees, teamsters—all have had YCW leaders on their union rosters as organizers, shop stewards, and local officers at one time or another over the years. The list could go on. Its length is a testimony to the extent to which the YCW movement of the fifties achieved its goal of becoming a Christian influence in the workplace and, more specifically, in the trade union movement.

Eddie O'Reilly, an officer in the Sheet Metal Workers Union in New York City for many years, was the coordinator of a committee of sheet metal workers who worked on the 1984-85 restoration of the Statue of Liberty in New York harbor. He said recently, "Three words that I learned in the YCW have been my guide and inspiration during life. They were Observe, Judge, Act! They have been my guide in hundreds of times I have taken action, on many matters. On many of these occasions I was alone in my position."[13]

Too Radical?

Union activity did not have the negative connotations that were often associated with "a workers' movement"—a term which to some Americans smacked of Marxism. Related to this perception was the paranoia that developed during the anti-Communist hysteria of the McCarthy era in the early fifties. Organizations and individuals who were concerned with changing the status quo or were considered too "liberal" were accused of being Communists or fellow travelers. The fallout from this was that any groups working for social change were viewed with suspicion.

And who were more apt to be alarmed by the threat of atheistic Communism than conservative Catholics, among them many Irish pastors who were less than polite to YCW organizers who knocked on their rectory doors? A movement of young "workers" was almost anathema. The irony of this is that one of the main reasons Pius XI so strongly supported the work of Canon Cardijn was that he perceived it as an answer to the Communist threat among the workers of Europe.

The idea of a "young worker movement" was viewed by many as something not really in tune with the American sentiment. David O'Shea, an English YCW organizer who came to the United States to help establish the movement here, acknowledged the failure of Europeans to comprehend what class meant in this country. "The Communist party blew it in this country. . . . They never really grew with the American reality. The really big social movements in the United States in the last fifty or sixty years were the Civil Rights movements. The big social struggles of the United States centered around access to status by successive waves of immigrants. . . . They had to fight to find their place in American society. It hasn't been a class thing; it was more of a cultural thing."[14]

College, the draft, the anti-Communist distrust of a worker movement image, the continued striving for social and economic advancement—all these worked against the building of a vibrant movement of young workers. America after emerging from a major depression and a world war was very confident in the fifties. With continued economic growth, a low level of unemployment, and a rising per capita income, is it any wonder that many young men and women when asked to consider the problems of working life as prospective Young Christian Workers would honestly say, "Problems? What problems? I don't see any problems."

This is not to say that the Young Christian Workers had no real role in America. The organization was concerned not just with economic problems but with the whole life of the young worker, as clearly stated in the introduction to a 1954 YCW handbook:

> When the working person leaves the protective confines of
> home and high school to enter the industrial, social, and

political life of the world, his Christian training all too often is challenged, mocked, and termed "kid stuff." It is not too long before he finds himself facing the task of re-evaluating his attitudes towards work, the family, marriage, the parish, community, and political life, in the face of the individualistic, depersonalized attitude of his fellow-workers and new-found companions.

Frequently this slowly changing young worker receives no help in sorting out the various ideas presented to him. He is left on his own to "pick and choose." But the social pressure in his environment is very often too strong for him to resist. He does not want to think or do anything that would be too different from his companions. He wants to be "in with the crowd." And so another Christian enters the world, but instead of changing it, he is changed by it. . . .

To counteract the tremendous social pressures present in the young worker's life is the job of the Young Christian Workers. Under the guidance of Christ and His Church—through his chaplain—the young worker unites with a small group of his fellows to discover how to bring about, through action, a more Christian social, political, and parish order. . . .

As a movement of the Church, the Young Christian Workers pledges itself to train young workingmen and girls as apostles for Christ.[15]

Pat Keegan, addressing a YCW meeting in San Francisco in 1954, spoke out strongly on this point.

The pivotal question confronting the Church is the struggle for the soul of the workingman. . . . It is imperative that lay people, irrespective of where they are and their background, should be mobilized in the lay apostolate; . . . all workers, blue- and white-collar, taking responsibility in those fields of work and daily life in which the average person must be a witness of Christianity. . . . The young workers themselves must be the apostles of their fellow young workers, not tight little groups for themselves, but to serve other workers.[16]

As time went by, the YCW adapted to the reality of American life. Efforts to maintain class distinctions were gradually abandoned. The common experience for young men and young women in the YCW was that they all worked for a living. Therefore, they could and should attack the problems of the working world with a unified approach. Even the onus of a college education faded and members were accepted in the movement if they earned a wage. By 1957, seventy-seven percent of the YCW members were white-collar workers and fifteen percent were blue collar. Twenty-one percent belonged to unions. Sixteen percent had completed college and seventeen percent were attending night school.

Jean Pew said in recalling the period when she was a full-time leader (1953-1959), "The 'worker' idea was discussed in gradually lessening degrees. It was felt that it could keep people out of the movement as most young people didn't think of themselves as such. However, it was felt that the doctrine of work and the whole social teaching of the Church had to remain an integral part of the movement. At one time we said that the movement would be aimed at reaching all those young people eligible for trade unions, which, of course, includes teachers and certain other so-called professionals."[17]

But the struggle to articulate the YCW's role continued. At a meeting of the National Council in 1957, discussion focused on the YCW commitment to being an apostolate in work life. It was agreed that most young workers lived in an unchristian environment where the Mystical Body must be represented and that, as an organization, it had to be concerned about the social injustices in all areas of work life and in the economic order. The question then revolved around the proportion of blue-collar workers and white-collar workers in the country and whether YCW sections truly represented all kinds of young workers. Most of the delegates observed that the young workers in their areas were fifty-fifty blue collar vs. white collar whereas the sections were seventy-five percent white collar. A few felt that the young people in their areas were mostly white collar. A motion was made to get accurate statistics on the actual status of the American young worker. It was also agreed to concentrate on reaching more blue-collar workers through personal contact in the recreational spots where they hung out. This was in the period when the United States was beginning to change from an industrial economy to one dominated by technology and the service industry.

Following the discussion, the national chaplain made the following remarks:

> I think YCW is the most important of all the lay apostolic movements. It has the best material in youth; one of its characteristics is that it is for people who *work* in comparison to students who will not always study; it is the only group putting a big emphasis on spreading the social doctrine of the Church; it has enlisted the most dedication from its members; it has had the best programming of the movements; it is the initiator and pioneer of all the movements. . . .
>
> We must be realistic in our approach and should accept that we should have some factory workers in our groups but not grind an axe on this. . . . We have put less stress on factory workers and more concentration on parishes. The parish concentration will engulf the factory workers right along with the other youth of the parish. We have to get into Negro and Puerto Rican parishes and we have to be attracting office workers too since they are becoming more and more numerous. . . .
>
> Now in the United States: The U.S. has a total of 16,000 parishes; we have YCW in 180. The U.S. has a total of 49,000 priests; we have 180 chaplains. We need *growth*. Concentrate on being the best parish organization. Make it a project to start more groups. We need more organizing teams. Pray for the day when an isolated priest can start and have enough literature available to help eliminate the need for organizers. Let's measure the success of the YCW by the future. . . . We are in a position to do it. We are alone in the field, have roots and experience behind us, plus 180 groups to start with.[18]

Reaching Out to Minority Workers

From the beginning, YCW leaders saw the need to develop the movement among young black workers. When Russ Tershy organized on the West Coast in the early fifties, he aided in the formation of several sections of blacks in the Fillmore district of San Francisco.

There were also sections among young black women in the early days in South Bend, Indiana, and in New York's Harlem. Dolores Grier, a black woman, was recruited for the movement by Gloria Kenny when they both worked as secretaries in the offices of Catholic Charities in New York City and she was a leader in a strong section at St. Aloysius parish for several years. After many years devoted to community service for the archdiocese, she was named as a vice chancellor of the New York Archdiocese in 1985, the first lay person, the first black, and the first woman to hold that position.

Millard Hughes, who became Chicago federation treasurer in 1957, and Lloyd St. James were black leaders in Chicago who worked long hours organizing sections in the black community. By the end of the fifties, they had five strong sections established. In Detroit, the archbishop specifically requested YCW leaders to recruit blacks.

Many of the black YCW members were not truly typical of the masses of young black men and women in the cities at that time, partly because they were Catholic, unlike most blacks, and partly because they tended to be better educated than their peers. One member who became a school teacher had been a Fulbright scholar and learned about the Jocists while studying at the Sorbonne in Paris. Another said recently, "I was a shoe salesman when I joined, and before I left the movement, my application for the police department was accepted. One of the girls in our section had a good civil service job. We really weren't peons."[19]

Minority workers in the black communities were not easily reached by white organizers. This is not surprising in view of the movement's emphasis on a like-to-like apostolate, and it did sometimes complicate matters for those blacks who did join. One former black leader in Chicago recalled recently how uncomfortable she felt for a long time being part of a largely white organization.

Gil Baylor, the black president of a section in Detroit, raised a criticism about the race relations inquiries in 1958 that were obviously written for and by whites. One "observe" question asked, "Are there members of minority groups living in your neighborhood?" The inquiry there was rewritten to embrace a black perspective on race. The point was raised at a council meeting later that year, and when the inquiries on racial problems were made in 1961, optional sets of inquiries on the subject were offered so that individual sections could choose the one most appropriate to their local needs.

A parallel can be drawn to the experience of Vince Geise, who after many years in YCS and YCW, became a priest. His first assignment was a black parish in Chicago where he organized teenagers in a section of Young Christian Students. After two years during which he took his black high school leaders to YCS gatherings in the city and to study weeks in the Midwest, he realized that they were frustrated trying to relate to the largely middle-class white students who constituted the bulk of YCS membership. Though the white leaders tried to interact with them, they did not really understand the problems of the young blacks. After the YCS convention in 1968, Fr. Geise's group decided to form their own movement of Black Christian Students because they had radically different problems from their white counterparts. Using the like-to-like concept of Cardijn when he organized his first working-class youth, they developed leadership skills to deal directly with the problems they saw in the black community. They established concrete services to meet the real needs they observed. The BCS spread to other parishes and continued until 1978. Many of the members went on to college and have become active community leaders.[20]

YCW recruitment among Hispanics was slightly easier because Hispanics were Catholic. Groups existed in Hispanic parishes in California almost from the beginning. There was a section of young women in Oakland in 1946. El Cajon, Hanford, Los Angeles, and Winslow, Arizona, had Hispanic groups by 1953. Later there were groups in Sacramento, Stockton, and San Jose. In addition to action on a variety of local problems, they became very much involved in the fight of the migrant workers to organize and marched in demonstrations led by Cesar Chavez, who in fact was strongly influenced in his own spiritual growth by a local YCW chaplain.[21]

However, language problems were a serious deterrent to the recruitment of Hispanics in many cities, especially in the Northeast and Midwest where many were recent immigrants. In Chicago in the late fifties and early sixties, there were a number of Spanish-speaking sections, but they were out of the mainstream of the Chicago federation because of the language barrier. They used the inquiry method to work on local problems they encountered in their communities, but they were unable to use the prescribed national inquiry program. It was not until the sixties that the YCW published materials in Spanish.

The Young Christian Workers movement was designed by its European founder to serve, educate, and represent working youth who were denied their God-given dignity because they were at the bottom of the socioeconomic ladder. The economy prospered during the fifties and though the Young Christian Workers tried to reach out to minority groups who had serious problems, most young American Catholics were no longer at the bottom of the heap. Free education beyond high school accompanied by upward social and occupational mobility was changing the world in which they lived. It was evident that the YCW must make adaptations to fit the movement to the reality of working life in this country.

Looking Back on Action at Work

I discovered YCW at a good time—I was beginning to feel like a lone ranger because I felt God was important—wasn't sure anyone else did. I believe it kept me in the right direction. I joined a union because of YCW and participated in its affairs. (Milwaukee)

I learned the importance and value of unions, experienced and learned how humans can abuse the ideal but also met people struggling to put the ideal into practice. I learned a good set of values and, hopefully, have been able to live that and pass it on to my family. (Chicago)

YCW offered me focus and support as I was going through some important years in my life and making independent decisions as a young adult—decisions that would have a significant impact on my future. This community of young lay people and religious exemplified Christian commitments and human concerns. For me, it presented the image of an exciting, dynamic, and dedicated church which still remains. In my community, many of my fellow YCWs are in positions of positive influence that continue to go on. (Milwaukee)

I enjoyed the YCW. I made good friends whom I still see. We share a bond that I don't have with other friends. I learned the dignity of work and all workers that has followed me to every job I've had. Because of it, I became the "trouble maker." I think I question things a lot more than my friends who were never involved. (New York City)

Because of my experience with YCW, I led an interracial group of Girl Scouts and chaired Chicago Focus—an interracial social justice group of women under forty. (Chicago)

The YCW had a very positive personal influence on me. As a picket, I helped to end racial discrimination at an amusement park and I became a union representative, although I don't think I accomplished very much in that position. I think the biggest weakness of the YCW was that it was designed for the European workplace and did not really basically relate to the reality of post-World War II conditions in the United States. (Baltimore)

The most important thing I learned in the YCW was that God had given me special talents and He expected me to use them not only to better myself but to help others. . . . As the only woman in my company to receive the title of vice-president, I had the opportunity to do things for workers in lower level jobs. (Chicago)

Notes

[1] George Sullivan, "State of the YCW," *YCW Bulletin for Priests*, January 1953, p. 7.

[2] Burton Bledstein, *The Culture of Professionalism* (New York: W.W. Norton, 1976), p. 3.

[3] *Ibid.*, p. 6.

[4] Eighty percent of fathers of YCW members responding to a survey conducted by the author had jobs identified as unskilled labor, semi-skilled labor, skilled tradespersons, farmers, and service workers. Fifty-one percent had no schooling beyond eighth grade; almost half their mothers did not finish eighth grade.

[5] Dennis Geaney, "YCW Roundup," *YCW Bulletin for Priests*, October 1952.

[6] Winifred Neville to author, March 8, 1987.

[7] Stephanie Dalidchik, letter to author, February 14, 1986.

[8] Joseph Kelly, recorded conversation at Frank Ardito's home, February 7, 1987.

[9] Edward Mitchinson, "The Doctrine of Work," *YCW Bulletin for Priests*, June 1951.

[10] Msgr. Reynold Hillenbrand at 1953 Study Week.

[11] Dorothy Curtin to Mrs. John Franz, December 16, 1957.

[12] Frank Ardito to author, February 7, 1987.

[13] Edward O'Reilly, letter to author, November 10, 1986.

[14] David O'Shea, taped conversation with author, October 6, 1985.

[15] Foreword, *This is the Young Christian Workers: A Manual* (Chicago: Young Christian Workers, 1954).

[16] Patrick Keegan, at YCW meeting, San Francisco, 1954.

[17] Jean Pew Tyacke to author, December 31, 1986.

[18] Hillenbrand, Council Meeting report, July 1957.

[19] Lou Shelley, Jr. in meeting at home of Lloyd St. James, November 15, 1987.

[20] Vincent Geise, *You Got It All: A Personal Account of a White Priest in a Chicago Ghetto* (Huntington, Indiana: Our Sunday Visitor, 1948).

[21] Russ Tershy to author, October 2, 1985.

7

The Americanization of a Worker Movement

As the YCW movement developed over the years, numerous adaptations were made to fit its image and method to the reality of American society. Gradually, adaptations were made with regard to age limits in the movement, the separation of the sexes, the training of leaders, the design of the national program, and the goal to encompass the huge masses of genuine workers—the stated European aim.

Age limits in the European movements were fourteen to twenty-five. Since single workers in the United States joined the movement later than the young workers in Europe, it was decided, early in the fifties, to change the upper age limit to thirty. Some national leaders stayed active for a few additional years. Because European Jocists joined in their early teens, they were seen as children compared to the Americans who were, in fact, young adults. This led to another major change in the American movement: young men and women in the same section.

Mixed Groups

From the beginning there had been concern about the shortage of male members. War conditions and the draft compounded the problem. Five years after the first general council meetings at Syosset and Childerly in 1947, there were sections of young men in only ten cities, whereas the young women had seventy-eight sections in twenty-five cities.

When plans were in process for the 1953 Study Week, the men and women decided to develop a common inquiry theme and present it at a joint study week, rather than hold separate study weeks as had been the practice. The theme was "One World, One Christ, One YCW." The joint meeting, attended by more than two hundred leaders of both sexes, was a great success.

Russ Tershy was one of those who began to push the idea that mixed groups might be the answer to the recruitment problem. He had initially been attracted to the YCW because of the dances and social activities organized by the St. Boniface section in San Francisco. The St. Boniface section had a long history as a joint YCW with mixed general meetings, though men and women met in separate groups for the gospel and social inquiry.

Why not develop a style that fits the American mentality? Tershy argued. Young men and women of American YCW age, the early twenties, are drawn to the opposite sex naturally. Why not take advantage of that attraction? Moreover, in this country both sexes were used to being in mixed groups. They should learn to meet together and exchange ideas freely and openly. Most of the problems in society were not based strictly on gender.

Fr. William Schackmuth, an energetic Chicago chaplain, worked with a large parish section at St. Andrew parish. Ten groups of leaders met each Thursday evening in his parish hall for their inquiry meetings. Afterwards they went to the back room of a local tavern to dance and talk. Many strong leaders from this section went on to leadership positions in the Chicago federation. Gradually, Fr. Schackmuth realized that the social camaraderie which followed the meetings and the friendships they formed were often what kept people coming. He sensed that social contact was important in the life of young people and a valid part of apostolic formation. When he first broached the idea of mixed sections to Msgr. Hillenbrand, the monsignor was strongly opposed. "That is not the Jocist way," he responded. Gradually, however, he became sold on the idea as a necessary adaptation of the American movement.

At the separate council meetings of the two branches which followed the study week held in July 1954, the leaders agreed to merge and start mixed sections in spite of the fact that many leaders in girls' sections were opposed. Jean Pew, the girls' president, spoke out for those who felt they would not have the same opportunity to develop

*Rev. Reynold Hillenbrand, national chaplain of
Specialized Catholic Action Movements, at Notre Dame, 1946.*

leadership skills in a mixed movement because men in those days relegated women to secondary roles. In the end, however, they accepted the change because it was presented as a necessary means for strengthening the total movement, a goal agreed upon by all. The first joint council meeting was held in January 1955.

In *Chaplain's Notes* the following year, Hillenbrand made the case for the mixed groups. Among his arguments were the following:

> We have clung too closely to what was done in Europe. This is true not only in the specialization of the sexes but in other ways. Pius XI spoke of the specialization of the sexes, but Pius XII has broadened the whole concept of the

apostolate. We have to try something that will fulfill our American needs in making the apostolate grow.

There is only one simple rule: as many or more fellows than girls.

The primary interest of the young people in the age group with which we work is marriage. By keeping our sections separate, we are, in a sense, working against the grain. At least we are not capitalizing on the natural tendencies which exist. This is very important, I think.

Granted that a chaplain does his work, I see no reason why the spiritual and apostolic formation cannot be secured in a mixed group. The tools are all still there. The mixed groups started this past year have been successful. They prove to be a good blend. The discussions are easy and natural and taking action is not hindered.[1]

Nonetheless, the truth of Jean Pew's concern turned out to be well-founded, as evidenced by what happened in one Chicago parish when a well-established section of young women was merged with the young men's group. The women learned to play dumb at meetings so the less experienced men could appear to be in control. Often, when a young woman expressed an idea to the chaplain, he passed it along to the male president of the section, who would then present it as his own at the next leaders' meeting. According to a former member of that group, many of the original young women quit out of frustration before long. They felt they were playing games and their ability to function as leaders was limited.[2]

In the prevailing thinking of the times, assertive behavior on the part of women was an indication of "unnatural" behavior and a poor preparation for marriage. Msgr. Hillenbrand was typical of many chaplains who had strong views about the role of women. He felt that men should be trained for their future positions in the labor unions and government where they would work to insure a life of dignity for all persons; women were supposed to marry and rear children who would be the apostles of the next generation. It was hard for him to accept outspoken young women who challenged male authority, which he saw as a sign of malformation. As late as 1961 he criticized Marylu Langan who had been vice-president in the late fifties as an example of one who was "too mannish" and "aggressive."[3] She was a vigorous leader who came from the same all-girls section in New York that had produced many strong leaders like Mary Tuohy and Caroline Pezzullo. Ironically, on another occasion he wondered why the movement in the sixties did not have strong leaders among the women like Caroline and Viola Brennan who were active in the late forties and early fifties.[4] He obviously did not see the contradiction in his own thinking, nor did he realize the women had developed as independent leaders in their own branch of the movement.

Joan Nett, the vice-president who had succeeded Jean Pew and Marylu Langan in 1959, had never been in an all-girls section. She acknowledged the male leadership role and seemed to accept a more submissive role than either of her predecessors, though not without some misgivings. On at least one occasion on record, she said she was at national headquarters merely "to create a presence." When she arrived at a training program, she thought the young women were being trained to be apostles and was surprised to discover they were, in effect, being trained for marriage because they were told how to communicate and be subordinate.[5]

This was still going on in the sixties, according to Nancy Diley Delaney, a secretary at the national office in 1964. "Once while leading a discussion on the subject, a national officer told us how to participate in meetings with men—to let them think our ideas were theirs," she recalls.[6]

There have been numerous stories told about women who were told to be quiet at meetings. One of these was Jo Jeske who had started in a girls' section in the early fifties and went on to become a successful YCW organizer in Chicago. She remembers one chaplain who always tried to shut her up when she visited his group. "I didn't see why," she recalls. "Then, one time, one of the fellows said, 'No, Father, you be quiet. If she has something to say, let her talk.'"[7] Since it was Bernie Kelly, a strong leader in the group who defended her, the chaplain relented, and she was allowed to continue.

Most of the male leaders in those days took it for granted that they should be in charge. One young man in the days following the changeover remembers how long it took him to get used to young women who voiced their opinions frankly and freely.[8]

Nancy Lee Conrad was another who was admonished for being too outspoken and taking too much leadership. When she was sent to New Orleans as an organizer in 1960, she was cautioned to stay "one step behind" the male leader of the organizing team. She tried hard, but it wasn't easy. When she attended an international meeting, after her election as vice-president in 1961, she met many strong leaders from the girls' movements of other countries. She wondered if it might have been better for the American women if they had continued as a separate branch. She felt the treatment of women in the mixed movement was unjust.

As national vice-president, Nancy Lee had come on the team expecting to be a partner with the president, sharing responsibility for the national program. She found she was often left out at meetings where important decisions were made and was relegated to lesser responsibilities with the "women." This became a particular problem when she challenged the design of the national program which she thought stressed education at the expense of formative action. Nancy Lee gradually developed a good working relationship with Mike Coleman who was president at that time, but her outspokenness caused her problems when dealing with Msgr. Hillenbrand.[9]

Jim Burke, a Chicago leader in the mid-sixties, recalls the fuss made about the seating at a council meeting when Milwaukee sent two women and no man. A woman always sat next to a man, and it was he who did most of the talking. How to seat the women was a major problem. "It was ridiculous," says Jim. "It didn't make any sense."[10]

Ann Ida Gannon, B.V.M., a leading exponent of women's rights and responsibilities, commented recently on the emergence of women in the lay movements who worked within the limits of established tradition.

> Many personally reassessed the role of women as they worked to further Catholic lay movements. In practice, it became clear to many that the concept of "sexual spheres" had little relation to actual experience and that, without denying the very real difference between the sexes, there was an expanding horizon of common fields of action and involvement. The traditional male-centered, clerical, and ecclesiastical culture of the Church became increasingly irrelevant to many of the men and women who were actively working to further the Church's apostolate. However, at this time women, more interested in achieving

results in spite of obstacles than in developing a feminine ideology, gave little attention to a concerted effort for equality.[11]

Some chaplains who had worked with the women's sections felt that the intensity of the movement was lessened in the mixed groups and that social considerations predominated. In some places the YCW came to be seen as a social club, though with a serious side.

The formation of mixed groups coincided with the return of hundreds of thousands of veterans at the end of the Korean War, and social clubs became a very popular activity in many parishes. The priests who drew their YCW membership from social clubs certainly had a much bigger pool of young people to draw from. In 1956 the national roster lists one hundred and nine sections of which seventy-one were mixed, and the total number of members throughout the country neared three thousand. How much of this resulted from the mixed sections and how much to the greater number of available young men is hard to determine. Whatever the case, numbers grew rapidly and membership in the last part of the decade reached an all-time high.

In 1958 there were fifty-two parish sections in Chicago. Millard Hughes, the federation treasurer, still speaks proudly of one month that year when there were over one thousand dues-paying members. This is particularly meaningful in light of Jack Dunne's statement at a council meeting in 1955 that only twenty-nine percent of known members nationally were regularly paying dues. Collecting dues was always a problem, so there were undoubtedly many uncounted members. This is why membership figures are unreliable. At the study week in 1958, it was announced that two hundred sections existed in thirty-five dioceses.

The change to mixed membership was not universally accepted. Many sections, especially in New York and Brooklyn, resisted the change. As late as 1960 more than half the sections in those cities were still organized by gender.

There was some concern in early 1957 when the International Bureau of the JOC circulated a proposed statement on "Fundamental Characteristics of the YCW" which seemed to ban mixed groups. Bob Olmstead, national president in 1957, wrote to Pat Keegan asking for clarification.[12] In answer, Pat stated that the International YCW was an association of national YCW organizations, not an international superstructure. Although two separate organizations of the JOC, one for men and one for women was the practice in Europe, he felt that the International YCW must now find "its expression and policy in a world where even if those things were desirable (which I do not believe), they are quite impossible." He proposed that the Americans apply for affiliation as two branches of one movement, the question of degree of separation being a domestic question and "your own national affair." He also suggested that at the coming meeting of the International Council an amendment be advanced to allow for a single mixed organization.[13]

When the *Fundamentals of the International YCW* was published later that year in Rome, no specific mention was made of separate organizations according to gender. Under the heading of "Organization," the following statement appears: "The YCW organization . . . need never take a rigid and static form which would paralyze the movement. The organization which exists to serve action, must be continually examined and adapted to take the shape required in life and action."[14]

The Lay Role in Formation

In Western Europe, where the Young Christian Workers were strongest, individual countries were no bigger than some of the American states. Interaction between leaders at conferences and study weeks could easily be arranged throughout the year. In the United States, the National Study Week played a major part in giving young workers the vision of a "new youth for a new world," but it was held only once a year. Its purpose was to introduce the theme of the inquiry program for the year ahead. Local study days and study weeks in the months that followed supplemented the national event.

At the National Study Week, many of the talks were given by the national leaders who developed the annual program themes; but experts in specialized fields were often brought in to speak on specific issues such as politics, unions, and international life. These talks were followed by questions from the floor and small group discussions. The hundreds of young adults who converged on the campus of the University of Notre Dame or St. Joseph's College in Rensselaer,

Indiana, were inspired and motivated to action. The enthusiasm of others dedicated to the same ideals, sharing experiences and ideas, gave the participants a sense of power and vitality. The study weeks were a source of hope and optimism to local section leaders who were sometimes overwhelmed by the problems they faced.

In the United States, however, great travel distances made it impossible for leaders from all sections to attend the National Study Weeks. Travel costs between the two coasts were beyond the means of the average young worker. In the early days, expenses for those who traveled far were subsidized by additional fees from those close by. This became a major logistic problem as numbers grew and only a token representation from the West Coast was able to attend. The answer: hold a separate study week for leaders west of the Rockies.

Rita Joseph and Russ Tershy set up a West Coast branch of the movement in 1951. From headquarters in San Francisco, they trained and sent organizers up and down the coast. They also planned a West Coast Study Week which followed a few months after the national meeting. Representatives from the West Coast continued to participate in the semi-annual national council meetings which set policy and directed the operation of the total movement, thus insuring that all YCW sections were part of a unified organization.

In time, certain differences of style and application of the inquiry method did arise. Some leaders on the West Coast felt that the programs developed at national headquarters did not fit their needs, and they argued for an independent program. The well-organized San Diego federation became very outspoken on this issue, to the point where they were perceived as mavericks by some in the national office. Because the International YCW office had stressed the importance of national unity from the beginning, the national office in Chicago was adamant. They rejected the suggestion that regional areas develop their own programs. Instead, they strove for unity. To achieve it, they continually sought the input of leaders from the western states. Some like Jack McCartney and Dick Delaney from California and Mike Woodruff from Portland served as national presidents. In addition, many young men and women from sections in the West were invited to work on the national staff. It can be said in retrospect, however, that the International YCW had no comprehension of the distances involved and the real differences which often existed in widely separated parts of the country.

Leadership Training Courses

Another key element in the formation of lay leaders was the establishment of a formal training program for leaders. The organizers who had initially been sent out to recruit and establish new sections were experienced leaders who were trained at the national headquarters. They knew the authentic organization of the YCW and were able to talk about it with a degree of authority. However, as the movement grew it became impossible to send organizers to all the areas asking for help.

Yet training remained essential. New priests trying to start sections on their own were apt to make inappropriate adaptations. It was important to train key individuals in the fundamental goals and methods which would insure solid lay leadership. After countless experiments in starting new sections, recruiting priests, training organizers, writing "How to Start" manuals, and dealing with the turnover in sections as young people left the movement due to marriage or age, the national leaders decided a new way was needed to give in-depth training to prospective leaders. Instead of sending organizers out, they would bring potential leaders into Chicago. A national training program would guarantee that all new leaders had a common understanding of the YCW.

Russ Tershy returned from California to take over the planning and direction of a three-month training school that would be run twice a year. He and Jean Pew worked out the ideas, and when she completed her term as national vice-president, she worked full time with him.

The purpose of the school was to train YCW people from different areas of the country so they could return as local officers and organizers, well-grounded in the principles of the movement. Russ said the program was based on the principle of the "loaves and fishes," the multiplying effect. Where before he might stay three months in an area and train leaders from a few sections, now people from twenty areas could be trained in the same amount of time. Moreover, leaders would be exposed to Msgr. Hillenbrand, who agreed to give a course on the social doctrine of the Church. They would live with the full-timers in Chicago, and a nearby Catholic community center was available for the training sessions. The cost would be two hundred dollars, including room and board. In some cities section members raised money to help pay the cost for their representative. Of course, the person chosen had to take a leave of absence from work or, as some did, quit their jobs.

Those who came were expected to be experienced YCW leaders, although in later years when the movement was growing rapidly and the need for formation was great, some came who had been in a section no more than six months. There were sessions on the apostolic spirit of the movement, its techniques and methodology, and group dynamics. Attendees learned how to run a meeting. They learned how to participate more actively in the Mass. They studied the labor movement and were exposed to international issues.

"We did intense training," says Russ. "We also taught them how to organize sections. It wasn't intended as a school to train and recruit full-time people for the national staff, but it helped some of them want to go full time. We had a lot of full-timers come through the training programs, but we were mainly interested in enriching the local scene with well-trained leaders sure of the fundamentals. We did things like having them attend local section meetings and talk to prospective chaplains. We wanted them to have experiences. We even took some of them to picket lines when a strike was going on."[15]

The first three-month training school was held in the spring of 1955, and the second began in September. A press release dated September 28, 1955, reads as follows:

> Eleven young people from seven cities in the United States and two in Canada are plunging into the Autumn Training Program of the Young Christian Workers at their general headquarters in Chicago. Learning to teach others how to make Christ the center of their lives at work, in the home, in the community, in politics, and during leisure time will be [and their names were listed].

By the following year it was decided to cut the training course to one month, because it was difficult for many who wanted to come to take so much time away from their jobs. Three-month training courses were still held for national organizers who assisted local sections and helped to recruit local chaplains.

Attendance at the month-long training courses ranged from twenty to thirty. The courses were held several times a year. One such course was described in an article in a national magazine by a young man who attended.

> There were twenty-six of us at this particular course, thirteen men and thirteen women. I marveled when I realized that eight different states were represented, stretching across the country from New Hampshire to California. . . . Getting to know the Young Christian Workers I met at this training course was to a great extent the best part of the education I received. Marguerite, a farm girl from Minnesota, was new in the YCW, but she wanted so much to learn in order to help spread the movement among the young workers in farm and rural areas. Ed from South Dakota and Roy from Montana had the same idea. These were levelheaded men who knew rural life, its bright and dark sides. They wanted to spread the brightness more and more.
>
> Joan was a nurse from Wisconsin. She wanted to help the YCW get started in the small towns. She also saw the great opportunity to get nurses interested. Ted and Joe were Chicago bricklayers. Joe's heart was set on getting Spanish-speaking Chicagoans into the YCW. Ted was concerned about the young working people in his parish who needed recreational resources.
>
> Don was a Chicago telephone man who had come to represent his parish group which had the shared the expenses of the course in order to advance themselves with leadership know-how.
>
> Each individual was wonderful. There were so many different backgrounds, but all were aiming at the same goal: better training and know-how in order to make Christ live in their lives and in their environment.[16]

Over two hundred fifty young men and women attended the training courses during the seven years that Russ Tershy was the director.[17] Jack McCartney took over from 1962 to 1966, assisted by vice-president Marie Powers and later Marian Kuzela and Linda Mann.

Jerry Curtis from Detroit, one of those who had to quit a good job because his employer would not give him the necessary time off, describes the training school as a highlight in his own personal development as a Young Christian Worker and one of the most important motivators in the YCW process.

> The training course was meant to be a final initiation into the fullest membership possible, or a stepping stone to it. One could achieve the same objective at the local level, but only through trial and error; whereas the national training course had a certain mystique. It had superb resources, experts, and was highly organized.
>
> The national training course also offered the advantage of meeting potential key leaders from all over the U.S.A. coming together in community for advanced training in skills, resources, and spirituality. Of itself, this one-month-long communal life was exhilarating and dynamic and, most of all, conveyed an understanding of what we were: people serving people. It provided the opportunity to live the YCW techniques and ideology in depth. It was the pinnacle of one's formation.[18]

The Seven Areas of Life

"Formation through Action" has almost become a cliché to describe the effect of the Observe, Judge, Act method of inquiry used by the Young Christian Workers in their weekly meetings. It changed their thinking patterns, helped develop a Christian conscience, and prepared them to accept responsibility. In its original use by the Jocists in Europe, daily life was examined principally in the areas of work, home, and neighborhood. Gradually, it became apparent to the Americans that there were pressing problems in other areas: race relations and civil rights, politics and citizenship.

When the two branches, male and female, of the movement merged in 1954 and a joint program was mapped out, a major decision was made. The national program should develop a Christian conscience in *all* the areas of life for which lay persons are responsible. With the help of Msgr. Hillenbrand, seven such areas were identified. They would form the basis for the annual program of weekly inquiries: (1) work and economic life, (2) marriage and family life, (3) political life and citizenship, (4) leisure, (5) international relations, (6) race relations, and (7) parish life. This last was insisted on by Msgr. Hillenbrand, who was convinced of the critical need for Catholics to be involved in the liturgical worship of the parish community.

Hillenbrand played a major role in developing the concept of the "seven areas of life." The germ of the idea dated back to 1939 when Donald Kanaly wrote, "domestic, economic, political, international," on a holy card from his breviary when the monsignor asked what areas of need young workers should address.

The seven areas of life were to be covered in a three-year cycle so that regardless of when a person came into the movement he or she would, over time, observe the problems and be formed in conscience on all seven. The timing and the specific problems in each area would vary; local sections were invited to give their input on what they saw as problems. Voting behavior was the topic of inquiry during months before major elections, for instance.

Hillenbrand defended the concept at a national team meeting several years later when he said, "Christ teaches salvation through full Christian living. Our movement must form a full Christian in as short a time as possible." Such a formation required about five years, he felt, but the length of time the average member stayed in the movement at that time averaged about three years.[19]

Such a system of inquiry, however admirable in theory, was open to criticism on the grounds that it failed to address the real needs of the membership. How did international relations affect the life of the young worker in a small town in Wisconsin? Why get into church matters in the parish when there was a real problem with local gangs in a Brooklyn neighborhood? Such arguments were brought up at regular intervals, especially when inquiries were on problems of attitude that were difficult to pin down. Section members remember actions like, "Talk to two persons about the this-or-that international issue."

On the other hand, inquiries on international issues did serve to increase the members' awareness of the rest of the world. In today's world with constant satellite communication with other countries on television, it is hard to remember that back in the fifties and sixties, most people didn't even know the names of countries like Kuwait or Iran. Inquiries on global topics were a small step on the way to world understanding. Many who criticized some of the programs based on the "seven areas of life" as being unrealistic or inappropriate later recognized that they did develop a conscience on matters that became more significant in later years.

Despite the criticism, the importance of leadership formation in the "seven areas" was generally agreed upon by the national leaders, who agreed with Msgr. Hillenbrand's view that the reconstruction of the social order was the major aim of the movement. This meant changing both institutions and people.

> Institutions are habits or accepted patterns of society that form people's attitudes and influence their behavior. We want to construct a social order that is human and Christian, where institutions help persons form Christian mentalities, giving them a more Christian human destiny and helping them to gain their eternal destiny with God.[20]

They also accepted Hillenbrand's belief that YCW's real value was in laying the groundwork for change in the future. To make that happen, they must train as many young working persons as possible in Christian principles. "That's our job," he stressed, "to train the leaders of tomorrow. They are the ones who will be responsible for the reconstruction of the social order."[21]

Another area of adaptation was based on changes in the American work force. The International YCW insisted that leaders must be truly representative of the working masses. For a long time the national leaders thought this meant a heavy concentration of workers in heavy industry and manufacturing. In the United States, however, the work force was changing from one primarily based in industry to one centering on technology and service. That, said the national leaders, along with the increased opportunities for education, accounted for a different kind of "genuine" worker. Fewer and fewer American workers were wearing hard hats and blue collars. Therefore, the American movement finally accepted the idea that any young men and women who held a job outside management were workers. Accountants and salesmen, nurses and stenographers were just as much workers as those who worked on an assembly line or in the steel mills.

Hillenbrand summarized the American thinking when he said:

> What we are in the process of doing is creating an American YCW while being part of a worldwide movement. If we

want the American YCW to be as natural as bacon and eggs or apple pie, if we want to be able to stand on our own two feet, then we have to get away from the fact that the YCW was created in Belgium. In the beginning we had European programs and foreign terminology. We must realize that in the United States, there are different working situations and a difference in the average age group. There is little class consciousness and little anti-clericalism in the United States, although we have grave social problems. Thus, our problems are not the same nor should our appeal be the same.[22]

The goal was clear: All kinds of young workers should be recruited into the YCW. The movement would develop in them a Christian social conscience based on the gospels and the social teaching of the encyclicals, provide education in the seven areas of lay responsibility, training in specific leadership skills, and the implantation of a habit of action in response to recognized needs.

In their adaptation of the YCW to the United States, the leaders moved in directions that seemed appropriate at the time, though there were some unfortunate by-products. The switch to sections of men and women together seemed necessary and appropriate to the American life-style, but unfortunately the "mixed" movement often failed to develop the full leadership potential of its young women.

Moreover the few years in which young men and women were eligible for membership often pressured the national leaders to cover the identified areas of social conscience formation in too short a time. In some sections "education" took precedence over a realistic response to community problems which arose at unpredictable times. "Formation through action" was easy to lose sight of in the attempt to focus on all areas of life in the few years between school and marriage. This tended to weaken the vitality of the movement in later years.

Former Leaders Reflect

YCW has on the whole had a positive effect on me. The Observe, Judge, Act approach to participating in life, I've found most practical. Also, a double message, about being a woman: Save the world, but let the men do it first. (St. Paul, Minnesota)

My husband and I both feel that YCW changed our lives completely. Even today, we find it difficult to live without involvement in the community, politics, social issues of today, and especially the formation of social consciousness in our sons and daughters. . . . Sometimes I wish I had not been indoctrinated with the Observe, Judge, and Act formula of the YCW because it does not let one stay out of the fray. (Chicago)

It was through my YCW experience that I came to realize that I had both rights and responsibilities. If I had the right to life, to respect, to education, to freedom of expression, to live according to my conscience, to economic justice, etc., I had a corresponding responsibility to do what I could to assure that others also had those same rights. The concept influenced the work I chose in community service, the direction my life took, and the volunteer activities I became involved in. The YCW also helped me to realize the importance of continuing to learn, to question, to listen, to think. (St. Paul, Minnesota)

Growing up in YCS and YCW was probably the single most importance influence in my conception of what a Christian should be. The idea of Action (doing) with a scriptural basis has been the foundation of what I have been doing over the years (although I wish I could have done better). There has been nothing of comparable value or influence in our children's lives—for which we are very sad and for which they are the losers. Vatican II was never a big surprise for me because it was what we had been talking about for years in YCW. . . . but whatever happened to the Christian world we thought we were building? It seems more elusive now than ever. (Chicago)

Notes

[1] Msgr. Reynold Hillenbrand, "About Mixed Groups," Chaplain's Notes, n.d.
[2] Mary Buckley to author, June 1986.
[3] Hillenbrand, handwritten notes at meeting, March 2, 1961. UND archives.
[4] Hillenbrand notes, n.d. UND archives.
[5] Notes from H.Q. team meeting, 1961. UND archives.
[6] Nancy Diley Delaney, letter to author, August 8, 1986.
[7] Jo Jeske Crosby to author, March 3, 1987.
[8] Frank Ardito to author, February 27, 1987.
[9] Nancy Lee Conrad, taped conversation with author, March 3, 1988.
[10] Jim Burke to author, January 3, 1988.
[11] Ann Ida Gannon, B.V.M., "Perspectives on Women in Business," *Chicago Studies*, April 1989, p. 59. Sr. Ann Ida is the former president of Mundelein College in Chicago, a college for women only. She has long been a concerned and active leader among Catholic women.
[12] Bob Olmstead to Pat Keegan, April 26, 1957. UND archives.
[13] Keegan to Olmstead, May 5, 1957. UND archives.
[14] Fundamentals of the International YCW, Rome, 1957. Zotti papers.
[15] Russ Tershy, taped conversation with author, October 1, 1985.
[16] *Liguorian*, February 1960.
[17] Russ Tershy has continued to train people. After the Peace Corps and the federal poverty program, he founded the Center for Employment Training in San Jose, which has grown to thirty centers in seven Western states. Besides teaching practical skills in small groups, a principal aim of CET is to develop in each person a sense of personal worth and dignity. Over 44,000 persons considered unemployable when they entered his program have been placed in jobs.
[18] Jerry Curtis, letter to author, May 16, 1989.
[19] Hillenbrand, national team meeting, 1956. UND archives.
[20] Hillenbrand, minutes of Headquarters Study Day, May 5, 1956.
[21] Hillenbrand, *Ibid.*
[22] Hillenbrand, National Council Meeting, July 1957.

8

The Formation of an Apostolic Leader

The aim of the Young Christian Workers to Christianize the world required that members have a realistic view of the world, develop a truly Christian conscience in order to make judgments, and cultivate the necessary skills to bring about change. Making a Christian judgment required an understanding of the Scriptures and a knowledge of the social teachings of the Church. Selfless action grew out of a hunger for social justice and a deep sense of obligation grounded in a solid spiritual life.

A deep-rooted habit of action based on an awareness of reality and a balanced social conscience in all areas of life became known, in the lexicon of the movement, as *formation*.

It differed from the traditional training young Catholics usually received from their families and in the Catholic schools. In the YCW, individuals became thinking, acting Christians rather than mere churchgoers with a code of personal moral behavior.

Cardijn described the process well in an article which appeared in the *Priests' Bulletin*.

> Leaders do not grow like mushrooms—they must be formed. Their formation must be constantly intensified and deepened. ... They are formed first of all by getting them to act, giving them small responsibilities. It is not necessary to take them apart and then give them a course of doctrine. ... First the action and then the responsibility, and only afterwards the talk.

It is because he is a human being, that his formation is absolutely essential. Animals can be broken in and trained to perform tricks, but human beings are not animals. They have intelligence, and their intelligence must be developed. They must know the purpose of what they are being taught to do and the reason why they have to do it. It is necessary to give them not merely a teaching of a doctrine, but a formation which is quite a different thing. People must be taught to act for love, and freely to suffer and fight for what they are taught. There is no other remedy against the regime of a dictator.

Leaders are not mass-produced, but formed personally, one by one.... We must have true revolutionaries, not tub-thumpers who work on crowds . . . but people who bring about a revolution by their testimony. Every leader must be such a witness—sincere, true witness to love, justice, charity, and respect for the young worker.[1]

The method and structure of the Jocist movement grew out of Cardijn's understanding of leadership formation. Proper use of the inquiry itself developed the prospective leader's ability to think realistically and motivated him to action. The reading of the Gospels and applying them in one's life was essential to understanding Christ and the Christian ethic. Leading the Gospel discussion, or Gospel inquiry as it was sometimes called, rotated among the members of the leaders' group. The individual who was to lead the Gospel inquiry was expected to meet with the chaplain before the meeting to prepare the points to be discussed. This meant that each member had an opportunity at least once every couple of months to sit down with the priest privately. This was a new experience for many young people and it provided an opportunity for him to ask for any personal guidance he might need. Often a new member's first real insight into what it meant to be a lay apostle was when he sat down with the priest to prepare the Gospel inquiry or lead the meeting.

One former section president said recently that without the support of his chaplain, he never could have continued. "They made me president, and quite honestly, I really shouldn't have been. Father was very helpful in that regard. Sometimes, I was carrying this thing around and I would have to sit down with Father and say, 'Hey, aside from being president, just the idea of being a Christian. . . . I don't know. It bothers me. I don't think I'm there.' We were fortunate to have a tremendous chaplain who was really supportive. He didn't wash over things. You really got to be more comfortable with Christ and with the faith. Then we would go on to prepare for leading the Gospel dis-cussion at the meeting."[2]

In a simple situation in one's daily life, like coming to the aid of a co-worker who became ill on the job, or talking to a lonely person, the teachings of the Gospel were clear. Many observed problems, however, were more complicated and a judgment required more study. The Gospels certainly were the primary source on which to know how a Christian should live, but often it was difficult to know how to apply the Gospels to the complexities of modern life. One source of guidance in this regard was the social doctrine of the Church developed in the papal encyclicals. We often studied and discussed them at study days so we could make better judgments on the facts we observed in the social inquiry.

On this point, Reynold Hillenbrand chastised the chaplains who sometimes were unacquainted with the social doctrine embodied in the papal encyclicals. In an article in the *Priests' Bulletin* in 1952, he strongly urged the chaplains to "close the gap between the teaching of the popes and the minds of the people. . . . We need to draw from the doctrine of the Church those things which apply specifically to the needs of our time."[3]

Another essential in the life of a Christian leader was the development of a personal spiritual life. A lay person trying to do the work of the Lord had to develop in his own life the Christian virtues taught by Jesus as well as a commitment to prayer. Msgr. Hillenbrand had long been a believer in liturgical worship—the Mass and the Sacraments—and he constantly stressed it as the best way for lay leaders to pray. It was he who insisted that a few minutes in each weekly meeting be devoted to a discussion of some aspect of the liturgy so that young workers could participate more intelligently and wholeheartedly in the worship of the Church.

The Role of the Chaplain

A sound apostolic formation did not occur quickly. Even though a member might be convinced of the need for apostolic action after a year or so, it generally took three or four years to develop a permanent habit of Christian action. This is why the role of the chaplain was so crucial.

Helping leaders to develop meaningful and practical Christian values was not a simple matter. It required a deep personal commitment on the chaplain's part as well as a clear vision of the lay apostolate. This did not happen overnight. The priest and the lay person grew together.

Many priests, frankly, were not prepared to provide the kinds of spiritual guidance that lay apostles needed. They had to learn to give evenings of reflection and days of recollection that were meaningful to young men and women who were immersed in the nitty-gritty routine of making a living. The priest had to make them realize that Jesus Christ really expected them to be concerned about others. He had to make their membership in the Mystical Body of Christ a conscious reality. And he had to bring them to the source of divine life in the Mass and the Sacraments where they would get the strength to persevere with their apostolic mission.

The formation of ordinary fellows and girls as apostolic leaders required priests who themselves had a strong faith and a deep prayer life, as well as an understanding of needs of Christians living in the world. Conscientious chaplains spent hours each week preparing for meetings with leaders and attending meetings. They never participated directly in the leaders' meetings; that was the domain of the lay people. Only afterwards were they given five or ten minutes for a short inspirational talk or clarification on a point of doctrine that came up at the meeting. This was not the time to tell the members what they did wrong at the meeting. If there were problems with the interaction of members in the group—one person who tried to dominate the discussion, or the tendency of another to go off on a tangent—these could better be discussed privately. Rather, this was the time to give confidence to the young people.

The Chicago Catholic Action Federation published a magazine, originally the *Priests' Bulletin*, later entitled *Apostolate*, which carried articles on all the specialized apostolic movements, as well as advice and ideas to help the priest-chaplain develop more effective apostolic leaders. Msgr. Hillenbrand also sent out a newsletter, *Chaplain's Notes*, which discussed issues of particular concern to YCW chaplains. When there were enough of them in a diocese, chaplains were encouraged to hold regular meetings where they could learn from each other. At national study weeks, there were always special meetings for the chaplains in attendance.

The Chaplain Role in Starting a Section

Though the YCW was a lay movement, it was visionary priests who sought out and invited the first young men and women to come to a YCW meeting. Many of them were seminarians when they heard about the lay movement of Catholic Action and they saw it as a challenging and realistic way to make their priesthood more meaningful. It was the priest who inspired and motivated and often times coaxed young people to get involved.

The prospective chaplain trying to start a section of young workingmen had to find a few young people in the parish who were potential leaders and could be challenged to try something new. Some priests spent months just getting to know a few young workers well enough to sit down and talk with them, much less interest them in becoming active Christians.

One chaplain tells the story of joining in a crap game on a local street corner, much to the amazement of the participants.[4] Another played cards every other week for six months with a young fellow before he broached the idea of starting a group. One just went through the parish records looking for names of families with sons that were of the right age and called them in to see him at the rectory.

Another chaplain tells the story of stopping to talk to a young fellow he met on the street who was obviously unemployed. "Hi, how are things going?" he inquired.

"Huh?"

"Want to shoot a few baskets?"

"Well, uh, o.k." After shooting baskets in the lot behind the school nearby, they sat down for a breather. Conversation eventually worked around to the subject of the young man's job-hunting problems. Suddenly, he looked at the priest and said, "Father, you're the first priest that ever talked to me without asking me first if I went to church last Sunday." The young man later became a Young Christian Worker and one of the key fellows around whom the priest built his section.[5]

Natural leadership talent was essential when a section was started. Cardijn continually said that it was important to find young people with the ability to attract and influence others. For his first group of girls in Laecken, he sought out girls with leadership ability who would bring the others in. His first male leaders, Fernand Tonnet, Paul Garcet, and Jacques Meert, were carefully chosen when he began what became the JOC after World War I.

> Being a leader is a quality and an aptitude—quite often a natural gift and aptitude. In any house or street, bus, or train, there is usually the boy who "rules the roost," who is the life and soul of the party, who attracts others, at whose house they naturally meet, to whom they all look, who carries them all along with him. He is a born leader with certain gifts, with more dash and go, who always takes the initiative and leads the others.
>
> Many a young worker has a wealth of character and driving force. He must make something of it, either for good or for evil. . . . Once he is won, it is necessary to supernaturalize his natural gifts and turn them into an apostolic force.
>
> This is what happened with all those who did anything great for the Church. St. Paul would have been a gangster, the greatest enemy of the Church, if Our Lord had not seized him and thrown him to the ground. He became the Lord's revolutionary. He had in him a driving force, a wealth of character, which he put to the service of Christ and the apostolate. . . . [6]

The early American chaplains were conscious of this. When Fr. Donald Runkle was faced with the problem of picking a new federation leader for the Chicago Business Girls in 1943, he had sent out Loretta Fenton, then working part time at 3 East, to visit all the cells and report back to him with her opinion of the girls she observed. Who were the best leaders in the cells? he asked. He trusted her judgment because she had met experienced leaders on her travels to established movements. From the two names she gave him, Father chose Edwina Hearn, an experienced natural leader with a strong personality and good common sense.[7]

Fr. Bill Quinn carefully observed the young men hanging around the street corners in his parish before approaching Tony Zivalich to be the leader of his first section of young men in 1946. Tony and Edwina both proved to have natural leadership talent that served them well when they became the first presidents of the Young Christian Workers.

Development of a Lay Spirituality

Another facet in the guidance of young people was the need to develop in them a spirituality that was appropriate to lay people in the world. Many of the early writers on the subject of spiritual formation for lay leaders were experienced chaplains of the English YCW such as Fr. Eugene Langdale, who wrote about lay spirituality in the *Priests' Bulletin.*

> The problem of the spiritual and apostolic formation of worker-leaders is not something new; it has existed ever since Catholics, in answer to the call of the Social Encyclicals, have concerned themselves with the problems of the working class. . . .
>
> One cannot insist too much in consequence on the importance of the spiritual training we give to our lads and girls. We are largely responsible for giving them a Christian vision of the world, the light that will illuminate the whole of their lives with Faith, Hope and Charity and give them the strength of Christ. . . .
>
> To be authentic, the spirituality of our worker leaders must be deeply traditional, finding its roots in the Old Testament, in the Gospels, in St. Paul, and in the Fathers of the Church. But it must be a spirituality that sets the perennial truths in the light of their vocation in the modern world; the traditional spirituality of the Church but of the Church incarnate in the twentieth century and in the modern world of work.[8]

In 1951 Fr. John Fitzsimons wrote on the need for "A New Spirituality for the Lay Apostle." He carefully outlined the theology of a lay spirituality that differed from the kind of spiritual life taught in the seminaries, based on the monastic spirit which draws persons away from the world and in which the priests themselves had been trained. He recommended that the lay apostle learn to know Christ in a personal way through the Gospels and participation in the liturgy in order that he can show Him to others. He pointed out there is no need in the layman's life to look for means of mortification and sacrifice. "If he is living an apostolic life as a member of a Catholic Action organization, such demands will be made on his time, goods, energy, attention, and goodwill that his whole day will be made up of a series of renunciations."[9]

Paul Marx, O.S.B., discussed the balanced harmony of the individual Christian and the community in terms of the Mystical Body of Christ.

> The Catholic layman who understands the Church as the continuation of Christ in the community life of His Mystical Body will understand that the graces are not meant just for himself but also for all those persons who come in contact with him, work with him, recreate with him, etc. . . . "Only in this light do Cardinal Suhard's words make sense: One cannot be a saint and live the gospel we preach without spending oneself to provide everyone with the housing, employment, goods, leisure, education, etc. without which life is no longer human."[10]

On the other hand, Cardinal Suhard, archbishop of Paris and a strong advocate of lay action, cautioned priests lest the idea of the Incarnation which brings the divinity of Christ into temporal society should become a means of "reducing the mystery of Christianity into a self-contained humanism."[11]

> If they are not careful, some Christians will remember only the first part of the Incarnation, the transfiguration of all profane things through Christ's descent on earth. By stopping halfway they are involved in divinizing the earthly state of things. . . . Of course, most of them would not get as far as this idolatrous glorification of worldly values. But the danger would remain of being too much attached to them and of reversing the right order by making them the end and not a means. . . . At this stage the priest must step in.

... He will always remember that although temporal realities have a real value, because they come from God. ... and have been redeemed in Christ, they still remain what they are, elementary and transitory. There is nothing in them to slake the thirst for the infinite of supernaturalized man.[12]

"We must help lay people to discover the spirituality of the ordinary, like the value of penance as the New York working girl rides the subway in the rush hour," said Francis Wendell, O.P. "Lay people must be given a sense of the Church—not a sense of belonging to the Church, but a sense of being the Church."[13]

"Do we teach them to pray at off moments during the day, remembering that they have given themselves to God at Mass?" asked Philip Kenney. "Do we really believe in the layman's competence in Catholic Action and are we willing to run the risk of laymen making mistakes? Do some of our leaders show more obedience than initiative?"[14]

They were challenged further by the high standards clearly described by Fr. Langdale.

Christian life can only become desirable through the witness of sanctity. One cannot stress too much the fact that the call to the apostolate is essentially a call to sanctity. The scandal of the world is the Christian who is not living his faith. . . . A Christian vision of the world demands a full human development all along the line. It is in the very name of our faith that we demand social progress. . . . If we have faith in the creation, in the supreme dignity of man, in the redemption of all things in Christ, our faith must find expression in our respect and service for men in the building of a human order. . . . Our struggle for justice and for charity is preparing men for the advent of God's kingdom in time and in eternity.[15]

Another put it succinctly: "The priest must convert the layman into being apostolic; the layman must convert the world to Christ."[16]

Strong words and a tall order for the priest working with ordinary fellows and girls. Small wonder that some of them became burned out, especially if they had to go through the process time and again, as leaders left to marry, or they themselves were transferred to another parish. But those who persisted were rewarded by seeing the formation of a strong spiritual base and apostolic zeal in many of the young men and women in their sections.

The Constant Need for Committed Chaplains

Leaders thus challenged and formed were constantly on the search for more priests to help in the expansion of the movement. It was not easy to find enough priests able to understand what was expected of a chaplain, much less willing to give themselves wholeheartedly to the training of lay leaders.

"Anywhere that the movement has produced leadership," wrote Caroline Pezzullo to a federation leader in New York, "there's a priest who through his own conviction started a section and formed leaders. Somehow, we have to make it possible to lay a plan before a great number of priests and allow them the free choice, because of some kind of conviction, to start a section."[17]

Sometimes there were problems with priests who became chaplains but did not understand the importance of giving the lay leaders freedom to make decisions about problems they observed in secular society. This sometimes happened in the local section, but it was more common at the federation level where more far-reaching decisions had to be made. Some priests worried about the ability of young people to make sound decisions, especially if they perceived them to be rash or imprudent. They feared that mistakes would bring down the wrath of pastors or others in positions of authority. The result was a curtailment of the leader's ability to grow as a responsible and confident Christian.

Fran Kelley, organizing in California in 1954, was concerned about this when she wrote to Msgr. Hillenbrand.

> The big problem here with the movement is one of the priests' misconceptions of the role of the laity, as expressed in things like Fr. H. insisting, at a federation meeting, that the priests have the final authority and responsibility in whatever goes on in the movement. When I heard this I nearly flipped. It made me a little sick, thinking how far we

have yet to go in making them understand that we are responsible for the temporal order and that both we and they have our own unique roles to play in the picture.

It seems to me that this point should be remembered at our study weeks and really blown up, discussed, studied and made clear. Otherwise everything we've been trying to do will ultimately fold up. It came as somewhat of a shock to me, but it's indicative of the general thinking among the clergy.

What they do is give us free rein, but attach so many strings to it that no one can grow fully in responsibility or have a basically sound and strong idea of what the real and total role of the lay person is in the social order.[18]

In answer to Fran, the monsignor wrote, "Your assessing of the situation of the priests' mentality is certainly correct. An awful lot of work has to be done. They simply do not understand what the lay people have to do, therefore do not trust them to do it. But learning this is going to be inevitable, given time. People will be forced into seeing it as they stand more and more helpless before the whole situation."[19]

As one experienced chaplain wrote, "Always the accent should be on counsel rather than command ('Do this, don't do that'). The person should be helped to make his own decisions. We are living in a time of Christian rejuvenation. Let us thank God and do our part in furthering it."[20]

More on Natural Leadership

The development of young people as Christian leaders was much easier when it could build on natural talent. Discernment of leadership potential was never easy, especially in young people. That is why the criterion of membership in the leader's group in the early days was the formation of a team. When a leader was able to recruit a team with whom he or she met informally but on a regular basis, it was an indication that that person was able to reach out and influence others.

In the early days, we didn't question this requirement. It made sense that if we were to be apostolic, we must get others involved. We didn't think about whether or not we were natural leaders. Forming a team was just a logical next step, so we did it.

Members in the leaders' group in Manhattan in the late forties, said Rita Joseph O'Shea, a leader there who later joined the national team, were also expected to have teams. It was an easy and natural way to sort members without creating hard feelings. If you had a team, you became a member of the leaders' group. If not, you weren't. That way everyone could find his or her niche in the organization.[21]

One member from the forties, responding to our survey of former members, said she was always a team member, but that never bothered her. She felt part of something important that gave her new understandings of what it meant to be a Christian and through it she made lifelong friends.

In the early fifties, the stress on organizational design, including team formation and monthly general meetings, gradually fell into disuse. In Europe, general meetings filled a need for young workers to enjoy leisure time together and build community spirit in the neighborhood, whereas the Americans found that their fellow workers had other social and recreational opportunities, and monthly general meetings for their own sake had little appeal. Such meetings were held only on special occasions or when particular action projects merited them. Reports from the late fifties also indicate that members thought it unrealistic to expect everyone to have a formal team. It was considered sufficient if members had two friends on whom they could depend for help in making observations or carrying out action. Some members of the section did have a group of followers they called an "action group." Gradually, the word "section" came to mean the group of members who met weekly with the chaplain to conduct the social inquiry. There was no longer a hierarchy of membership participation.

This may have come about because there was a growing sentiment that no one should be excluded from the YCW section. It was not the democratic way. Were we not trying to reach out to everybody? It is a fact that most YCW groups were very friendly and newcomers always felt welcome.[22] The flip side of this is that in later years many persons joined the YCW section for their own personal needs, rather than because of a desire to reach out to others. Many of these persons did not have the leadership skills to form a team. Gradually the term "leader" was replaced simply by "member."

Officers of the section or the federation were generally identified as leaders.

A former Chicago leader commented on this when he described his section in the sixties.

> As I understood YCW, its chief purpose was "formation"—the molding of its members through prayer, study and action—people who lived in the world as conscious, deliberate followers of Christ and who attempted to bring about social change in the world in accordance with Christian values. . . .
>
> Our section was typical, I suppose. It had its periods of growth and decline; it sponsored various events in the parish—social events for young adults, Lenten forums on the social teachings of the Church, a political debate with candidates for city and state governments (one of its more ambitious projects); and it persevered in its attempts to form its members. This activity, which was, after all, the most important one for a YCW section was the most frustrating, at least as far as I was concerned. A great variety of people came into our YCW group, and I am not sure that the movement had much of a transforming effect in their lives. For those with natural abilities and idealism, it offered a means of putting those abilities to work. For those with various kinds of emotional and psychological problems—there were many such—it accomplished very little, I'm afraid.[23]

This problem was also alluded to by a section president who wrote to the national office about the membership potential for apostolic and social action.

> Too many people in the movement give little to YCW yet derive considerable benefit. We have people with us who might not be accepted elsewhere because of social or psychological difficulties. We have many people who use the section as a point of gravitation, hanging on to it as a social outlet until they drag the section down. This situation occurs often with the girls. Too many have few friends

outside the YCW; they would have no place to go if it were not for the movement's social functions. Thus, many of our sections become "isolated" and "special." They do not blend in with the community.[24]

Peter Foote, a Chicago federation president in the sixties, commenting on this statement in 1963, said that if this parish president was right, there was a large theory and practice gap in the YCW, "more probably than the YCW would like to admit." "No doubt," he added, "this is because the YCW is charged by its founder as an outgoing, apostolic movement."[25]

Cardijn apparently noticed this when he toured the United States about that time, for he noted that the YCW must overcome the natural tendency of young fellows and girls to meet together in a closed way and to forget the needs of others. "We have observed that the CFM [Christian Family Movement] seems to progress more than the YCW. The CFM seems always to organize new teams and new sections. The same tendency must exist in the YCW. . . . Too many leaders seem to forget a few elementary means of friendship, of contact, of simpler responsibilities which . . . orientate youth, with the grace of God, towards a greater apostolic responsibility."[26]

Another aspect of leadership development surfaced from time to time. Well-formed leaders were not formed overnight and sometimes individuals were brought into positions of greater responsibility who were not ready. This was especially true in the case of some who came onto the national leadership team.

Some of them were very capable in the local section or federation and others were excellent organizers in the field; but heading a movement which became quite large by the late fifties required leaders who were more than generous, well-intentioned persons. It required stable persons with mature judgment, emotional stamina, good physical health, and a sound spirituality. National leaders had to make great personal sacrifices when they left home and moved to Chicago to work long hours for very little money in a very demanding situation. As idealistic as they might be, they were still very young. What is truly amazing is that so many men and women in their twenties did develop the apostolic spirit and leadership skills required at the forefront of a national movement. It is testimony to the dedicated chaplains who saw in them the potential to make a difference and gave them the moral and spiritual support that was so necessary.

Looking Back on YCW Formation

Our parish priest who had a boys' group was starting one for girls and asked me to join. That priest is still one of my best friends. The YCW had and still has a positive effect on me. It directed me to be active in the community, Church, and world affairs. It sparked my interest in what was happening in the Church and the world. I became a progressive Catholic and have lived to see many issues that I fought for become standard in my parish. It was partly responsible for my reading the Bible, nurtured my love of the liturgy, made me aware that "we are the Church." Gave me a need for community and fellowship with God's people that is still with me. I guess YCW made me willing to serve and ready for leadership. (Brooklyn)

Observe, Judge, Act together, basic to formation and community. YCW inspired spiritual and sociopolitical growth, giving a sense of individual and community responsiveness to involvement. (New Orleans)

My main appreciation was the Gospel related to everyday life— that the Church had a say-so in economic life, as a guide to make judgments. It provided continuing religious education for the adult: able to see the complexities of life; willingness to be patient and accept small successes; sow and let others reap; excellent training of the will. Rejoiced when Mater et Magistra *was written. Regretted the small number of chaplains who really understood the movement. Wish I could have worked more closely with those who did.* (Inglewood, California)

YCW did for me what Vatican II did for the Church—it was a breath of fresh air, the Holy Spirit, that empowered me on my life course. Like Vatican II, there have been rocky roads, but I still believe in the basic vision—the possibility—that I got from YCW. I still sit down with small groups of peers (as part of my work with adults in parish groups) and lead them to Observe what's going on in life; Judge what does scripture say; and take Action. (New Orleans)

My view of YCW is positive. I did go through a burnout period in the early seventies, but as my faith was rejuvenated, my interest in issues rose. YCW was formative for me in terms of a love for liturgy (Msgr. Hillenbrand's input) and interest in issues. I was active in civil rights—impetus from YCW—and my interest in unions was strongly influenced by YCW. And probably the fact that I attach a religious imperative to supporting candidates and programs that tend to reflect the Church's social teachings. (Detroit)

Notes

1. Msgr. Joseph Cardijn, "The Young Worker Faces Life, Part II," *YCW Bulletin for Priests*, April 1950, pp. 11–13.
2. Frank Ardito to author, February 27, 1987.
3. Msgr. Reynold Hillenbrand, "The Priesthood and the World," *YCW Bulletin for Priests*, March 1952, p. 3.
4. William Quinn to author, November 30, 1986.
5. Edward Hogan to author, March 8, 1986.
6. Cardijn, *op. cit.*, p. 12.
7. Loretta Fenton Brislen to author, September 15, 1985.
8. Eugene Langdale, "The Spirituality of Worker Leaders," *YCW Bulletin for Priests*, September 1950, pp. 1, 2, 6.
9. John Fitzsimons, "New Spirituality for Lay Apostles," *YCW Bulletin for Priests*, December 1951, p. 12.
10. Paul Marx, O.S.B., "Spiritual Formation and the Social Action Apostolate," *Apostolate*, Fall 1959, pp. 7–8.
11. Cardinal Suhard, *The Priest in the Modern World*, quoted in *YCW Bulletin for Priests*, December 1951, p. 3.
12. *Ibid.*
13. Francis Wendell, O.P., "Priests and the Spirituality of Lay People," *Apostolate*, Summer 1956, p. 2.
14. Philip Kenney, "Thoughts on the YCW Chaplain's Job," *Apostolate*, Spring 1956, p. 18.
15. Langdale, *op. cit.*, p. 11.
16. Marx, *op. cit.*, p. 10.
17. Caroline Pezzullo to Mary Mannix, April 11, 1952.
18. Fran Kelley to Hillenbrand, March 28, 1954.
19. Hillenbrand to Kelley, May 4, 1954.
20. James Voss, "Thoughts for Chaplains," *Apostolate*, Winter 1953, p. 36.
21. Rita Joseph O'Shea to author, October 4, 1985.
22. Seventy-five percent of those who responded to a survey of former members conducted by the author in 1985 to 1988 said they were attracted to the YCW by the friendliness of its members.
23. John McCudden, letter to author, March 7, 1987.
24. Gerald Hanley, quoted by Peter Foote. "New Light on the Young Adult Movement," *Apostolate*, Fall 1963, p. 17.
25. Foote, *ibid.*, p. 22.
26. Joseph Cardijn, "Thoughts About the United States YCW," *Apostolate*, Fall 1963, p. 10.

9

People in Action

It was the young people who got involved, tens of thousands of them over thirty years, who made the YCW movement what it was. It was the young man who spent one night a week sitting around a table with six or eight others working on a social inquiry, another evening with a couple of friends he was trying to involve in a service project, and maybe a third night stopping by the rectory to see Father to prepare to lead the gospel inquiry at the next meeting. It was the young woman who carefully wrote facts she observed in a notebook so she could report at the next meeting. It was the person who was constantly on the lookout for people with problems that needed solving. It was Barbara and Claire, Albert and Fred, and the others like them for whom living as a committed Young Christian Worker became the norm of daily life.

Most of them were not particularly interested in getting involved in anything serious until someone, a friend or a friendly priest, invited them to attend a meeting with a few other young persons. Why did they go? Mostly because they liked the person who asked them. Sometimes they were curious. Sometimes they just didn't know how to say no. What could they lose by going along for a night or two to see what was going on?

Why did they stay? Some didn't, of course. Those who did were usually intrigued by the fact that someone thought they and their ideas were important and that they were needed. They liked the other people in the group, and they were impressed by what they heard.

Many of them had gone to Catholic schools, and they knew something about their religion, but this was different. It was a new way of looking at everyday life. A few were aware of social problems and were looking for answers and a way do something useful. Generally, they were idealistic young people who were challenged by the idea that they could play a part in making the world a better place. "A new youth for a new world" was an appealing idea.

Getting a New Section Started

After the first introductory meeting in which they got a brief idea of what the YCW was, new members were given a book which contained weekly meeting outlines for the next six months. Over the years programs for beginning sections were written, refined and updated, as the movement itself developed and adapted to the changing times. By following the meeting outlines in the beginning manuals, YCW members discovered what the movement was all about and got a broad view of what was expected of them.

When *Introducing YCW* was published in 1960, the movement had adopted the "Seven Areas of Life" in its program format, and so the beginning book touched on all these areas briefly. It also described the kind of education provided in the movement.

> The YCW is a school-in-life through which its members learn to Observe, Judge and Act in the light of what Christ wants. This education is concerned with the *whole* life of the young person, not just part of it: his home, neighborhood, work, leisure, and preparation for marriage.
>
> This education does not come primarily from lectures and books, but through the discussions, decisions, actions and activities of the movement. Working together to solve problems, YCW members develop a social sense and a social conduct. They see the greatness of God's plan for them, and they develop a deep conviction about this.
>
> But this education does not stop with the YCW members. Their action must be aimed at educating other young people, showing them God's love for them, and showing them their dignity.[1]

"They see the greatness of God's plan for them, and they develop a deep conviction about this. . . . Their action must be aimed at educating other young people." These are key statements about the training of the Young Christian Worker. Most young people who stayed in the movement long enough did develop such a conviction. Sometimes an awareness of what it meant to be part of the Mystical Body of Christ with the responsibility to serve God by serving other people came as a kind of conversion. Those who heard the soft-spoken Msgr. Hillenbrand talk intensely about the reality of Christ in the Mystical Body at a study week often came away imbued with a deep sense of commitment. He gave them a vision of a Christ-centered world and a personal call to the lay apostolate.

Action Results from the Annual Program[2]

After completing the introductory program and learning about the organizational aspects of the movement, a new section then used the annual program of inquiry written by the national team in Chicago. Each year had a theme and inquiries centered on two or three of the "seven areas."

Reports in the YCW archives show the wide range of action members engaged in. After an inquiry on the draft, a pre-induction night was held in 1953 for Milwaukee draftees. Inquiries on work that year led to general meetings in San Francisco and Decoto, California, where union leaders were invited to speak. In Brooklyn and New York, the womens' sections compiled statistics on the situation of workers in the garment industry to present to the garment workers' union. The sale of Christian Christmas cards as a fund-raising project through the late forties and early fifties was also seen as a way to give members a chance to spread a more Christian understanding of the holiday.

Unity was the theme of the inquiry program in 1957. Members looked at problems in daily life which separated people: racial discrimination, communism, and mixed marriage, lack of understanding of people in and from other countries around the world. Leaders examined life in the parish and the neighborhood, unions at work and even the United Nations. Actions on international concerns included talking to friends on the need for understanding the situation in other countries, helping immigrants to adjust to American life, and sending CARE packages to the poor overseas.

Major action followed the examination of the facts of racial discrimination. In Omaha, observation revealed that a Nebraska law prohibiting discrimination in restaurants was often ignored. When YCW members learned that the city council had invited the Urban League and a Baptist convention to meet in Omaha that summer, they decided to take a survey on the extent of discrimination in all the restaurants in the city. They distributed the list to all convention goers.

AIM, the new national YCW newspaper, reported on the results of that action in its issue of July 1958.

> The YCW leaders agreed, "It was not a survey just to determine statistics about discrimination, but also a means of determining where, how, and when we personally could Christianize and educate our fine All-American City, our friends in it, and especially the restaurant people."
>
> The results surprised even themselves. . . .
>
> They talked to 76 restaurant proprietors about discrimination and put together a fact sheet on Nebraska Civil rights laws. . . .
>
> The results of the survey caused quite a small stir. Said George Robinson, Omaha Urban League president, "The group's impact on restaurant owners was most interesting."
>
> It seems that more than two-thirds of the restaurants told the YCWs they served Negroes under the same conditions as anyone else, but, when it came to putting their name on a list for convention use, less than half were willing to do so. . . . [3]

The Holy Cross YCW section in Omaha won a national citation for its constructive action the following year at the National Catholic Interracial Conference, the first award to a lay group in the NCIC's history. Ray Horn, the project leader, started the Catholic Interracial Council of Omaha when he left the movement to get married.

In San Francisco, YCW members, incensed by the facts they discovered about racial discrimination on the job, waged a major campaign to establish a Fair Employment Practices Commission in their city. Public meetings, petitions, letters to newspapers, state legislators, and local officials brought about the passage of fair employment legislation. A YCW leader was appointed a commissioner on the newly instituted FEPC. The organization was commended by a public official who gave the YCW credit for mobilizing public opinion to get the legislation passed.

By 1961, when the inquiries again focused on the problems of racial discrimination, the national program devoted five months to the problem, with much more sophisticated guidelines for action. A major part of the suggested action was a neighborhood survey to be taken by all YCW sections on discrimination in housing, employment, education, and public places including restaurants, theaters, and hospitals. In Covington, Kentucky, 1,017 families were surveyed regarding their attitudes on minority groups and the results were presented, on request, to the Governor's Conference on Human Rights. The Covington YCW also played a major role in integrating their local parish churches.

Civil rights was becoming an issue throughout the country and YCW leaders participated in sit-ins, wade-ins, and Freedom Rides. Some developed interracial discussion groups and social events, aided families in need, painting the house of an elderly black couple in Milwaukee, for example. In St. Cloud, Minnesota, YCW helped Indians on the nearby reservations prepare for jobs in the city. Migrant families were helped in Racine, Wisconsin. Other YCW leaders worked in community organizations and encouraged open occupancy laws. In New Orleans, a fellow and a girl impersonated a married couple, at considerable danger to themselves, to see what was going on in a segregationist group. In Baltimore, YCW leaders were in a group arrested trying to integrate a local amusement park. Members in Oklahoma were also arrested for participating in demonstrations for racial justice. Individual actions were taken by members everywhere.

In a summary of Civil Rights Action resulting from the 1961 program, YCW President Mike Coleman wrote:

> The program served as an instrument of education for all members in the YCW, helping them to uncover truth regarding the problems of minority groups. They learned to work with other groups like NAACP, Catholic Interracial Council, Urban League, and B'nai B'rith. Our members discovered that many people were afraid of the race issue,

but slowly through education, they found it easier to converse about it. They began to understand the Negro and his contribution to our society. They realized, also, they had to begin to know Negroes as people and not as problems.[4]

The stand of the Young Christian Workers on the issue of civil rights by the mid-sixties became so well-known that Jim Burke, then a YCW organizer in Chicago, recalls being thrown out of more than one Southwest Side rectory by pastors facing the prospect of rapidly changing neighborhoods. The first time he was told, "I don't want your nigger-loving group in my parish," he returned to his own chaplain in tears of dismay.[5]

In 1958, "Love, Man, and Society" focused the attention of members on problems related to politics and voter participation. Candidates were invited to general meetings to address young workers about their views on the issues of the day. In many places Young Christian Workers undertook campaigns to register new voters.

After the elections were over, the sections spent the next six months on problems related to dating and marriage. In the spring of 1959 preparation for marriage courses were held in over fifteen cities and reached thousands of young men and women. In Chicago a series of six talks was held in twelve parishes that were attended by an estimated fifteen thousand young people. This was a repeat of a similar program that had been initiated the previous year as a Lenten Forum entitled "Countdown on Love" in conjunction with the Christian Family Movement.

Twelve hundred persons attended similar sessions in fourteen locations in Brooklyn, eight hundred in New York City. New Ulm, Covington, San Francisco, Baltimore, Omaha, Milwaukee, Portland, South Bend, St. Paul, and Oklahoma City were among the cities that ran successful premarriage courses. In Rochester, Minnesota, the courses were so successful, the bishop asked the YCW chaplain to take over the marriage program for the diocese. The special course for young couples planning to marry within a year was so strongly encouraged by the bishop that he gave each couple who completed six hours a personally signed certificate.

The title for the 1959-60 program, "Man in Work and Leisure," clearly identifies its focus. Job preparation programs for high school

*Jack McCartney and Marylu Langan, president and vice-president in 1959,
in front of national headquarters on Jackson Boulevard in Chicago.*

seniors was a common action. Detroit held workshops on job opportunities for seniors with speakers from various companies. Baltimore
organized a work preparation course for high school students. In some
cities Young Christian Workers spoke at career days held in local high
schools. Some sections had parish programs for graduating seniors
with talks and discussions on rights and responsibilities in work life,
and practical pointers on finding the right job, followed by refresh-
ments and a dance. Besides helping the students prepare for work, this
service was seen as a way to get to know prospective YCW members.

Leisure time actions included organizing dances, sports programs, and summer outings for young working adults. In Brooklyn,
YCW members helped teenagers organize a summer club in the
parish. They got the pastor's permission and left the responsibility for
details to the teenagers themselves, acting only in a supervisory role.
In turn some of the teenagers helped the YCW with projects, one of

which was taking underprivileged children to the beach on Saturdays. Two crowds in the neighborhood who were considered "wild" joined in the action and accepted responsibility for organizing sports and other social activities.

A popular project in many cities over the years was renting summer cottages for inexpensive vacations for young workers. This was done in Cleveland, Toledo, and Chicago in the forties and in New York City, San Diego, and Portland in the fifties. A YCW group in San Jose, California, went to the Office of Economic Opportunity in their town and presented the case for the establishment of a local youth center which was eventually built.

Along with the actions based on the weekly inquiries, actions were constantly undertaken on individual needs. In the late fifties, a special meeting each month was set aside to look at particular local problems that did not fit in with the annual inquiry theme. The "Facts" meetings replaced the ten-minute Review of Influence which had previously been the time when facts on random problems were presented. Actions on local problems included a Sunday School for mentally retarded children, baby-sitting so parents could get to mass on Sunday, campaigns against indecent literature, a parish newsletter for servicemen, and monthly visits to hospital patients. One section in Brooklyn helped to establish a community action organization in their neighborhood.

In the late sixties, two young women from a San Jose section found themselves picking onions one day because a section member came to the meeting with information about a nearby farm that was allegedly exploiting farm workers. To get proof for the investigators, the two volunteered to work as onion pickers for a day. They were hired and had their timecards punched each time they filled a basket. They found out that several laws were being violated: Children were working in the fields and there were no proper restroom facilities. At the end of the day when they were to turn in their timecards, the investigators arrived with cameras and they produced their timecards which proved that the wages were incorrectly computed. The growers were getting away with the violations because they were paying cash by the day and kept no records. The young women recall that their total pay for that day in the sun was just enough to buy a hamburger and a milkshake.[6]

Federations: A Sign of Strength

Federations to coordinate the work of the sections existed where the movement was strong, but only about five had federations which lasted most of the life of the movement: Brooklyn, New York City, Chicago, Milwaukee, and San Francisco. Federations in Cleveland, Toledo, South Bend, Lowell, and Wilmington lasted through the early fifties but a shortage of interested priests willing to serve as chaplains caused the sections to decline. In some cases, the priests had difficulty finding single young men and women and they opted to work with students in the high schools and couples in the Christian Family Movement who were more involved in parish life. CFM membership in the late fifties reached more than twenty thousand families. Another factor which kept CFM membership figures high was the fact that families stayed in the parish many years, whereas YCW membership was limited to the few years when workers were young and single, resulting in a constant turnover.

Nonetheless, cities like Detroit, Los Angeles, Minneapolis and St. Paul, San Diego, and Portland, Oregon, developed strong federations in the fifties and formed many young workers as lay apostles with a lifetime commitment as Christian witnesses and leaders in social action. By the late fifties when the movement was reaching its peak strength, with upwards of three thousand dues-paying members, cities like Baltimore, Maryland; Covington, Kentucky; Indianapolis, Indiana; Omaha and Lincoln, Nebraska; Ramsey, New Jersey; and New Ulm, Minnesota established federations.

In dozens of other cities individual sections were started by interested priests. Some of them lasted a year or two, some as many as four or five years. Some were in small cities like Youngstown, Ohio, and Davenport, Iowa, and never really took hold. Others were started by the national organizers in places like St. Louis, Washington, D.C., and Cincinnati. Many such groups, however, did not receive strong local support and they withered when the original members left.

When there were several sections in an area, they were able to give moral support to each other and get involved in significant actions that built spirit among the leaders and drew in new recruits. In the absence of such support, chaplains often sent new leaders to the national study weeks to get them fired up, but it didn't always have a lasting effect. It got so that national leaders, concerned about the many brand new recruits who arrived at the study weeks each year, set up special sessions for them on the fundamentals of the movement.

One midwestern city that had a strong federation for many years was St. Paul, Minnesota, where the movement was started by Fr. Blaine Barr and Fr. Oliver DuFresne. In 1953-54, twenty-five parish groups were in the federation. The YCW operated as many as four residences for young men and young women who came to the city from the surrounding rural areas. They also ran popular biweekly dances which met a leisure time need and attracted recruits to the movement. Many energetic leaders from St. Paul came to Chicago for the national training program and later joined the national team.

The notable fact about this active federation was its lack of support from the hierarchy. At one time, it was forbidden by the archbishop to have contact with the national organization. One priest there tells the story of being in a seminarians' Catholic Action study group that was forced to discontinue meeting in the late fifties because it was "subversive."

Support from Bishops

In cities where the YCW was recognized by the bishop, it was easier for priests to work with sections. Brooklyn was one of these. In 1952, Bishop Malloy appointed Rev. John Berkery and Rev. Joseph Nolan as regional chaplains in Queens county, Rev. John Mahoney and Msgr. Francis Donnelly in Kings, although they were expected at the same time to continue with their previous clerical duties. By 1957, when the Brooklyn Federation celebrated its tenth anniversary, it had sections in twenty-five parishes with a combined membership over five hundred.

Fr. Ed Hogan spoke of its many accomplishments at the anniversary mass.

> From it have come vocations to the priesthood and the sisterhood, fellows and girls properly prepared for marriage and family responsibilities; from its ranks have come fellows and girls who have taken positions of leadership in the various institutions and associations of the social order.

Its real accomplishments are very often in the world of the invisible, in the world of the supernatural. For who can measure the graces received as a Gospel passage was discussed? Who can count the convictions made as a social inquiry was made and acted upon? Who can number the prayers and sacrifices which went into the preparation of study days, of nights of recollection, and of weekend retreats. Yes, who can tell how many priests became better priests and how many laymen became better laymen as a result of their contact with and work in the Young Christian Workers movement?

Indeed, on such an occasion as this, it is good to keep in mind that Christ and His Church have gone forward, even in the smallest action of a Young Christian Worker apostle, as well as in the greatest action of the national movement.[7]

In Chicago, Samuel Cardinal Stritch, who first expressed his support by appointing a full-time chaplain for the Specialized Catholic Action federations in 1947, continued his support behind the scenes, giving financial aid to the national office when expenses outstripped income. He also arranged for the YCW to get an interest-free loan from Catholic Charities in the archdiocese to buy a house where the full-time women could live. By the mid-fifties when the cardinal apparently had more confidence in the maturity of the movement, the restrictions on publicity were loosened.

In some major cities where the bishop was not sympathetic, the YCW was not allowed to exist at all. In the cities where active federations did exist, they usually reported to their bishops annually in a written form. Personal contact was very infrequent. In general, the attitude of the bishops was permissive rather than enthusiastic and truly supportive. Their customary procedure was to allow the YCW to become active on a small scale without the fanfare or promotion which groups like the CYO enjoyed.

Adding to this somewhat casual interest of the bishops was the lack of attention in the seminaries to the study of social problems, especially as they related to urban ministry. Though young men in some seminaries were exposed to the idea of Catholic Action, the treatment of the laity as an entity was sadly neglected. YCW organizers tried to remedy this by visiting the seminaries and talking to those preparing for the priesthood, but this was not always permitted. On more than one occasion, YCW leaders were sneaked into a basement room in the seminary at Mundelein, Illinois, by seminarians who wanted to learn about the problems faced by young working men and women and what the YCW was trying to do about them.[8]

Heroes and Heroines

For more than thirty years ordinary young men and women came into sections with little more than average intelligence, a bit of idealism, and a spirit of generosity. Challenged by the vision of the Young Christian Workers and strengthened by a growing spirituality, some of them made major personal sacrifices and acquired virtue and leadership skills that made them role models for those who followed. Several who died while still in the movement set an example that had a powerful effect on those they left behind.

One of these was Charlotte Smith, a bright-eyed college graduate who learned about Catholic Action as a student. On her second visit to the Chicago headquarters at 3 East Chicago Avenue in 1947, she offered to lend a hand in the work and joined the YCW. She soon learned that in the local YCW slang, "la-de-da," meant snooty and having false pride and she became concerned about the world's la-de-da attitude about manual work. In an article in *Impact*, the girls' magazine for which she became business manager, she wrote: "We judge the job according to its dress, overalls or serge suit, instead of whether it serves other people or helps to make life more truly livable for them."[9]

When *Impact* folded late in 1949, she became an organizer for the AFL retail clerks' union. Her college friends couldn't understand why she didn't work in advertising or, if she had to "poke her nose" into social problems, social work. Her answer was easy. "Social workers try to put out fires. More people are needed to keep the fires from starting."

Her job was to organize the salesgirls at Marshall Field's downtown department store. During the day, she roamed around the store, trying to interest salesclerks in the union, and at night she visited them in their homes trying to collect signatures so that the union could represent the clerks in bargaining talks. Store detectives followed her around constantly and eventually ordered her out of the store along with the other organizers. After that, her work was largely restricted to handing out leaflets outside the employees' entrance.

One day in early November 1950, Charlotte noticed large black and blue spots on her skin. Her doctor immediately hospitalized her and a few days later she learned she had acute leukemia. To the chaplain who gave her the diagnosis, she said, "Father, you gotta help me. How can I learn to love God more?" She was a girl who loved life but she knew that the best was yet to come. She refused blood transfusions as merely delaying the inevitable and asked that all her friends come to see her. She was going home to God and she wanted to take their messages with her. On a cold Sunday afternoon, my new husband and I joined hundreds of Chicago Young Christian Workers and other friends in line on the stairway and in the hall at the hospital, waiting to say goodbye to Charlotte. She told us, "Listen, I wouldn't trade places with any of you." And to a fellow organizer in the line, "Tell the girls at Field's they'll soon have an organizer working with them out of Heaven—and no store detective will be able to stop it."

At her funeral later that week, Fr. William Quinn said, "She dedicated her life to love of God and love of neighbor." A few days later, several of her friends volunteered to do her duty at her old post— the employees' entrance at Fields. The union application cards came in as never before, sixty on one day, seventy on another. Charlotte was helping in a way she never could before. Needless to say, her tremendous faith in God gave new energy to the many Young Christian Workers she left behind.[10]

Another heroine of the movement was Dolores Kozlowski, a YCW member in New York City. When she joined the Manhattan section in 1945, it was she who located the store on Second Avenue that became the first YCW headquarters in New York. It was she who led in the scrubbing and cleaning and even found an old stove so the girls could cook and eat together before the meeting. After several years in that section, she left to start a section in her home parish in the Bronx and also helped to organize the first black section at Resurrection parish. One year she was in charge of the summer vacation house which the New York YCW ran for young workers. She organized a union at one of the places where she worked as a stenographer, determined as she was to put the papal social encyclicals into action.

With all the energy and joy she exerted in her apostolic efforts, many people did not know that she had suffered from diabetes since a child. I remember seeing Dolores at a YCW Study Week in 1947 with an orange that looked very appetizing. When I asked her where she got it, I was chagrined to learn that she always carried it in case she had a reaction to the insulin she had to inject every day.

Dolores was excited when Canon Cardijn came to New York in 1947. Later she was teased by the others because, in every picture they took, there was Dolores next to or right behind the canon. In the spring of 1953, a few months before Dolores died, the canon was again in New York on a world tour of the Young Christian Workers. He visited Dolores in her home and thanked her for all her efforts on behalf of the movement. (By this time, she was blind and confined to bed.) He assured her that her sufferings were of more benefit to the apostolate than any amount of action. "I give big speeches all over the world," he said, "but you are more important. You are on the cross with Christ."

Dolores told a friend that it was the YCW that brought her out of herself and helped her to see the needs of other people. The friend didn't dare contradict her but said later that Dolores already had zeal and generosity and compassion.[11] It was the YCW which directed it into useful channels. YCW did do a lot for Dolores, but the movement gained more from her and her shining example.

In 1957 the movement lost another great leader when Bernie Kelly died. Bernie heard about the Young Christian Workers in Chicago from a co-worker. For months he traveled to St. Andrew's parish on the North Side to meet with the section he asked to join. As soon as he knew enough, he started a group in his own parish on the South Side of the city.

In 1955 he took the leadership training course run by Russ Tershy and joined the national team as an organizer. When Bernie decided to leave a good job as sales manager, he told his mother that although he was unable to serve his country in the armed forces, there was no reason he shouldn't give several years of his life to the service of the Church. At age sixteen, Bernie had contracted the deadly Hodgkin's disease, but it had not deterred him from living an active life. He had worked summers in the steel mills to earn money for college, where he even played football. His concern for the needs of young workers and his enthusiasm in their service was evidence of his determination to make his life meaningful. He spoke often about the first Apostles who laid down what they were doing and followed Christ completely. This was his motivating ideal.

In the summer of 1956 Bernie was elected national president. Shortly before Christmas, just a few months into his term, he became seriously ill while attending a meeting in St. Paul. Upon his return to Chicago, he entered the hospital for the last time. Msgr. Cardijn, again on a visit to the United States, learned of Bernie's illness and went to his bedside. "On this hospital bed," he said, "you are now with Christ on the Cross. It may be that you will get up from this bed, or it may not be. If you get up, you must die through your work with Christ for all the young workers all over the world. If you do not, you must die for them here with Christ on the Cross. You are a lucky man."[12]

As a tribute to him and in recognition of his tremendous apostolic spirit, the parish section at St. Andrew's in Chicago opened a parish YCW center which they named the Bernie Kelly Center. For four years, a group of young men lived in the upstairs apartment and their rent helped finance the storefront center. Until they left to get married, the center was an active place where the name of Bernie lived on as a model for Young Christian Workers in Chicago.

The Cardijn Centers

In several cities centers were established and named in honor of the movement's founder, Joseph Cardijn. The Cardijn Center in San Diego was headquarters for all the specialized movements there. It published a newsletter for all the local groups and developed special actions and services for personnel in the large military bases in the area. In June 1954, for example, they cosponsored a Study Day for members of AFA from the nearby naval air station and the amphibious base at Coronado at the summer camp operated by the YCW.

Even after the YCW itself ceased to function, Fr. Leo Davis with the help of Fr. Jim Anderson, and a small corps of former leaders continued to operate the center to foster Christian social thinking and to serve the needy. As recently as November 1985, its newsletter had an article on the YCW method of social inquiry and suggested its use in small groups with a common bond who were concerned with problems in society.[13]

The Cardijn Center in Milwaukee, Wisconsin was opened in 1949 by Fr. John Beix, who taught at the minor seminary. He was deeply interested in social action in the archdiocese and was the first to organize Catholic Action cells there in the early forties. When he saw the need for a gathering place where local groups could meet and give each other moral support, he was given permission by Archbishop Moses Kiley, though the archbishop had misgivings about such lay groups and insisted on monthly reports. With the financial help of other priests and lay people, he rented a one-time flophouse on Water Street in the shadow of city hall. Armed with scrub pails and paintbrushes, volunteers set to work and the second floor headquarters soon housed a bookstore, a library, meeting rooms, and a kitchen. It brought members together from all over the city.

Over the twelve years of its existence, the Milwaukee Cardijn Center reached out to hundreds of young adults and was the meeting place for many young workers from the factories and offices in town. Before long, thirteen parish sections with more than one hundred fifty members were established. Among the services the center offered, besides the library and bookstore, were adult education courses and lecture series featuring such speakers as Dorothy Day, Dan Herr, Ed Marciniak, and Jacques Maritain. The lectures and classes reached an estimated sixteen thousand persons.[14] When Cardinal Meyer became archbishop in 1953, he gave benign support for the work of the lay apostolate, but he never gave it the support he gave to other archdiocesan organizations. When he visited the center in 1956, he requested that his picture not be taken there and he cautioned the enthusiastic members lest they become involved in "the heresy of good work" at the expense of their own personal sanctification.[15]

When it was decided to close the center in 1961 because its adult education programs had been taken over by the archdiocese and the parish sections no longer felt the need for a downtown center, its then director, Fr. Daniel York, said, "The Center has done many things over the past years. It has introduced and emphasized many ideas, the most important of which is that the layman has a role to play in the Church. Because of this idea, the Young Christian Workers are firmly established. They will continue."[16]

The Milwaukee Cardijn Center is fondly remembered by many of those whose lives were profoundly affected by their experiences at the center, but none speaks more eloquently than Thelma Schreiner.

My first awareness of YCW was only the door—a bright red-orange with a huge chi rho in gold on the front door. This door fascinated me and I knew something Christian was happening on the other side. At the time, I was in high school and passed it on Water Street while riding the streetcar. Water Street, in the fifties, consisted of bars and flophouses. I decided to investigate the place a year after I was out of high school and up for some adventure.

After entering the beckoning door and going up a long stairway, I was invited into a room on the left where a group had gathered around a table with a lighted single candle in the center. The group commenced with a Bible reading for each to ponder. Then each mentioned the line or thought that most struck the person. Having never done this in a group before, I was satisfied that I had found the right group to be involved with. I continued meeting with them each week.

Then the center moved to its own "YCW House"—a gray, clapboard mansion type on 13th and Wisconsin Avenue in the midst of Marquette University. It was here that I offered to cook for twenty people on an upcoming leadership summer program to be held there. They came from all over and were destined for national team work, and so was I. We all moved to Chicago after the YCW Convention in Rensselaer, Indiana, at St. Joseph's College (where the Chicago Bears also held summer camp). It was 1958 and I was nineteen years old. . . .

Life was fast-paced in Chicago, so my chance to return to organizing in Milwaukee came when a road organizer wanted to settle down in Chicago on the national team as an office worker rather than organize in Milwaukee or anywhere else. We were paid eight dollars a week, with room and board!

After all of these years wondering who had the "wit and wisdom" to paint a red-orange door with a huge golden chi rho for the YCW Center here, just several weeks ago I discovered from Rosemary Budisch that her father was the creator of the amazing door. Bless his soul.[17]

Life on the National Staff

Over the years, several hundred young men and women made a personal sacrifice when they gave up their jobs for two or more years to work for a pittance as a full-time organizer or national staff worker for the YCW. Thoroughly convinced that the Young Christian Workers were the wave of the future, that lay persons could really bring about major change in the world, and that Jesus Christ needed them to do His work, they followed—like Peter and John and the other fishers of men.

Some of them, like Paul, had to be convinced the hard way (although there is no evidence any of them were knocked off a horse), but once they made the commitment they gave it their all.

It was not easy to leave home, come to a strange city, live in a beat-up apartment in a poor section of the city or a crowded house on the outskirts, and share meager resources with strangers.

> Headquarters in Chicago was located on Jackson and Paulina, a few blocks from famed Maxwell Street (the hot item market!). The building was condemned and given to the YCW rent-free. It looked like a Random House logo. Higher than wide, and four floors of small rooms, suggesting a history of hotel life, with even a bed in each room on the third and fourth floor. The kitchen and dining room were located in the basement which was cool. A Dixie funeral parlor was next door and at funeral time, Dixieland jazz filled the air as the procession came through the street.

> We girls (women) lived in a 3-story dark red brick YCW-owned house on Midway Drive close to Oak Park. There were twenty of us living in the "Girls' House." Ten moved out and ten moved in each year, as the two-year commitment ended for ten and began for ten others. All this happened on the same day with some suitcases staying that should have left and others leaving that should have stayed![18]

They came from big cities and small towns. New York, Brooklyn, St. Paul, St. Cloud, Milwaukee, Green Bay, San Francisco, Indianapolis, Portland, New Orleans, Detroit, Baltimore, New Hampshire, and

New Jersey—all were represented on the national team at one time or another. Making the adjustment to the intense and busy life of the national office was very difficult. They worked in the central office all day and went home with the same people at night. Twenty-four hours a day, seven days a week, except when they were out on the road organizing, they lived together. They argued about their goals and the ways to achieve them. Sometimes, they got on each other's nerves. It was a strenuous life under the best of conditions but somehow they survived, often became close friends and grew in strength and the love of God and their fellows.

The strain of meeting deadlines on publications, putting out reports, planning meetings and study weeks, chasing around the country meeting with groups of young men and women to sell them on the good news of YCW, knocking on rectory doors and often being rejected, a way of life that no one in their right mind would consider; but these were young people with a dream and a spiritual conviction. Tough as it was, most of them thrived on the challenge, and looking back today, realize it was one of the greatest times in their lives. "We never worried about the future," said Russ Tershy recently. "It was a great experience. It made me what I am today. I think sometimes that I could have been a millionaire today, if I used that energy in other ways!"[19]

People in action. All kinds of people. Young people in their twenties. They had a dream of a "new youth for a new world" and a commitment to apostolic action. They were Young Christian Workers.

People Remember

In the years before I joined YCW I had been interested in people and movements that tried to incarnate Christianity in the world—Dorothy Day and the Catholic Worker movement seemed to me to be one of the best examples of this attempt. It was in this way that YCW and its members struck me: here were authentic Christians, here was Christianity lived in the world. The intellectual aspect of YCW also attracted me. The Church as the Mystical Body of Christ presented itself to me as an immensely appealing reality. . . .

The insistence in the YCW on the value of each person's contribution and its forward-looking outlook—its assumption that its members would change themselves and their world—probably made it easier for me than it would otherwise have been to join with others in efforts to bring about change in our parishes and our communities. (Chicago)

I had a blast while in YCW!! We did many good things but we had such a fun time doing it. (Omaha)

It changed my life. I have since had meaning and purpose in life and a desire to serve. Very conscious of peace and justice issues because of YCW study of social encyclicals. One of the frustrations in YCW was fulfilling the action after discussing the Observe and Judge. However, I believe that the technique of O-J-A prepared us to act many times in our future life as husbands, wives, parents, citizens, parishioners, etc. (Chicago)

That damn YCW! I still can't say no, when I see a problem. (St. Paul, Minnesota)

Notes

1 *Introducing YCW: A Program for Beginning Groups,* Young Christian Workers, Chicago, Illinois, May 24, 1960.
2 All the actions reported in this chapter have been taken from YCW reports of action sent to the national office. UND archives.
3 Bob Olmstead, "Omaha's Young Christian Workers Pinpoint Discrimination in Restaurants," *AIM,* July 1958, p. 1.
4 Mike Coleman, "Young Christian Workers Activities in the Field of Human Rights," 1961. Zotti papers.
5 Jim Burke to author, January 3, 1988.
6 Hortensia Alvarado Wohlsfield and Carmen Ponce in recorded conversation with author, San Jose, California, October 2, 1985.
7 "Tenth Anniversary of YCW Marked," *The Tablet,* October 26, 1957, pp. 1, 24.
8 Jim Burke to author, *op. cit.*
9 Charlotte Smith, "Her Father is a Janitor," *Impact,* April 1948, pp. 1–3.
10 "The Girl Who Made Good," *Work,* December 1950, pp. 1, 8.
11 Dorothy Dohen, "Portrait of a Young Worker: Dolores Kozlowski," *The Torch,* March 1954.
12 Vince Geise, *Training for Leadership* (Notre Dame: Fides), 1953, pp. 7–10.
13 *Cardijn Center Bulletin,* San Diego, California, November 1985, pp. 7–8.
14 *The First Years of Cardijn Center,* (leaflet) Milwaukee: Cardijn Center, n.d.
15 Steven M. Avilla, "Milwaukee's Middle Prime," *Salesianum,* Spring–Summer 1989, p. 17.
16 "Center to Close," *Come Unity,* published bimonthly by the Cardijn Center, Milwaukee, April 1961, p. 1.
17 Thelma Schreiner, letter to author, February 17, 1988.
18 *Ibid.*
19 Russ Tershy to author, October 1, 1985.

10

Speaking Out for Young Workers

Though representing young workers had long been an aim of the YCW, it was many years before the American YCW was strong enough to allow its national leaders to speak out publicly in the name of working youth before public bodies which had the power to bring about major change. In the early years the leaders were so concerned with building a national YCW and fitting it to American working life they did not have the vision and the energy to take on the problems of the larger world. That was not true of the European leaders. They had been training and developing leaders since the mid-twenties, and they knew that many of the social and economic problems that affected young workers were global in scope.

To effectively Christianize the whole of society, said the Europeans, the movement must be spread to all countries. Because the United States was seen, even before World War II, as a rich and powerful presence on the international scene, they were convinced that a strong YCW in the United States was essential. It was on the mind of Canon Cardijn when he visited the American seminarians in Louvain when Donald Kanaly was a student there in the thirties. It was the message Edwina Hearn and I were asked to take home when we visited Europe in 1946. Cardijn, on his very first visit to the United States that same summer, constantly stressed, "We cannot be strong in our international movement without America."

Gradually the American YCW began to understand the importance of international understanding and involvement. In 1953, after completing her term as girls' president, Caroline Pezzullo returned to her home in New York where she supported herself with part-time jobs while serving as the representative of the International YCW before the Economic and Social Council of the United Nations (ECOSOC), speaking out on issues which affected young workers. She served in that capacity until 1960. During that time she visited regularly at the national headquarters, bringing the international dimension to the national leaders and those in attendance at the leadership training programs.

At a study week in 1954 Caroline conducted a session on her work at the United Nations representing the International YCW and suggested that the American members become involved in the "work of extending Christ's body to persons in other lands" by such things as reading about foreign affairs in the newspapers, subscribing to the YCW International Bulletin, corresponding with persons in other countries, and supporting the work of ECOSOC and the International Labor Organization (ILO).

In the early fifties a few American leaders, including Ursula Belley from Lowell, Kay Weber from New York, and Florence Triendl from Toledo, went to Brussels to work in the International YCW Office as translators and office workers. They were followed in later years by others, including Martha Roman from Chicago and Mary Mulvey of Milwaukee. From time to time European and South American leaders visited in the United States and were invited into the homes of American YCW leaders. These were beginning steps in developing international awareness.

In 1955 it was announced that there would be a great international pilgrimage to Rome in 1957 to mark the official launching of the International YCW. Though the International Bureau had been functioning in Brussels for many years, the International YCW organization had never been formally legitimized. As the movement had grown over the years, it depended greatly on the charismatic inspiration of Joseph Cardijn, and he was nearing the age of seventy-five. The lay leaders felt that a written constitution was needed. Cardijn himself was concerned that the written word might limit and imprison the spirit of the movement, but he recognized that it had to be done. After lengthy consultations with the leaders of the various national YCWs and with church leaders in Rome, a constitution was drawn up.

"Come to Rome"

The International Bureau wanted to have a meeting of delegates from each of the national organizations to vote on the new Constitution, but that was not Cardijn's way. He wanted to launch the new plan in Rome with a giant gathering of YCW members from around the world.

Jack Dunne, who had been national treasurer of the United States YCW for two years, was appointed to coordinate the plans for sending as many American YCW leaders as possible to the pilgrimage. This included getting the word out to local leaders as well as major fund-raising for expenses. Pat Keegan, visiting in New York on business of the International YCW a few months later, arranged for Jack Dunne to meet with David Davis of the Foundation for Youth and Student Affairs in hopes of securing a grant to cover travel expenses to Rome for the national leaders. The foundation had been established in 1952 when many Americans were concerned with the importance of building up a positive American presence abroad to counter the influence of Eastern bloc countries. The chairman of its board of directors was Arthur Houghton, president of the Steuben Glass Company. Its purpose was to encourage the development of international friendship, cooperation, and cultural exchange among young adults.

"He [Davis] showed quite an interest in the project of the American YCW and my inclination is to feel that he is very favorable to it," said Pat in a letter to Bob Olmstead and Marylu Langan, then national president and vice-president. "He is certainly most anxious to have more American representation in the international life, and he realizes that the American YCW is unique in the fact that it consists of young adult workers and is in a better position than any other to have a human contact with the movements of young adult workers in other countries."[1]

The international office of the movement had long been adept at getting funds from outside the movement. As early as 1951, Marguerite Fievez from the international office in Brussels had written to Caroline asking the cooperation of the American leaders in making proposals to American foundations for money to finance the work of the international movement. In Belgium, as the JOC had gained in strength, it received funds from a variety of governmental agencies, trade unions, and wealthy individuals who saw the movement as a positive, constructive force. Certainly there must be rich Americans who could be prevailed upon to support the international work of the movement. Appeals were made to a few wealthy American Catholics, but no money was ever forthcoming.

American members were enthused about the idea of going to the International Pilgrimage in Rome. Many paid for the trip from their own savings and funds were raised for many others. In all, 215 made the trip in August 1957. Romeo Maione, then the Canadian national YCW president, described the meeting years later: "Rome in August of 1957 became a temporary home for 32,000 young workers from eighty-seven countries. He (Cardijn) understood that every once in a while, young workers must feel their collective strength. Large manifestations without the work at the local level are so much mist, but local action once in a while must come together. I have never attended a more joyful and spiritual event."[2]

The Americans who attended still have vivid memories of the experience and the words of Pius XII when he addressed the thousands gathered in St. Peter's Square.

> As young workingmen and women from more than eighty nations, united in the great Christian brotherhood, you proclaim loudly that you have come here to assert your Catholic faith, your limitless love for Christ, your filial confidence in His Vicar and in His Church, your will for justice and peace. You have come to renew in Our presence, your magnanimous promise to bring all workers back to the Church. . . .
>
> You wish to live an intense, authentically Christian life, not only in the secret depths of your conscience but also openly—in your families, in the neighborhood, in the factory, the workshop, or the office, thus showing that you belong fully and sincerely to Christ and to the Church.
>
> Your strong organization, your method which the well-known formula summarizes as See, Judge, Act; your activities on the local, regional, national, and international

levels—all these enable you to contribute towards the extension of God's Kingdom in modern society, and to permeate that society with the teachings of Christianity in all their vigor and originality. . . .

As you experience in yourselves the benefits of Young Christian Workers training—that new ardor which permeates your lives—you yearn to bring these to others, and above all to those who, being deprived of the means of training and culture, have not learned as you have personal discipline of living and the methods of social and religious action.

Beloved sons and daughters, may you on your return home continue, each in the field of apostolate assigned to him, an even more decided and vigorous action, since you will have understood better the incalculable value of the cause you defend. Now as in the past we count upon you, and we expect great things of you.[3]

Following the great rally, six workers from each country in the movement met in Rome to establish the World Council of the YCW. They adopted the international constitution and elected Romeo Maione from Canada as international president. After hearing reports on the situation of young workers throughout the world, they adopted a manifesto which summarized the aims and fundamental positions of the YCW with regard to the great problems facing young workers. It updated previous manifestos of the movement approved in 1947 in Montreal and 1950 in Belgium.[4]

After the Rome pilgrimage, the American representatives attended a special reception in Brussels with Cardijn. He told them, "We must understand the importance of our missionary movement in all the countries of the world, not only in one country, not only for a little number of young workers, but more and more for all the young workers in the world, all races, all delegates from Africa, South America, all countries of the world united in Christ. And we must become more convinced of our mission here on earth."

He then reminded them of the great importance of the United States in the world and charged them with a tremendous responsibility: "You must be at the head of our movement. You must show the way for the youth of tomorrow."[5]

Some had misgivings about the ability of the Americans to work on the international level. In a memo from Rome after the pilgrimage, Marylu Langan, vice-president in those years, wrote: "The strong influence of European ideas and their ways of doing things—we seemed so different—I sometimes wondered if we could ever co-ordinate thinking and planning on an international level."[6]

The contact of so many YCW leaders with their counterparts in other parts of the world did have the effect of making the world a little smaller and its problems more real. The president and vice-president of the American YCW continued to participate in all meetings of the international movement from then on: in Rio de Janiero in 1961, Bangkok in 1965, and Beirut, Lebanon in 1969. YCW sections helped to raise money to pay for the trips, but the principal travel funds came from foundation grants. On these occasions the current American president and vice-president shared ideas with their counterparts in other countries and helped to evaluate the global progress of the YCW movement.

Representation on the National Level

In the late fifties and early sixties the YCW participated in a variety of national conferences and meetings to represent the needs and concerns of young workers. One of these was the 1960 White House Conference on Youth where the YCW reported on a survey of the conditions among young workers. They participated in meetings of the Bishop's Committee for Migrant Workers, the President's Committee on Children and Youth, the National Council for Interracial Justice, the National Catholic Social Action Conference, and the National Conference on Lay Mission Work. The YCW also maintained relationships with the National Committee on Agricultural Labor, the NAACP, and CORE.

Local federation leaders in 1960 represented the needs and views of young people at the Chicago Youth Committee for Civil Rights, the Chicago Young Adult Forum, the Interracial Council in New York, the Young Adult Council in New York, the Marriage and Human Relations Board in Omaha, the State Council of AFL and CIO in Indiana, and the Urban League in California, to name a few. When the opportunity arose, the YCW spoke up.

The International Project

When the national council met in January 1958, Bob Olmstead gave a report on the "International Project." A grant had been received from the Foundation for Youth and Student Affairs which paid for the printing of the national program and subsidized the first six issues of the new national YCW newspaper, *AIM*, by paying the salary of its editor and a secretary. Money from the foundation was also used to pay the fare for leaders attending the International Lay Apostolate Meeting in Rome which followed the YCW pilgrimage. Two South American leaders were also financed on a tour of the United States.

The foundation had expressed an interest in future international exchanges planned by the YCW. Bob stressed that the heart of the current proposal was the sending of YCW leaders to other countries to provide technical assistance to developing movements, something very much encouraged by the international YCW leaders. It was hoped to send the first team overseas by March of 1959. The national leadership training school directed by Russ Tershy was authorized to train the leaders going overseas, and Russ's salary was paid by the foundation. Pat Keegan spent several months working with Russ to develop a training program for extension workers that would bring them up-to-date on the International YCW as well as the particular needs of the countries to which they would be going.

To support the growth of the YCW in underdeveloped countries, the international office set up a solidarity fund to which the developed countries could contribute financial aid for those countries in need. The United States leaders decided to set aside a week each spring as International Week when local sections would focus on the needs of their neighbors in other countries and plan some kind of fund-raising activity.

Russ Tershy initiated the fund-raising plans in a letter to all members of the YCW National Council on March 12, 1959.

Because Christ needs you, and us, to carry Him to the four corners of the world, we now ask you, we plead with you, to organize an International Week in your diocese. Through International Week these important goals will be accomplished:

—We will be united with Young Christian Workers in eighty-five countries and territories.

—We will support the International YCW. From the proceeds raised during the week, one-half will be sent to the International Office in Brussels to assist the YCW all over the world.

—We will learn more about people in other countries— how they live and work, what problems they face, and what the YCW is doing to help them.

—We will support the international program of the U.S. YCW. The second half of proceeds raised during the week will be used in particular for the training and sending of American leaders to newly-developing countries.

Accompanying the letter was a flyer for each section member in which Russ described meeting South American YCW members in Rome, who walked five miles to attend a YCW meeting, and he listed some facts about the impoverished conditions of their lives. "A struggle of ideas is going on beneath all the poverty. Will it be Christianity or Communism which will capture the souls of millions? The question must be answered by Christianity, not for the purpose of defeating Communism, but because we must manifest Christ in His charity and mercy and justice." He announced that five leaders were going to South America and Africa in 1959, and more would go overseas in 1960.[7]

YCW members interested in going overseas to aid in the spread of the YCW were expected to make the commitment for two years. The Foundation for Youth and Student Affairs agreed to help with the funding. But they were only interested in supporting extension workers for South America and South Africa, though the international office had plans to send workers to other parts of the world as well.

When the project was discussed by the national team, leaders stressed the need for prudent planning. Several expressed the importance of a missionary spirit among all the members and suggested that it must start on the basic section level, one member bringing a friend into a section, one section starting another section, one diocese trying to open the next diocese, as well as Americans reaching out to other countries.

The first extension team left for Bogotá, Colombia, in September 1959. It consisted of Bill Cosby, a national organizer originally from Massachusetts; his wife, the former Jo Jeske from Chicago; Inez

Alfonso, a secretary from Queens; and Teddy Horn, a nurse from Omaha. Bill was provided with language training, and the fares of all were paid by the foundation. When they reached Colombia, they found jobs to earn their daily living expenses. Bill was unemployed for six months and Jo was pregnant, but they lived in a working-class neighborhood and survived for two years. Teddy worked in a local clinic and later a home for unwed mothers. Bill worked with local JOC members in the neighborhood where they lived, and the young women assisted young women Jocistas in the women's branch.

Teddy described her experiences in a letter home.

> Our parish, San Ignacio, has had a girls' section on and off for several years. During this time the group never had a chaplain and from our observations lacked practically all the fundamentals of the movement. . . . The team decided that I should go ahead with the federation secretary, Edilma, and together we would begin a San Ignacio group. From the "Supermarket" we had made friends with one of the young workers, Mercedes, and I knew another friend who worked in a beauty salon, so with those two, we were able to assemble ten workers from a very close area. Edilma and I write inquiries because the national Bulletin [in Colombia] is very unsatisfactory in many ways, but especially for beginning groups, not to mention the fact that it is written by boys, for boys. Our chaplain is doing a superb job including preparation, attending the meetings, getting to know the girls, and forever seeking ways and means for him to be a better chaplain. This is also the first section experience for Edilma, and it is tremendous to see the growth of her understanding of the girls' problems and the JOC; it will undoubtedly reflect in her work with the federation.[8]

Bill, who became a community organizer when he returned to the States, talked later about his experience helping the local JOC movement to train leaders in Colombia, "We did what we were supposed to do. We worked our asses off. We didn't run around being the American saviors. We did a good job."[9]

Six months later Frank and Barbara Chiancone from the Brooklyn YCW went to Caracas, Venezuela, as YCW extension workers.

Frank had been a high school dropout who joined the YCW after two years in the army. After four years in the movement during which he earned his high school diploma at night school, Frank became a construction worker, diesel mechanic, and then shop steward for his union. The foundation financed his tuition in a trade union course at Harvard before he and his new wife, a practical nurse, left for South America. There they worked with the local YCW and Frank worked at his trade and with various trade union leaders.

Local YCW groups raised funds to help others go overseas. Among these was Connie Rojas who was subsidized by the Omaha sections when she went to Bogotá to work as a nurse. Jean Pew, Sally Doherty, and Janice Wandmader went to Capetown in South Africa. The money for Jean's fare was raised through donations from section members and priests in Chicago, and the other two were subsidized by the St. Paul YCW. Carol Jean Fredericks and Dolores Bernards from Portland, Oregon, went to Peru in 1960. Purificación Mercada, a nurse from San Francisco, left in March 1960 for Guatemala City. She paid her own transportation, but the YCW in San Francisco agreed to send monthly stipends to pay for her support during her two years there.

International committees in five dioceses raised and sent money to national YCW leaders in Africa to assist their organizing efforts. Nine YCW sections in Chicago raised money for a motor bike for the Rhodesian YCW, and San Diego sent money to Nyasaland in Central Africa to buy a jeep to be used in organizing efforts there. The sections in Ramsey, New Jersey, developed and funded a summer program which sent teams of young workers and students to El Salvador for six weeks each summer to assist in service projects of many kinds.[10]

When the Peace Corps was established by President Kennedy, YCW members were recruited for positions of responsibility because of their training and experience with organized groups. At the council meeting in January 1964, Jack McCartney, then in charge of the YCW training program, announced that the Peace Corps was looking for people to fill staff supervisory positions and urged anyone with extensive YCW training and possibly some college to consider applying. Sargent Shriver, the director of the Peace Corps, lived in Chicago and knew the local YCW leaders there. At his request, Bill Kruse, Chicago federation president, became director of the Peace Corps in Ethiopia and later Nigeria. There he was joined by Fran and David McGrath from the Los Angeles YCW, who directed a teacher-training project. Russ and Ellie Tershy spent two years in Bolivia when Russ directed the Peace Corps there.

Many other Young Christian Workers joined the Peace Corps, and others went later to South America for a year or two with PAVLA (Papal Volunteers in Latin America) and to Africa with Catholic Relief Service. Thus the missionary spirit engendered by their YCW training became evident as Pat Keegan prophesied it would when he said at a study week in 1954 in San Francisco, "I believe that if a strong YCW can develop in the U.S.A., it will be a strong reservoir for helping other countries, apart from dealing with the problems here."[11]

Representation in Other International Organizations

Caroline Pezzullo initiated the membership of the Young Christian Workers in the Young Adult Council (YAC), the United States member of the World Assembly of Youth (WAY). Pat Keegan was involved in establishing the World Assembly of Youth in the late forties. He had joined with leaders of the British postwar Labour government who promoted the development of a democratic world assembly of youth to counteract Communist initiatives. In those years youth organizations with a Marxist ideology, such as the World Federation of Democratic Youth (WFDY), made public statements and took a stand on many international issues, such as the European Common Market which they opposed. Such statements got attention from many European political parties.[12]

The YCW application for membership in YAC was accepted in June 1956. YAC was represented on the United States National Commission at the United Nations and promoted youth support for the United Nations and its specialized agencies through conferences, publications, and educational travel.

At the Third World Convention held by WAY in New Delhi during August 1958, four hundred delegates from eighty countries approved a Charter of Youth Workers which in many ways expressed the same convictions as the YCW International Manifesto of 1957. In language which echoed the YCW thinking, the resolution of the WAY charter insisted "that the future of the world depends on the future of the working masses." The charter itself emphasized the duty to "reaffirm the rights of youth and their willingness to accept responsibilities." At the New Delhi conference twenty Young Christian Workers were present from five countries.[13]

In 1960 an American Commission for International Development (CID) was established by former YCW leaders for the purpose of expanding international activities in this country and conducting an exchange with YCW leaders and former leaders from other countries. George "Red" Sullivan was named as director of the CID, but on his return flight from his first overseas trip, he was killed in a plane crash over Long Island. The loss of George, president of the movement in the early fifties, was a grievous one for all who knew him but especially for Msgr. Hillenbrand who had been his first chaplain in a high school YCS group in Chicago. At his funeral, Monsignor said:

> He is the only one I can recall who was in all four movements [High school YCS, College YCS, YCW, and CFM]. This makes him unique in the record of the apostolate. In this first generation of the specialized movements, he is the most luminous figure. . . . He saw the apostolate as something that Christ wanted of him. No one in this country ever gave more to the YCW than he, when he saw it through the days of the Korean War, days which reduced the men's groups to the vanishing point, days in which he adapted the approaches to the circumstances, wrote the manuals for servicemen, and then doggedly directed its recovery. . . . In the eyes of faith, he stood at the heart of things. . . . Christ said last Friday, over the Narrows in New York Harbor, "I come quickly, I come lovingly to gather you into my everlasting embrace, so that where I am you may always be." And George: "Come, Lord Jesus."[14]

After George's death, his place as head of the CID was taken over by Caroline Pezzullo who was already planning to leave the United Nations. She was assisted by Mike Coleman when he completed his term as YCW president in January 1962. The emphasis of the commission was on dialogue and technical exchange between fledgling national leaders in Third World countries and their counterparts from the developed countries, as well as among union organizers in those countries, many of whom were former Young Christian Workers.

As the YCW became more involved in participation in international conferences, Msgr. Hillenbrand had some misgivings. Though expenses for such travel were paid for by others, usually the Foundation for Youth and Student Affairs, he felt that more emphasis should be placed on national development. Moreover, he felt it was a mistake to be taking money from unknown sources. He and Mike Coleman had some dispute about this when Mike was national president in 1960 and 1961. The lay leaders, backed by Pat Keegan, stressed the importance of an American YCW voice on the international level and continued to accept foundation funds.

Monsignor's concern turned out to be well-founded when an exposé in *Ramparts* magazine in 1967 revealed that the National Student Association (NSA), a highly regarded organization of college students, received a large part of its funding from foundations that were conduits for money from the CIA. The NSA admitted after the story broke that certain individuals on the NSA international committee had done intelligence work for the CIA by reporting on the political tendencies of up-and-coming student leaders. They had been receiving CIA funds since 1952. One of the foundations that had been used as a conduit was the Foundation for Youth and Student Affairs.

In the intensive government investigation which followed, it was revealed that the CIA had channeled over twenty million dollars to more than forty foundations as part of a strategy of the National Security Council to establish an American presence in critical areas around the world where Communism was a threat. Many legitimate organizations were given travel money to send members overseas, but no other spy activity was reported. What the YCW had received was comparatively small, and the YCW was never publicly listed among the recipients.[15]

Looking at the Bright Side

In a 1963 report on Representative Action, Jerry King, then national president of the movement, wrote:

YAC is the United States affiliate of the World Assembly of Youth. As such it is regarded internationally as the voice of

American Youth. Within YAC, the YCW potentially can have considerable influence. We are among the most respected, most active groups in YAC. We are the only ones representing working people. Of the thirty-two organizations, twenty-four are student groups. The eight non-student groups are often represented by students. YAC looks to us to provide working people for their programs, international tours and the like.[16]

Delegations from Europe and South America sponsored by YAC were hosted by the American YCW and American leaders were recommended for tours overseas. Ted Zelewsky went to northern Africa in 1963 on an exchange visit sponsored by YAC where, with representatives from other organizations represented on the council, he visited with leaders of local trade unions in Morocco, Tunisia, Liberia, Algeria, and Egypt. Dick Delaney traveled with another group of YAC representatives to Central Africa in 1965, visiting and interviewing worker-leaders.

In 1963 Jerry King and Mike Coleman, both former YCW national presidents, represented the United States in Geneva at a seminar on trade unionism for young workers sponsored by WAY. The aim of the conference was to bring together the leaders of young worker organizations and trade union youth movements so that the unions could better understand the needs of young workers. It also enabled them to spot young union members who could be groomed for a future role in the union leadership. Youth leaders from twenty-six countries on five continents participated.[17]

One hoped-for development in the YCW organization was cooperation between the local sections and federations and the national headquarters on large-scale problems. The assumption was that local initiative coupled with the national leaders' knowledge of the big picture would enable the YCW to take effective representative action. Often, however, local members were more concerned about local problems and did not understand the larger issues promoted by the national office.

On at least one occasion, though, a major national action developed out of facts uncovered by a local section. YCW members in Ramsey, New Jersey, observed that migrant workers on the small farms outside the city were living in sordid conditions. After a survey óf the facts and a study of state law, they helped to form a community council to deal with the problems they discovered. United States Senator Harrison Williams of New Jersey, who headed a Senate subcommittee on migrant workers, spoke at an open meeting organized by the Ramsey YCW attended by 175 persons including farm workers, merchants, business men, and church leaders. The leaders then requested the national officers to use their influence to stimulate action in other areas where migrant workers lived. Using material gathered in surveys conducted across the country, Mike Coleman represented the Young Christian Workers in testimony on the *bracero* problem and domestic migrants before a subcommittee of the House Committee on Agriculture on March 2, 1961. Although the fight for legislation at that time was unsuccessful, YCW continued to monitor migrant laws and maintained close contact with Senator Williams, a leading proponent of migrant worker legislation.[18]

Support for undertakings such as the Commission for International Development and the International Solidarity Fund required cooperative efforts from many YCW sections whose membership had not necessarily arrived at a full understanding of Young Christian Worker thinking on economic and social problems. Msgr. Hillenbrand wrote in 1962, "The YCW works on problems of young working people. It is wrong if it means only the immediate, local, personal problems. It is right if it includes the large dislocations of our times which affect all people and especially working people. We must show them that they are members of Christ. . . . We begin with the small, personal, and local problems, but we must move on to the larger problems by which they are affected, in which they are contributing members."[19]

Progress in achieving social awareness at the lower echelons of the organization depended very much on local leadership. The apathy of young adults not faced with obvious or immediate social problems in their own lives, plus the constant turnover in membership characteristic of a youth organization, placed a large burden on the formative role of the chaplain.

The national headquarters continued to stress that the local membership must develop a social conscience through the inquiry and education on issues coupled with an energetic program of action. The national leaders, meanwhile, would continue to speak out and represent young workers on the large-scale issues. It was the constant hope that their visibility before public bodies would strengthen the prestige of the movement and attract additional members who would understand and support the need for Christian social action. Expansion of local sections and the education of members on major issues of social justice continued to be a high priority because effective action everywhere in the country depended on grass-roots effort. This was especially true when meaningful representative action was needed.

Reminiscing

I was a Young Christian Worker during some of the most formative years of my life—age 18 through 22. My association with YCW made the most astounding impact on me.

First let me tell you what I was like at the time I joined YCW. I was a flighty, shallow person—interested only in boys and clothes and having a good time. I was what you'd call a "Sunday morning Catholic." Religious and spiritual things played a very insignificant role in my life. I acquiesced with my parents' prejudices toward minorities. I never harbored a single serious thought in my head. I was that totally unformed lump of clay. At the first several YCW meetings, I had not one opinion, idea, view, or belief to contribute.

Why I stuck with it, I don't know. Perhaps I sensed a need, felt an emptiness that yearned to be filled. My friend Bob counseled me, consoled me, and encouraged me to continue. Thank God for him and many others like him.

Slowly, painfully, through the meetings, the spiritual guidance of our chaplain, the many YCW activities, the caring and the camaraderie, the total acceptance of me as wonderful and worthy, I blossomed into a whole person—all that I could be.

I've not changed the world to any great extent or really made a difference, but I have personally been changed and been made a different person by YCW.

In discussions with my children, even they realize the indirect impact YCW has had on them—their rich liturgical life, spiritual life, their awareness of social injustice, the absence of prejudice, their Christian attitudes, their ability to judge situations on moral levels, etc. They realize that through me, they have learned and they use the Observe, Judge, and Act method in many aspects of their lives. (Los Angeles)

We all know that we were not perfect and that the world today does not seem to be what we were hoping for. However, I am so thankful for having been part of the movement. At times, I try to imagine what it would have been like if I had not experienced YCW, and I shudder. Life would probably have been very ordinary. Instead, I believe that my life has been rich and exciting as a result of YCW. . . .

I was especially fortunate, having had such rich experiences while a part of the movement. Involvement locally, regionally, nationally, and internationally, afforded me with unique opportunities to see and get to know people, their lives, joys, and sorrows, with a Christian perspective.

As a result of the movement, my way of seeing the world and life around me is forever changed; my way of making decisions is forever changed; I was changed. And I really do not regret any of this. (Baltimore)

Notes

1   Pat Keegan to Bob Olmstead and Marylu Langan, February 21, 1957.
2   Romeo Maione, Summary Report, YCW reunion, July 27, 1987.
3   "Pope Pius XII Addresses Thirty Thousand Young Christian Workers at the International Pilgrimage," reprint from *The Torch*, n.d. Zotti papers.
4   Manifesto of the International YCW (draft), 1957. Zotti papers.
5   DeSanto, Bernice, "Msgr. Cardijn Tells Americans: 'You Must Be Head of YCW,'" *The Chicago Challenge*, Vol. 1, No. 6, October 1957, p. 6.
6   Marylu Langan to Bob Olmstead, handwritten memo, after 1957 pilgrimage, n.d.
7   Russ Tershy, letter to council members, March 12, 1959.
8   Theodora Horn, report to YCW National Office, February 1960.
9   Bill Cosby to author, Framingham, Massachusetts, March 13, 1987.
10 Reports of Action, council meeting, 1960 through 1968.
11 Pat Keegan, talk at San Francisco Study Week, 1954. On tape. Zotti papers.
12 Pat Keegan's role in formation of WAY was verified by his close friend and former English YCW chaplain, Rev. John Fitzsimons, in interview with author, June 1988.
13 Report on WAY Conference in New Delhi, 1958. UND archives.
14 Msgr. Reynold Hillenbrand, homily at funeral of George Sullivan, December 21, 1960. Zotti papers.
15 Sol Stern, "NSA and the CIA," *Ramparts*, Vol. 5, No. 9, March 1967.

An article in the *Congressional Quarterly Weekly Report*, March 10, 1967, reported on the preliminary findings of a committee named by President Johnson to study the CIA's role in providing funds for organizations with overseas operations. The committee reported that "the CIA did not act on its own initiative" but in accord with policies established by the National Security Council, dating back to the Eisenhower administration.

Organizations receiving funds through the various foundations used by the CIA included the American Newspaper Guild, the American Society of African Culture, the International Confederation of Free Trade Unions, the International Student Conference, the National Council of Churches, the National Education Association, the Retail Clerks International Association, the United States Youth Council, and the World Assembly of Youth.

At no time was the YCW named as a recipient of any CIA funds, but the effect of being tainted "by association" was unavoidable. Young Christian Workers who had received funds from the Foundation for Youth and Student Affairs for international travel expressed shock and disbelief, then anger. They felt they had been duped.

Other organizations who had received money from the foundations named as CIA "dummies" were equally upset over the implication that they had engaged in intelligence activity. The Young Adult Council, for instance, held a meeting in New York to clear its name. It had no government agenda for its international activities, and the only reports required were statements on expenditures of money received.

Bill Cosby, recipient of foundation funds, speaking in conversation on

March 13, 1987, about the rumors that circulated after the CIA story emerged, said, "Let's put things straight. The YCW was not involved in any spy activity."

[16] Jerry King, Headquarters Report on Representative Action, National Council Meeting, July 1963.

[17] "Report of the Seminar for Leaders of Young Workers and Trade Union Youth Movements," *The WAY Review*, Vol. VII, No. 6, 1963.

[18] "Ramsey, New Jersey, YCW and the Migrant Worker Problem," *Impetus*, March 1961.

[19] Hillenbrand, handwritten notes at officers' meeting, May 22, 1962.

11

Emerging Problems

When the sixties began there was every reason to think that the future of the Young Christian Workers was bright. It was a time of optimism. When John F. Kennedy was elected president in 1960, many of his supporters were convinced that America was embarking on a Golden Age. Not the least of these supporters were American Catholics who finally saw one of their own reach the nation's highest office. Kennedy's election, helped along by the countless actions of Young Christian Workers who worked to get out the vote and participate in the electoral process, seemed to fulfill Catholic aspirations in America. Here was a Catholic out to save America and the world, just as Young Christian Workers and other Catholics had been aiming to do for decades.

In his inaugural address President Kennedy captured the imagination of his young supporters when he said, "The torch has been passed to a new generation of Americans." He went on to describe a program of change he called "The New Frontier." In March 1961 Kennedy launched the Peace Corps, which sent thousands of Americans to help people in developing countries improve their standard of living. In April Congress approved aid to economically depressed areas in the United States. An increase in the minimum wage and a request to Congress to pass sweeping civil rights legislation soon followed. Kennedy's idealistic program sought many of the same visionary goals as the YCW. Hopes ran high.

Another election that was to have a dramatic effect on Catholic life had occurred in 1958 when the College of Cardinals chose John XXIII to succeed Pius XII. Shortly after his election, the new Holy Father called for a general ecumenical council of the Church to begin in 1962. Americans did not get very excited at this because Vatican Councils did not have much meaning for most Catholics at the time. Little did they know what would follow the pope's call to open the windows of the Church to the world.

Official Church Affiliation

What did seem significant to the American Young Christian Workers was the announcement in 1960 that the specialized Catholic Action movements in the United States, including YCW, YCS, and CFM, were to become part of the official church structure under the umbrella of the National Catholic Welfare Conference. This represented quite a turnabout. Years earlier, the YCW leaders had decided not to identify their organization as official Catholic Action which was under the control of the hierarchy, so that they could remain free to go their own way. Even so, attempts to organize in certain dioceses were blocked by bishops who did not approve of the YCW's views on social reform, views which some pastors and bishops considered to be imprudent, even radical. Many in the hierarchy were also uneasy about and even critical of lay action that was independent of direct clerical control. Bishops preferred traditional organizations like the Catholic Youth Organization (CYO) or the Confraternity of Christian Doctrine (CCD).

Some chaplains felt the movement would have greater support from the bishops if it were affiliated with the National Catholic Welfare Conference. Msgr. Hillenbrand conceded that such recognition could give status to the movement, but insisted that the specialized movements, including the Young Christian Students and the Christian Family Movement, be accepted as a unit. The national offices of high school and college YCS, YCW, and CFM shared headquarters on Jackson Boulevard and, though they operated independently, they did have the characteristics of a loosely knit family. More important, they shared a common view of the apostolate and a common method. For this reason, YCW could not accept membership in the Youth

Department for that would leave out CFM; nor, since all the organizations were mixed, could they fit under the Council of Catholic Men or the Council of Catholic Women. Finally, in the fall of 1960, a solution was found and the joint movements were affiliated as a unit with the Department of Lay Organizations.

On hearing the news, Fr. John Kean, a leading Brooklyn chaplain, wrote to Msgr. Hillenbrand, "I want to congratulate you on the affiliation with NCWC. It was great news . . . and I am sure very heartening to you after all these years."[1]

Official recognition didn't change things much, however. Bishops weren't suddenly inspired to push the movement in their dioceses and large numbers of priests still did not understand or support the idea of an active laity.

Cardijn found this to be true in Europe as well. Returning from a trip to a traditionally Catholic country in 1958, he had exclaimed, "In spite of the repeated insistence of the last popes, the clergy in general do not understand the importance or the meaning of the apostolate of the laity, the necessity of formation and an apostolic organization for the laity. . . ."[2]

The Pope's Call to Action

Perhaps the most emphatic and public stamp of church approval for the ideas of the Young Christian Workers at this time came in Pope John XXIII's encyclical, *Mater et Magistra*, in May 1961. In his annual personal report to the Holy Father the previous year, Cardijn had reminded the pontiff that 1961 would be the seventieth anniversary of *Rerum Novarum*. He suggested that it might be an appropriate time to update the social doctrine of the Church in light of current conditions. At the Holy Father's request, Cardijn wrote out, on his return home, a twenty-page tract on his ideas and sent them to Rome. After receiving a very cool response from the secretary of state some weeks later, he told his friends in Brussels, "This is what happens to those who think they are going to advise the pope. My paper has been put somewhere, probably hidden away in a drawer."

But Cardijn's paper was more influential than he thought. A year after the publication of the encyclical, when Cardijn was attending a general audience in St. Peter's with some Jocist leaders, John XXIII called him to the podium and whispered, "Thank you very much for the inspiration you gave me to publish the encyclical *Mater et Magistra*. It's done a lot of good. I thank you for the YCW. Keep on. I'm counting on you."[3]

The final section of *Mater et Magistra* was a call to action, to reconstruct social relationships in truth, justice, and love. "We affirm strongly that this Christian social doctrine is an integral part of the Christian conception of life," John wrote; and he urged that all Catholics should learn it and put it into practice. The method the pope suggested for this was the one long associated with the Young Christian Workers: Observe, Judge, and Act. "Knowledge acquired in this way," he said, "does not remain in the realm of the abstract but is something to be translated into deeds."

Msgr. Hillenbrand, always attuned to the words of the Holy Father and the social teachings of the Church, expected that the new encyclical would encourage greater support for the YCW in the United States. He was convinced that the movement would soon take its rightful place as a major Catholic instrument to form young working people as apostolic Christians. It was only a matter of time.

Expansion Problems Develop

In spite of such encouraging developments, problems at the local level were beginning to surface. Membership in the movement was not growing as might have been expected. From a peak somewhat over 3,000 at the end of the fifties, it dropped to 2,500 in the early sixties. Moreover, rapid turnover in the membership was becoming apparent. For every ten new sections, ten or twelve were folding. As the United States shifted from an industrial economy to a service economy and more young people opted for higher education, it was hard to attract new members who would or could stay in a section the recommended three years. Moreover, the average marrying age by the late fifties reached an all-time low.[4] This seriously reduced the number of available single young workers.

Leaders who had come into the movement during the heyday of the movement in the late fifties were slow to grasp what the real problems were. They did not understand the growing complacency of many young workers and their lack of interest in social problems. When reporting on the turnover in membership and the lack of lasting commitment among new members at the council meeting in 1960, they laid the blame on chaplains who did not give sufficient time to their important role in forming leaders. There was some truth to this, of course. The search for more priests who would understand the goals of the YCW and devote sufficient time to the formation of young adults seemed never ending. The shortage of committed chaplains, however, was only part of the problem.

Theory vs. Real Life

One difficulty was the rigid social inquiry program. When Tom Trost from St. Paul stood up at the 1961 council meeting and vehemently cried out, "The movement is becoming an educational movement," he was speaking for many local sections who were becoming frustrated trying to carry out a national program that did not fit their needs. He went on to say that the educational thrust of the movement was actually taking members away from their friends instead of sending them back to Christianize their friends. In the heated exchange that followed, Jerry King, the newly elected president, defended the national program, saying it was necessary for national unity.[5]

Many were upset by the national office's inflexibility. "It appeared to me that progressively tighter control was emerging at a time when we were asking that the YCW's direction should be to decentralize and respond to growing local need for help to effect stronger initiative there," Jerry Curtis recalls.[6] Dissension at the 1961 council meeting prompted the federations in the Midwest—Michigan, Ohio, Wisconsin, Illinois, and Minnesota—to form an experimental regional YCW working within the national structure to seek solutions for common recruitment problems and offer grassroots input to those who wrote the national inquiry program. The Midwest experiment was discouraged by the national officers who saw it as a move toward disunity and it eventually was discontinued. The East Coast and West Coast continued to have regional meetings, but the national leaders viewed them as a practical way to reach local members unable to travel to the Midwest for the national study weeks.

Complaints about the national program continued to come from many parts of the country. Many felt the program did not deal sufficiently with the real problems of young workers—work, leisure, and dating. Denver reported at the August 1962 council meeting that they had not followed the national program in 1961 on international problems, but instead had worked on problems of migrant workers and school dropouts in their area.

Mike Colavecchio then read a joint statement from the Brooklyn and New York federations.

> We have found that the national program has been of an educative nature and [is] not really dealing with the needs of the young people in a way that they may grow, develop, and seek answers to the problems that relate to their daily lives. We also feel that it would be impossible for a national program to meet the needs in all areas because of the varied problems, so that by its very nature it must be educative.
>
> Because of these reasons, we are planning to write our own inquiries. They will retain a relationship with the national program in that we will program every fourth meeting on the area that the national is programming. We feel that this is essential to the national YCW.[7]

The inquiries on international issues caused the most problems. One leader complained that they were "too advanced" for many sections and thought it depended somewhat on how well educated the members were. One inquiry in 1961 did, in fact, read like a schoolroom test. The Observe section read, "This week question your friends to see if they can tell you . . . ," and there followed a list of ten questions starting with "How many nations (are) now in the United Nations?" and ending with "What are two prominent neutral nations?" The judgment asked, "Why should we be well posted on these things at this particular time? Why does belonging to the Mystical Body mean we must have an interest in people over the world? What effect does your ignorance have on people who talk with you?" (Shades of the "intellectual questions on religion" noted in the minutes of the girls' group in 1940!)

The success of Spanish-speaking sections doing their own programming on local problems was seen as evidence that members could be formed in Christian action without the national program. It was finally agreed that there could be flexibility in using the program in various cities, but the national leaders continued to look for the solution in better-written national inquiries.

In 1961, when Mike Coleman and Nancy Lee Conrad attended the International YCW meeting in Rio de Janeiro, they discovered that the national programs in other countries were much less structured than the American program. On their return, they argued that the movement should be forming members through action, not education. "You don't stop one thing because it's time to go into your education for the next area," said Nancy Lee.

Nancy Lee later spent a month observing the Canadian national program. She learned that they had a flexible program based on a general theme for a year, with each group molding it to suit their group and area. Moreover, a "Review of Life" which dealt with any and all sorts of problems encountered among one's friends and co-workers was a regular part of each meeting. The Review of Life, called "Review of Influence" by the Americans, had once been an important part of the YCW program in this country but had fallen into neglect when education on social issues became dominant or when sections with a strong social club emphasis lost their apostolic thrust. The Review of Life kept members focused on real facts and conditions in everyday life.

Furthermore she found that no other countries offered educational programs anywhere near as elaborate as Msgr. Hillenbrand's seven areas of life, which was based on the presumption that lay persons must develop a full and rounded social conscience in three years. Nancy Lee's strong opposition to the rigid format of the national inquiry program was one of the primary reasons Msgr. Hillenbrand asked her to resign early from the vice-presidency. To his mind, she had lost sight of the movement's main mission, which he saw as the formation of leaders who would eventually lead the way to major changes in the social order: "YCW is training for the future."[8]

Monsignor was so sure of the wisdom of the American style of programming that he thought it was something other countries eventually would want to emulate. The ironic thing is that in his early days, Monsignor recognized the need for action which grew out of life experience. The Jocist movement impressed him because it was action-oriented and promised to be much more effective in reconstructing the social order than the study clubs advocated by many in the thirties.

From his earliest contact with the American YCW in the forties, Canon Cardijn had cautioned the leaders lest they become too theoretical in their approach to problems. I remember his comments at our 1947 Study Week in Syosset, when he stressed the importance of looking first at the facts. Judgment should follow. He was not happy when the American YCW strayed from this straightforward approach. In the early sixties, when he spoke about the American program to Mike Coleman, then national president, Nancy Lee Conrad, vice-president, and Fr. John Hill, assistant chaplain at the headquarters, he said the situation was hopeless. He was very concerned about what he saw—a tightly structured, rigidly controlled approach in the national inquiry program.[9]

In a recent visit in Brussels with Marguerite Fievez, Cardijn's secretary, I was surprised to learn from her that Cardijn and the monsignor never really got along. Cardijn sensed that the monsignor did not fully understood the inquiry method and the need for lay leaders to learn by doing. They needed encouragement and positive reinforcement rather than close direction. Although the monsignor preached freedom of action by the leaders, he was quick to point out their mistakes, particularly in the development of the inquiry program. Leaders in the late fifties recall his careful review and their worry about his editorial blue pencil when they submitted their written inquiry drafts for his imprimatur. In effect, this was a form of control.

Jack McCartney, who ran the training program in the early sixties, has said of the monsignor's insistence on the educational thrust of the movement, "I think he made kind of a hazy adaptation to the very rapid turnover in the movement and leaned toward indoctrination rather than development through discovery. I think he sensed that we had to move quickly. . . . How do you speed up this process of discovery working one-to-one with friends?"[10]

Andrew Greeley, a chaplain in the specialized movements, also took issue with the use of the inquiry to educate the members in Christian social principles. In an article to chaplains he said that most young people using the inquiry program are not fully formed and they need the stimulus of obvious personal involvement to get excited.

> If Catholics do not approach the encyclicals in the context of concrete situations, the papal teachings, no matter how important, will seem irrelevant. To expect things to be different is to repeal human nature. . . .
>
> If our purpose is to instruct the members in matters of fact and principle, the inquiry framework is a cumbersome

and awkward tool. Discussion leading to action is an extremely efficient technique when the facts are readily available and the principles are fairly well known. . . . be treated in special study nights, not in social inquiries. The difference between an inquiry on neighborhood recreational facilities and a pseudo inquiry on foreign economic aid is one of kind and not of degree. To put them side by side is to confuse people and give the impression that they are the same kind of problem. . . .

It would seem that for the inquiry technique to lead to true apostolic formation, each inquiry should be as open and permissive as possible. The inquirers must observe and judge for themselves. They must not go through the motions on a subject that has already been prejudged by the program committee which drew up the questions. Thus, the "slanted" inquiry which is aimed at one sort of judgment and one type of action is not going to offer much information. The group members are being led to a predetermined conclusion, no matter how democratic the process may appear. . . .

We must constantly be aware of artificial actions, i.e., actions unconnected with the problem revealed in the observations and discussed in the judgments. If the inquiry concerns situations that the membership perceives as problems there will be no difficulty. But the forced actions which often come when a group gets beyond its depth do very little good either in transforming the social order or developing the apostolicity of the group. . . . The initial purpose of an apostolic movement, it would seem, is not to solve any list of problems culled from papal writings but to form a state of mind and will in the people who should and must solve the problems.[11]

An Age of Abundance?

But the YCW's problems went deeper still. When the participants in the council meetings in the early sixties asked why the YCW was not attracting and holding young workers, they assumed that somehow the movement itself was at fault. They did not realize that many young workers failed to see the relevance of a problem-solving organization because life was good to them. The early sixties were an extraordinarily self-confident time.

Social scientists of the day shared in the general optimism. Many felt America was entering an age of abundance when the struggle for survival would no longer be a concern. Machines would take over most manual labor, education would be available to all, and citizens would enjoy greater leisure time. Whatever poverty remained could be solved by a benign government.

> The expansion of production and productivity resulted in a much greater economic pie. The graduated income tax, expanded welfare services, and education were equitably distributing this larger pie. Continued increase in aggregate economic wealth would invariably filter down, more or less equitably, to all income groupings. Marginal economic groups, it was assumed, would in time gracefully succumb to continued economic growth and small residual groups not covered by expanded welfare and social security programs would be handily cared for by the public dole.[12]

The economist John Kenneth Galbraith called the emerging new order the "Affluent Society." It was his idea that the "scarcity consciousness" of an earlier age was a thing of the past and poverty was no longer a major problem. Continuous growth in the gross national product, the low level of unemployment, and the highest per capita income in the world were proof of America's bright economic future. Technological advancement and education would transform American society.

At the turn of the century, only about four percent of the eligible population graduated from high school. By 1960, this figure was more than sixty percent. Higher education especially underwent rapid change. Between 1940 and 1960, college enrollment more than doubled. The emergence of free colleges made it possible for many young men and women to attend college who could never have afforded it previously.

The American Catholic community reflected the nationwide change. In the first half of the century, Catholics had advanced from immigrant poverty to middle-class respectability. The moral idealism of American patriotism became intertwined with the absolute confidence Catholics had in their religious faith. In the late fifties and early sixties, everything seemed to be going well. It was increasingly difficult to convince young adults that they had the kind of problems the YCW movement was designed to solve. Where was the appeal of a "school in life" when free education in the rapidly expanding junior colleges held out the promise of a better job?

As more young people took advantage of public education, "the leadership was taken out of the base of ordinary workers," recalls Peter Foote, president of the Chicago YCW federation in the late fifties. He cited, as an example, what happened in a strong section at St. Francis of Assisi parish on the west side of Chicago. The leaders' group, with six or seven action groups reaching out to an orbit of approximately five hundred young Mexican-Americans, was decimated when a new in-city branch of the University of Illinois opened up in their neighborhood in the late fifties and scooped up all the key leaders. Those left behind were team members who did not have the ability to attract new members and rejuvenate the section.[13]

Occupational and Social Mobility

Foote was concerned about the loss of sections in Chicago in the early sixties and the rapid turnover among members and decided to look for answers. He made a carefully researched study of the composition and approach of the Young Christian Workers in the Chicago area, restricted to young men because of the census materials available to him. He concluded that there were three major changes in the population of young working men that affected the growth of the movement: (1) occupational mobility—young people, particularly those in the service occupations like insurance, were being transferred to other parts of the country on a regular basis; (2) social mobility—people with more money in their pocket bought cars, got their own apartments "away from Ma," and drifted away from the neighborhoods that were the base of the movement; and (3) an earlier marriage age and the continuing impact of the Selective Service System further reduced the number of eligible single young workingmen in a given parish.[14]

The problem of mobility has been confirmed by others. One chaplain in St. Cloud, Minnesota, said that sections there were weakened by the fact that many of the brighter, more aggressive young men left home to seek work in the larger cities. As a result, and since the movement *had to have a man as president*, its leadership was often weak. The earlier emphasis on seeking strong, natural leaders often went by the board. It was a case of working with whomever was available.

The problem of leadership quality was compounded by rapid turnover in the membership. Foote's study discovered that the likelihood of developing a cadre of young workers who would stay around long enough to go through the three-year training cycle and then lead and administer a subsequent cycle was extremely small. There was just too few young people in the neighborhood who stayed around long enough.

The study clearly implied that the parish base of the movement was no longer practical. The time was too short and the numbers were just too small. But efforts to establish interparish or regional groupings were often resisted by the local clergy. Pastors were only interested, if then, in supporting activities that would enhance their own parish. Several instances have been cited where a pastor in Chicago objected when he found that the YCW section in his parish included members from other parishes.[15] The fact that a chaplain was often transferred to another parish, leaving a section floundering, only compounded the problem.

The Detroit YCW hailed Foote's study and felt it shed considerable light on their own situation.

> His study was invaluable. It identified statistics, facts, and situations which we could not see with such insight or within such a broad context. We did study days for section leaders who had raised the kinds of concerns Foote identified and analyzed. Long before Foote's study, the Detroit YCW had abandoned the strict parish base and adjusted itself to organizing sections so that fewer leaders with longevity could serve several sections in an indigenous region. One way was to have a central section serving a broad area with no boundaries, a natural response to the inability of every parish to be totally independent and self-sufficient.[16]

Sections that developed in Phoenix, Indianapolis, Covington, and New Jersey in the late fifties and early sixties did not limit themselves to parish boundaries as had been insisted on in earlier days. The section in Ramsey, New Jersey, started in 1958 by an energetic chaplain, Fr. Edward Cook, was centered at St. Paul's parish, but its members came from a wide surrounding area. As its apostolic spirit developed, however, more than a dozen other groups were formed in the surrounding Newark diocese by its leaders. The original groups were primarily composed of suburban white-collar workers, but in 1965 several of the Ramsey leaders moved into Irvington, a blue-collar area, to start groups. Several groups were also started in the heavily black city of Newark itself where social and economic problems were more apparent.

The view that the YCW was a movement of young workers primarily involved in improving working conditions by advancing the trade union movement began to change in sections everywhere.

As more and more young workers moved up the socioeconomic ladder and became more affluent, they became less interested in social problems that did not concern their personal lives. A writer doing a study of the American YCW in the early sixties pointed this out.

> Presently, there appears to be a gap between the individual member's personal development and the response to the YCW and its "grand objectives" of social justice for all, the brotherhood of man, etc. A middle range of effective collaborative action is less well developed. Partially, this difficulty accounts for a certain lack of dynamic character in the American movement. . . . The American YCW is distinctively middle-class in membership and did not have to fight for basic bread-and-butter advantages for its members. A large measure of its concern is, therefore, with the plight of others such as minority groups, migrant workers, et cetera. The resulting danger of haziness of aim, the "do-gooder" weakness is apparent. . . .
>
> The aims of the YCW are relevant to the totality of the young worker's life, his religious practice, his leisure, his housing conditions, his social relationships, his political ideology, as well as his conditions of work. Thus, the YCW has a place in the future, even though some of its traditional concerns may diminish; however, this is contingent on the

regular reevaluation of the meaningfulness and effectiveness of its programs. The YCW offers an attraction to young
people—the opportunity to synthesize and direct their
energies and enthusiasms toward intelligible goals.[17]

Middle-class affluence and upward social mobility, coupled with
the movement of young people away from the parish setting, have
been cited by most of the former chaplains I questioned as major
reasons for the decline of the American YCW in the early sixties. These
priests had had successful sections in the earlier days and struggled to
maintain the spirit of the movement, when change was in the air.
"Social evils were no longer recognized as giants to be toppled;
government would solve society's problems with new programs," said
one. And another, "Our group became much more a social, recreational group." Still another said, "Many members were not attracted
because of the great discipline of weekly meetings and weekly action."

In spite of the problems in recruiting large numbers, however,
many leaders in the early sixties continued to find social problems
that needed attention. Jerry Curtis, president of the Detroit Federation
at the time, still has a positive view.

The paramount observation here is that the YCW continued
to turn out competent leaders. How? Because YCW taught us
how to organize, to lead if we wished and to grow continu-
ously—to be wide open. . . . Growth and change are the
characteristics of youth. The YCW role was to bring together
the young to make sense out of life, and get it done.[18]

A Change of Name

Those who felt there was still a need for an apostolic movement
began to question whether the YCW name was a deterrent.

White collar and blue collar workers alike did not feel comfortable being identified as "workers." At the 1964 Study Week, Al
Eisenmenger reported that his discussion group talked about the
YCW's public image. This led to a serious exchange about the
possibility of a name change. It was decided to discuss the matter at
an open meeting on the last day. The conversation, according to one

participant, became a "semantic symposium on how we could best market the YCW image . . . to make it more palatable to everyone."[19]

At the council meeting which followed the study week, changing the name was on the agenda. Members also questioned the use of certain words in the YCW prayer which had been written in Europe in the early days of the movement.

> Lord Jesus, we offer You this day all our work, our hopes and struggles, our joys and sorrows. Grant to us and all our fellow workers the grace to think like You, to work with You, to live in You. Make us able to love You with all our hearts and serve You with all your strength. Your Kingdom come in all our factories, workshops, offices and in all our homes. May those of us who have died on labor's field of honor rest in peace.

The line about "labor's field of honor" was a concept meaningless to young Americans of the sixties. By the same token, most Americans did not use the term "workshop." The words, "Stand steadfast, comrades, for your rights," in the chorus of the YCW international song, certainly did not reflect the American idiom. "We're used to it," said one, "but those outside do not like it." The prayer was revised soon after and work began on the song.

As to changing the name YCW, that was more difficult. Would a name change be a liability or an advantage? Most didn't like the name because it didn't convey an image and was hard to explain. But no one had a good suggestion for an alternative. Msgr. Hillenbrand agreed with the general sentiment when he said, "The state of the movement is static; this year, there is a decline. The YCW is not fully accepted. If we are not getting our job done, we are losing our identity."[20]

After discussion at headquarters, the national leaders decided to put the vote for a name change on the agenda at the Winter Council meeting. There is no evidence that any serious research on the wisdom of a name change was done. The decision was apparently based on the simple presumption that the worker identity of the movement was the problem. A different name would make the movement more attractive to young adults of the sixties. Those who attended the council meeting were asked to come with suggestions.

The January council meeting was opened by President Dick Delaney with the statement that he felt this was a very important meeting.

> We should realize that we in the movement are ahead of our time—we are leading in many ways. The areas we program on are controversial; we have been active in revitalizing the liturgy; we have been pioneers in this country. We should not lose the sense of where we are in history. . . . We at this council should be prepared to take on the responsibilities for reaching more young people— training young people. We should take up our responsibility for change: responsibilities to the Church, responsibilities to society. We have this responsibility in changing the name of the movement. We should not cling to terminology of the past, but change with the times. We should attempt to put ourselves in step with the our times and our culture.[21]

A total of sixty names were suggested by the twenty-eight council members present. When the first vote was taken on the opening day, the name "Christian Action Movement" received twenty votes, "Young Christian Movement" received nineteen votes and "Christian Young Adult Movement" received six votes. Other names received a few votes. The delegates were asked to think about the choices and, after more discussion, a final vote would be taken on the top names on Sunday morning. Debate raged furiously as proponents of the two top choices gave the reasons for their choice. The idea of retaining the YCW name was not even considered a choice, although a few sections went on record opposing a change. Dick Delaney expressed the thinking of many when he said, "The term 'worker' to many people in the United States has a bad connotation. We have no 'working class' as such. We want to reach average young people like ourselves. General office workers do not look upon themselves as workers. The term 'worker' has held us back."[22]

Msgr. Hillenbrand spoke out in agreement.

> We have been in this country since 1939 and (in recent years) the movement has not grown. We really haven't held our own when you count the sections operating with

more than four people paying dues. We must look for the obstacles to growth. The name has become an obstacle. People shied off because of the name—this is true of priests. People do not regard themselves as workers. There is a spirit of equality in this country. We don't have a mentality in this country to build upon the word "worker." Other countries are thinking of changing the term worker also.

Dick mentioned that the change was discussed with the International YCW. "They respect our right to do this. We would still be united with the International movement. . . . Unity is much deeper than a name."

Everybody seemed to agree that the name should be something members could identify with. Some felt that "Christian Action Movement" might intimidate young people coming into the movement. "Some people come into the YCW not ready to act or afraid to act. . . . We get them in quietly and train them for action." Another objection to "Christian Action" was its similarity to "Catholic Action" which implied a purely religious organization rather than a movement which also stressed social action in the world. It was argued that the new name should be similar to the old one in order to make the transition easier.

When the vote was taken, "Young Christian Movement" received twenty-five votes and "Christian Action Movement" received only three. The Council then voted by acclamation to unanimously accept "Young Christian Movement" as the new name. A few participants felt that the name was changed from one that was controversial to one that had no image at all. One participant scribbled on his notes, "YCM?—mushers, mastiffs, mutts, muledrivers!"[23]

Sheila Smith Hebein, who became vice-president in 1968, does not agree.

We used a democratic process and we tried to stay in tune with the rapid changes that were occurring in our society. We had the Civil Rights Movement, the Peace Movement, the Women's Movement. All these growing movements were *action* groups. Actually, many of our YCM members belonged to them. In addition, we were closely affiliated with the Christian Family Movement and so I think the choice of the name "Young Christian Movement" made good sense. From my point of view, the name change was a good thing, made for the right reasons—but we needed more than a name change to save the YCW in the sixties.[24]

When Msgr. Hillenbrand gave his customary closing remarks at the end of the council, he thanked the participants for their thorough discussion on the name change. With his usual confidence in the young leaders present, he continued:

> Our movement is still only a beachhead simply because there hasn't been a great breakthrough in the apostolate. We stand for training lay apostles; we have the method and apparatus to do it.
>
> The popes have been calling for participation in the Mass. It wasn't until the breakthrough in the Council that it became a reality. The trend will not stop now and the YCW will stand forth as the group which is the most efficiently trained apostolate. Even though we are a small movement, we shouldn't be overwhelmed by our large burden.[25]

In spite of its struggles and concerns, the newly named Young Christian Movement continued to have a hopeful view of the future. One positive sign was the growing recognition by many outside observers that the movement was developing strong, active leaders. Many single issue organizations were coming to the YCM in search of trained leaders for their particular agendas. The Independent Voters of Illinois was typical. It approached its members to work in local political precincts to gather support for local progressive candidates. Others like the Alinsky-inspired community action programs sought individuals for positions of leadership in neighborhood programs in various cities.

At the same council meeting which had changed the name, Barney Offerman, a former member and resource person, introduced George Koch from the Office of Economic Opportunity. Mr. Koch explained the programs of the OEO which had been established in August 1964, with Sargent Shriver as its director. He described the Job Corps, Community Action programs, and VISTA (Volunteers in Service To America, the domestic version of the Peace Corps) and asked the support of the YCM in recruiting volunteers. Barney then commented that the movement had a reputation for involvement and that the VISTA program was trying to get at the causes of poverty, not just the effects. He also suggested that members read *The Other America*, Michael Harrington's eye-opening book about the reality of poverty in the United States. This was a cogent argument against the facade of the Affluent Society.

Many members did go into VISTA and other poverty-related programs as well as community action organizations after they left the movement. Others took jobs with local government agencies serving community needs where they continued to use the skills they had developed in the YCW.

When Dick Delaney and Linda Mann were preparing to go to Bangkok, Thailand, for the Third World Council of the international movement in the fall of 1965, they were informed that one of the main topics of discussion would be the worker character of the movement. "The changes in working life and the attitude of young people toward work is changing throughout the world. In Europe and North America, the problem of most young working people is not that of extreme poverty and intolerable working conditions, while throughout Asia, Africa, and Latin America, there are these extreme conditions. These realities prompted the discussions of the worker character of YCW. The YCW is challenged throughout the world to constantly adapt to such changes."[26] The international movement was interested in learning how the American movement was adapting. Clearly, the status of the YCW as a worker movement was not just an American problem.

The early sixties were paradoxical for the Young Christian Workers. On the one hand, they were encouraged by the words of John XXIII who promoted the See, Judge, Act method in his 1962 encyclical and the acceptance of the specialized movements by the NCWC. On the other hand, the movement was not expanding. There seemed to be two main reasons: (1) The rigid educational program was out of touch with the real needs of young people, and (2) affluent young Americans didn't think of themselves as workers.

Was the movement failing because it was becoming irrelevant? This is a question the YCW/YCM leaders of the early sixties did not ask, in fact could not ask, so totally committed were they to the need for a lay apostolate among young workers.

Members from the Sixties Look Back

I was a YCW member in Brooklyn from 1959 to 1963, finding application of Catholicism with the social order plus Gospel spirituality very forward and rewarding in terms of Christian humanist formation. With others we formed a local community council and organized seminars toward community betterment. I was an electronic technician and my interest in my fellow workers led me into a supervisory position. . . .

When I entered YCW in 1959, it was in its phaseout stage. As far as I know, the organization ceased to exist [in Brooklyn] by 1965 or so. I was meeting young priests then whose attitudes toward the papal encyclicals was, "Since they are not infallibly declared, you don't have to believe them." This was so childish on their part, there being no effort to read and appreciate the wisdom therein. . . . I personally owe much to the YCW experience and many people in the organization. (Brooklyn)

The YCM awakened in me a sense of the importance of social justice. As teenagers we had been told to "mind our own business." YCW taught us what is our business. There are certain things you just can't keep quiet about. Everybody wins in a roundabout way—the ones being helped, the helper who feels good about herself, and the victimizer, if there is one, is given another chance to rethink or redirect his policy, hopefully for the good. (San Jose, California)

After my training in the YCW, I was recalled to the army in the Berlin crisis. While in the army, I was stationed near St. Louis, Missouri, and helped establish a beginning group in a parish there. Part of the action of that group was to picket a restaurant in Webster Groves which would not serve blacks. The YCW group, CORE, and two other soldiers from my company picketed the restaurant. The three of us from camp were arrested by the police as we were picketing in uniform. This incident gained some attention and we were defended by a local congresswoman.

After leaving the Army, I returned home to find the YCW almost dead. We hung on for a year or two but with no real expansion. Over the years, I have been involved in labor unions, political campaigns and parish councils. It if were not for the YCW, I would not have had any interest in these organizations. I feel that the YCW was a good learning experience and remember it fondly.

My only criticism is that [some of] the "left wingers" we turned out became ultraconservative. In addition, the YCW concept of a woman's role is rather ludicrous. The YCW really missed the boat on women in modern society. (New York City)

The YCW has had and continues to have a great influence in my life. My values and concerns in life were greatly influenced by the movement. My commitment to social change and to improving the lives of individuals is a direct result of YCW. The change to social work, a direct result of YCW, has been rewarding and fulfilling. (Milwaukee)

YCW was important in the formation of my character, life, direction. . . . Our groups (in the early sixties) were able to manage well. It was another job for the clerics to deal with, and their own basis was not always in line with the development of lay leaders. There were needed more people with leadership to help develop the members. But, overall, it was an exciting time of commitment, involvement, and a chance to be in the movement that reflected so much of the new social thinking, encyclicals, growth in the Church. It was a chance to meet people on a deeper level than was possible in religious or social circles. (Los Angeles)

It was a time when youthful enthusiasm could be tapped and channeled to develop strong Christian values, to spread the gospel through actions without proselytizing, and to involve individuals in the lives of others, their neighbors, community, nation, and even the world. My eyes were opened a great deal and I had the opportunity to be a part of some memorable and character-building experiences, such as the civil rights movement and greater lay participation in the Church. (Chicago)

Notes

1. Msgr. John Kean to Msgr. Reynold Hillenbrand, 1961.
2. Marguerite Fievez, *Cardijn* (Bruxelles: Editions Vie Ouvriere, 1978), p. 210.
3. *Ibid.*, p. 201.
4. The age of first marriage for men in the United States dropped from 24.3 in 1940 to 22.6 in 1955. For women, the figure dropped from 23.5 to 22.6 in those same years. Statistics cited in *World Almanac and Book of Facts, 1990*.
5. National Council proceedings, August 1961. UND archives.
6. Jerry Curtis, letter to author, May 16, 1989.
7. Mike Colavecchio at Summer Council meeting, August 1960.
8. Nancy Lee Conrad to author, March 3, 1988.
9. John Hill and Nancy Lee Conrad referred to Cardijn's comments in separate conversations with author in 1987 and 1988.
10. Jack McCartney to author, July 1989.
11. Andrew Greeley, "Problem Approach to the Social Inquiry," *Apostolate*, Spring 1959, p. 4.
12. S.M. Miller and Martin Rein, "Poverty and Social Change," in Louis Ferman, et al., *Poverty in America* (Ann Arbor: University of Michigan Press, 1967), p. 497.
13. Peter Foote to author, December 6, 1987.
14. Peter Foote, "Study of the Composition and Approach of the YCW in the Chicago Area," *Apostolate*, Spring 1964, pp. 17–22.
15. Ardito, et. al., conversation with author, February 27, 1987.
16. Jerry Curtis, "Commentary on YCW in the 60s," received by author, July 1989, p. 18.
17. Margaret Soderburg, *The Politics of Catholic Youth, A Comparative Study of the YCW*, doctoral dissertation for Washington University, St. Louis, Missouri, p. 12.
18. Jerry Curtis, *op. cit.* p. 20.
19. *Ibid.*, p. 21.
20. Hillenbrand, council meeting, January 1965.
21. Richard Delaney, council meeting, January 1965.
22. All comments on the name change discussion are taken from the minutes of the Winter Council meeting, January 1965.
23. Handwritten notes seen on copy of 1965 minutes in the University of Notre Dame archives, council meeting, January 1965.
24. Sheila Smith Hebein, "YCW to YCM in the Sixties," *Cardijn Newsletter*, January-February 1990, p. 3.
25. Hillenbrand, minutes of council meeting, January 1965.
26. To the national YCWs—Australia, United States, India, Malaysia, Korea, Philippines, England, "The Reality of the YCW in the World," A 2311/34 Annex 4. YCW International Secretariat, Brussels. n.d. UND archives.

12

YCW at the Grass Roots

The frustration felt by the national leaders was merely an echo of what was happening in local sections around the country. A picture of what happened and why at the all-important local level is useful for a full understanding of the emergence, growth, and ultimate deterioration of the movement nationwide. Though the YCW in each city had a unique setting and coloration, each shared a common spirit and a common apostolic goal. We have chosen to tell the story of the Detroit YCW because its achievements and problems were typical of the mainstream YCW in many communities across the country.

Detroit was a large, industrial city with strong ethnic diversity that should have been fertile ground for a movement of young workingmen and women. The earliest glimmerings of YCW appears to have been around the time Paul McGuire was stirring the hearts of so many across the United States. According to Detroit sources, it was Fr. Clare Murphy and some of his priest friends who initiated the first Catholic Action cells. Dorothy LeLonde, a cell leader from Detroit, was present at the Girls' Study Week held in Chicago in 1946. Bob Trautman and several young men from a Dearborn cell attended the first national men's organizing meeting in 1947. Growth was erratic, however, and it was difficult to recruit chaplains.

Despite concentrated efforts by David O'Shea, an experienced organizer from England, to recruit members and start sections in the mid-fifties, progress was slow. A half dozen sections were started, and one Fr. Kolch accepted responsibility as overall chaplain for the specialized movements. Though small (one hundred or so members in a Catholic population in excess of one million), the Detroit YCW was an effective movement that got things done and developed a sound leadership cadre. The regular meetings of members to inquire into the problems of young workers led to individual actions, study days, and various spiritual enterprises. Some of those involved have been located and attest that the YCW experience increased their intensity as Christians after they left the movement.[1]

A serious deterrent, as in many other dioceses at the time, was the lack of interest by church authorities. The Catholic Youth Organization (CYO) was the designated organization for youth in the archdiocese. With the approval of Edward Cardinal Mooney, Msgr. Markey, the head of the CYO, had a virtual monopoly on youth activity in parishes and schools. The CYO was so firmly in place that it was hard to convert clergy to other kinds of youth activity. They had been imbued with the belief that the CYO was the ultimate solution to the youth formation question. Moreover, the CYO had a very large budget, full-time priests, and full-time laity. David O'Shea was told when he organized in Detroit that the YCW must operate as part of the CYO, but it was not a good, workable relationship.

Jerry Curtis, a former Detroit leader, described the situation between the two organizations in very strong terms.

> Much to the CYO's chagrin, the fledgling YCW upstart did get off the ground and provoked an ongoing animosity with the CYO which perennially strove to get the YCW under its jurisdiction. The YCW's forte was action rooted in formation, whereas the CYO program centered on strong Catholics turning inward, building a monolithic youth culture whose experience, outlook, and expectations were parochial. The YCW was such a radical contrast with its ecumenical name, its social ideology, and its outreach beyond defensive Catholic apologetics so popular at the time, it was a proverbial sitting duck.[2]

The effectiveness of YCW formation is reflected in the 1957 attendance of Detroit's Harvey Kuehn and Mary Hammer at the international pilgrimage in Rome. Their great effort to make the trip at a time when local sections were few testifies to their YCW spirit, a spirit greatly enhanced by the thrill of that tumultuous gathering of committed, apostolic young workers and the ringing endorsement of the YCW's mission by Pope Pius XII. So moved were they by their experience that upon their return to Detroit, they went to see Cardinal Dearden, the new archbishop. He gave permission for the YCW to exist as an autonomous organization which would report directly to him. This allowed them to bypass the CYO.[3]

Fr. Jerome Fraser, a young priest who had actively worked with the movement since his seminary days, prevailed upon the archbishop to appoint him YCW chaplain for the archdiocese in addition to his duties as faculty member at Sacred Heart Seminary and part-time parish priest. By the time he took over the chaplaincy in 1958, there was only one section and that met secretly because its chaplain had died and the pastor didn't approve of the YCW.[4] Fr. Fraser sought out priests to become chaplains and new sections began. He organized regular priests' meetings to help them grow as chaplains by sharing their experiences and learning from one another. His strategy yielded a cohesive spirit for the Detroit movement and a harvest of strong leaders.

The presence of a committed chaplain at this time points up another important feature of the YCW. Cardijn insisted that the presence of a good priest was essential in the development of strong worker-leaders. In every city where the YCW grew strong, one finds a dedicated chaplain who motivated the young lay people. Fraser was such a priest, a tireless enthusiast who bred a dynamic spirit among the leaders, insisting that if they were well-organized and efficient, virtually nothing was out of reach. He was a scripture scholar and a liturgist as well as a counselor and spiritual advisor to the young people. The Detroit chaplains he recruited shared his personal commitment and initiative. They also developed a skillfulness in protecting the movement from pastors and laity who found the YCW unconventional or radical at a time when many Catholics were threatened by the rising tide of change in the sixties.

When the local sections decided to form a federation, Kenan Heise became its first president. He had long been active in social action, in the Catholic Interracial Council and the Catholic Social Action conference. As editor of *The Wage Earner*, the publication of the Detroit Catholic Labor Conference, he interviewed Harvey Kuehn when he returned from Rome. He was impressed by the YCW as an action movement that could be more effective than the discussion-oriented groups with which he had been involved. He determined to see it grow.[5]

Kenan moved into the city from his suburban home and, with Fr. Fraser's help, found an abandoned thirteen-room house in St. Boniface parish in a deteriorating neighborhood that could be used as a Cardijn Center. The YCW occupied the house in return for repairing it and paying all utilities. YCW members from around the city made local headlines by restoring the abandoned slum dwelling to its Victorian splendor, tearing out basement partitions and decades of trash to create an adequate meeting place and social center, while the upper part of the building provided living quarters for full-time leaders. Kenan was able to work almost full-time because of his "creative" work schedule as a journalist. When Ted Zelewsky went to Detroit as a national YCW organizer later that year, he lived in the house with Kenan.

The center became a rallying place for the federation and before long, *The Link*, a newsletter, first mimeographed and then a printed tabloid, began to circulate among the members and their contacts. The original Cardijn Center on Vermont Street was taken back by the pastor of St. Boniface after it was in good shape and the leaders then rented another "fixer-upper" on Leverett Street. The YCW renovation there inspired an upgrading in other buildings nearby and another downtown block was saved from the wrecking ball.

Patti Ryan and Joe Kelly followed Ted as national full-time organizers. Patti lived with Marylu Langan who had moved to Detroit after her term as national vice-president and Joe lived at the center. Later, he was joined by Dan Shay, a local member who volunteered for full-time organizing. In 1961 Kenan moved to Chicago to work on the national YCW staff and Jerry Curtis was elected to replace him as federation president. After a brief period as president, Jerry decided to attend the leadership training course in Chicago. General Motors wouldn't give him time off, so he quit his job. This turned out to be providential for the YCW because, upon his return, he spent two years as a full-time officer, supporting himself with a variety of part-time work.

By the mid-sixties, though the groups were still not extensive in numbers, their total apostolic commitment and energy had become a potent force. The number of sections grew from six in 1959 to a peak of seventeen in 1966. In the early sixties, many new sections were quickly organized by the full-time leaders, but they soon realized that large numbers of uncommitted members didn't do much good.

Though they wanted to attract as many as possible to give them the opportunity for growth provided by the YCW, they opted instead for a vital, effective nucleus which would truly be a leaven.

The federation leaders found that a section in every parish was unrealistic and they began to organize regional sections in parishes near the member's work and recreational centers. Membership was largely composed of office workers, although sections included laborers, UAW members, and teachers, as well as persons involved in sales and the trades. The diversity did not seem to present a problem. Members from the various socioeconomic groups learned from one another. It has been estimated that Detroit, during the peak years, had 160 active and committed members who had a direct influence on at least one thousand persons.

Pat Petit, who was brought in from St. Paul by the Detroiters to serve as an organizer, often used unorthodox methods to reach out to prospective members and others who could be influenced by the ideals of the movement, including gang members and street people. Some sections were highly organized, did in-depth research on inquiries, and planned complex actions, while another section in the central city might be at the level, literally, of figuring out how to survive in life. With the annual national inquiry theme as a backdrop, the Detroit YCW improvised to meet the needs seen in particular sections. Pat converted traditional leaders to the view that the inquiries should evolve from people's lives and not be entirely dependent upon the formal program developed by the national office. He saw the program as a unifying dynamic which should serve the members and their peers rather than the members serving the program. This was especially necessary in ghetto neighborhoods where the YCW was attempting to establish a foothold.[6]

Roughly a third of Detroit sections were in the suburbs, another third in the then stable outer city, and the balance in the inner city. The membership was a variegated tapestry of middle-class whites in the outlying areas, and blacks, Mexican-Americans, and Puerto Ricans in the inner city. One section was in a Maltese neighborhood and another in a Polish ethnic parish. There was also a group of nurses at Henry Ford hospital who functioned under the YCW umbrella.

During the turbulent sixties, a high priority in the affluent white parishes of the outer city was race, so YCW sections fought energetically to halt blockbusting by cynical real estate agents who played on racial fears for the sake of profits. Along with like-minded community groups, they developed ambitious programs to educate the people to accept integration and learn to live with blacks.

In the inner city, sections were grappling with swiftly decaying neighborhoods, the astronomical rise of crime, and the weakening of community services and education. The YCW organized activities such as sports teams and tutoring programs for teen-agers. The most urgent task of the YCW in such places was to instill a sense of hope in crisis-ridden areas by making people feel they were not alone.

One technique for bringing the members together was having local sections host federation meetings and other events at different locations throughout the city and suburbs. In several instances, this meant that a black or a Hispanic would be among the first minorities to enter a given suburban parish. YCW members in all-white communities often took abuse because of this. On the other hand, white members conquered their fears and began making routine trips into the inner city parishes to show solidarity with their counterparts there. Social events and leisure time activities always strove to include everyone.

The federation officers worked closely with each section to insure that formation through action on the program was constantly ongoing. The monthly federation meeting which brought together the leaders of each section was carefully prepared with the chaplain, just as section meetings were.

Given the immaturity of youth, the Detroit leaders were fortunate to have a wide spectrum of people and resources to draw on. These ad hoc consultants included former national YCW leaders who lived in Detroit, Jim and Cathy Rose and Marylu Langan Zobel who were always available for consultation and moral support, as were the CFM leaders. The Catholic Interracial Council and the Detroit Catholic Labor Conference offered cooperation and expertise. Justine Murphy, who with her husband ran a Catholic Worker House of Hospitality, was in a Catholic Action cell in the forties. The Catholic Worker House was near the Cardijn Center on Leverett Street and the Murphys became good friends. The presence of experienced advisors served to keep the young leaders focused on the needs of others and prevented them from growing inward. A self-centered approach was always a danger in an inexperienced section.

The federation leaders also maintained contact with leaders in civic positions, like Bill Ryan, publisher of *The Wage Earner*, who became a state representative and then House leader for many years. He was called on when issues came up which involved state politics. The editors of *The Michigan Catholic* were also supportive and gave good publicity to the work of the movement.

Labor Day was a multisection effort that centered on a mass near downtown Detroit to enable members to participate in the annual UAW-Democratic political rally held in Cadillac Square. In collaboration with the Catholic Labor Conference, they also participated in a liturgy on the feast of St. Joseph the Worker in May. This was hosted by the federation each year at a different parish church.

Also on the federation agenda were three study days during the year, on the subject of the current inquiry program. The study days were organized by individual sections who ran them entirely, though with in-depth training provided by the federation team in the preparatory stages. This freed the federation team from detail planning so that they were able to direct a full annual program of activity with just a handful of full-time leaders.

Leisure activities such as ski trips and picnics were planned by alternating sections and members were encouraged to invite their friends and acquaintances. Individual sections sponsored trips to the opera, the theater, jazz and rock concerts, as well as to museums and local ethnic festivals. These events, often the result of inquiries on the use of leisure time, helped to build group solidarity and enabled YCW leaders to reach out to nonmembers.

The YCW participated in the Detroit Committee for Fair Housing Practices and helped lobby the legislature for fair housing laws. They invited foreign exchange students into their homes and did research on United States immigration laws. They began to follow foreign affairs in the newspapers. Because he spoke Spanish, Hank Vasquez was asked to accompany international leaders attending a WAY conference in New Jersey when they traveled around the country. "My bosses gave me time off," he said later. "It was a great experience."

While working on major social issues, YCW members also helped persons with individual problems. Jobs were found for the unemployed. Individuals returned to the Sacraments as a result of YCW influence; others began to take instructions in the Catholic faith. The members' own spiritual development was strengthened by the annual retreat and several days of recollection each year. In 1964, the Detroit YCW was booming.

Because of its involvement in social issues, the YCW was considered radical at a time when social involvement was not popular. The Detroit YCS in fact became quite radical, according to one observer, and the YCW was linked with that in some minds. One of those who argued about the views and tactics of the movement was Fr. Thomas Gumbleton, who later became an outspoken bishop deeply concerned with social issues and who has actively supported organizations like Pax Christi and Bread for the World. At that time, he was vice-chancellor of the archdiocese. Jerry Curtis remembers one strong argument when Gumbleton said, "I personally agree with you, but as vice-chancellor, I cannot." This was not an unusual position for a church leader in those days.[7]

The movement began to change significantly around 1966 when the time came for the leaders of the late fifties and early sixties to move on as they reached age thirty or thereabouts. The generation of leaders who joined the YCW after 1960 felt the organization could be run without full-time leaders. In 1966, the Cardijn Center was closed because no one was able to live there and take care of it. This coincided with the reassignment of many chaplains to other parishes. It was always difficult to replace a good chaplain and sometimes a section would have to merge with another. This was before the priest-exodus crisis which began by the end of the decade.

When I visited Detroit in 1989, I asked former members to recall their YCW days.[8] "We had lots of fun doing all kinds of things," they said. "And we became good friends."

"Is that why you joined?" I asked.

"No, no," they chorused. "That came after. We absorbed the apostolic spirit almost unconsciously. Social action became part of our lives. The fun part of it was extra. That's what's easier to remember now."

"What went wrong? Why did the movement fade away?"

One member said that the YCW required an enormous commitment of time and energy. At best, it appealed to only a minority of young people who would accept its challenging ideals. By the mid-sixties, many did not see the need to make that kind of effort. "It was very difficult to get people involved in wanting to take responsibility for their own lives, much less take responsibility for society," said

George McMahon, one of the last remaining members at the Cardijn Center.

"The rigid national program was also part of it," said Helene Mrokowski Evans. "In the sixties, you could get involved in something like the civil rights movement that was happening and was historic. If you were in the YCW, you switched topics from week to week and you had to do those different things in the program. It was more interesting to get involved in a group doing something that sparked your interest and you could see results."

"I think it had something to do with the Church coming of age," said Bob Saenz. "Catholics no longer needed a church organization to get involved in those things. They could go out and do them on their own. When you're young, you have to be in a group to feel secure in social protest. Those other groups were doing the same things. In the older days, they weren't there. Catholic social philosophy has been adopted by a lot of other organizations, . . . but not calling it Catholic social philosophy."

"Union groups, civil rights groups, anti-abortion groups, family life groups. All these organizations now take care of the things that we were looking at. There are other channels now," said Patti Ryan Zobel, "and you don't have to concentrate on as many different issues as we did."

"Other groups replaced us, but not well," responded Helene. "I remember people later on who were union-minded but anti-civil rights. And some of the anti-abortion people seem ready to kill everyone that doesn't agree with them! I look back and I say, thank God for YCW because it gave us a well-rounded approach. The seven areas had their validity."

The dynamism generated among those young people resulted in many productive activities in later years. Kenan Heise initiated a column in the *Chicago Tribune* called "Action Line" which, for seventeen years, helped people to solve personal and communitywide problems. Tomás Gonzales, who had recruited numerous Hispanics in Detroit, left a budding career at General Motors to move to the San Joaquín valley of California where he formed an action movement among farm workers using the YCW techniques. He founded a two-year college, Colegio de la Tierra, affiliated with a local college, bought a communally owned and maintained ranch-farm, and established a cooperative food store/warehouse for the region.

Others who stayed in Detroit found other ways to serve. Chuck and Charlene List, for example, adopted several hard-to-place children. Lucy and Howard Weathington worked in the public schools doing remedial teaching and working with handicapped children. Most of the others have been involved in some kind of social action.

Jim Lamb, one of the last remaining officers in 1968, has poignant memories of the final days:

> When I joined St. Alphonsus section, it was wonderful. There was always something going on and there were always the three words: Observe, Judge, and Act. We were in the right place at the right time. It was a happening. If a person was a doer, he or she stayed to find out that life is a great challenge. The same things were going on in other sections. It was a time of great changes in the Church and we were part of that change.
>
> But let's look at the bottom line. We were not part of the structured Church of that day. We were unique and did not fit in. . . . What fools we were at this time. I remember trying to convince people that we need ourselves and not the structure. Yet at that point, I did not know where we were going or perhaps what I was saying. Something was dying and the ship was sinking. There was not a day without a crisis.
>
> This was the saddest time for Anita (Leonard McDonald) and myself. We sat together one night and said, "It's over," and we gave up the ship. We were alone and had nothing to grab on to anymore. (Anita was vice-president, and I was secretary-treasurer. We didn't have a president.)
>
> We dissolved the Detroit Federation and sold all assets for $600, all of which was donated to Holy Trinity Church. It was finally over. Sometimes I look back and say maybe we could have done differently. . . . I would not change the decision we had to make. In retrospect, Detroit was different. We held out longer than some of the others.[9]

The Detroit YCW reached its peak in the days when it had strong, committed leaders who gave their whole energy to building and maintaining it as a Christian social action movement. A developing shortage of chaplains and a lack of enough leaders willing and able to sacrifice their personal goals for a year or two, as their predecessors had done, affected the vitality of the Detroit YCW. It was also getting harder and harder to get new members. In the late fifties and early sixties, there was no other organization able to interest and train idealistic young people who wanted to be involved in social action. Later in the decade, other single-issue organizations were taking over that required a less demanding commitment.

The Detroit story could be duplicated in many other cities. It was a small core of dedicated leaders struggling against great odds, a community of faith dedicated to serving the needs of young adults, the Church in action in the world.

Voices from the Sixties

Let us all thank all those priests who worked with and supported us. They were wonderful. At the national convention in Indiana, a priest from Houma, Louisiana, said to us when we were all assembled, "Do you realize how good you are?" That was so helpful to me. They were witnesses to God's love, mercy, care, and forgiveness. . . . We learned to search out the best and hope for the best in each other. The work life and unions theme was very formative for me. Now, 27 years later, I am a member of the carpenters' union and I value it and what it takes to keep it going. I still have my YCW pin. (Detroit)

Many of the former YCWs still in San Diego continued YCW work in unions, public schools, environmental and various civil rights and social justice organizations. For the past 20 years, ex-YCWs have been/are active in MANO, the Mexican American Neighbor Organization, originally formed in 1963. (San Diego)

I not only have fond memories of the many activities that I was involved in, but the people—their dedication, their awareness, and their caring—made a profound influence in my life. I feel very fortunate to have been a part of the movement. Our old section still keeps in touch. (Chicago)

At first the joining of YCW was negative to me mainly because I was not a leader, a brain, or socially liked. I loved living in the YCW house and, although I did not give much of myself then, it did help me a lot in later life with my marriage, my slowly acquired values, and knowing how Christians should live their lives. . . . I feel I am a stronger Christian today and have had some valuable influence on the lives of many who are now doing God's work. I feel I am a very important part in God's plan for his Mystical Body, in work and in my daily dealings with people. (Portland, Oregon)

The YCW gave me a valuable, contemporary Christian approach to life and a methodology for responding to my environment as a problem-solver and opinion-influencer. Though I am no longer conscious of the source on a day-to-day basis, I believe it affects virtually all of my behavior. (Milwaukee)

I think young adult groups are important, but the YCW was more than just a social club. It gave us formation in issues, helped us to examine important things together. It would be good if something similar were reinstated today which relates scriptural principles to current affairs. (New Hampshire)

Notes

1. Robert Trautman and Justine Murphy, in separate conversations with author, September 16, 1989.
2. Jerome Curtis, letter to author, October 14, 1989.
3. Ted Zelewsky to author, September 18, 1989.
4. Kenan Heise in letter to Helene Evans, September 13, 1989.
5. Kenan Heise to author, October 12, 1989.
6. Jerome Curtis, "Commentary on the 60s," May 16, 1987.
7. *Ibid.*
8. Facts and quotes in this section from taped discussion with former Detroit YCWs, September 16, 1989.
9. Jim Lamb, letter to author, September 30, 1989.

13

The Final Days

While the American YCW was struggling with its role as a lay movement, the Church itself was evolving. Since 1962 the bishops had been meeting in the Second Vatican Council to discuss the nature of the Church and its role in the modern world. One topic on the agenda was the role of the laity. When *Lumen Gentium*, the Constitution on the Church, was issued, the role of the laity in the world was clearly identified.

> These faithful are by baptism made one body with Christ and are established among the People of God. They are in their own way made sharers in the priestly, prophetic, and kingly functions of Christ. They carry out their own part in the mission of the whole Christian people with respect to the Church and the world. . . .
>
> The laity, by their very vocation, seek the kingdom of God by engaging in temporal affairs and by ordering them according to the plan of God. They live in the world, that is, in each and all of the secular professions and occupations. They live in the ordinary circumstances of family and social life, from which the very web of their existence is woven.
>
> They are called there by God so that by exercising their proper function and being led by the spirit of the Gospel, they can work for the sanctification of the world from within, in the manner of leaven.[1]

The old formulation of Catholic Action as the "participation of the laity in the apostolate of the hierarchy" was no longer justifiable. Where before "the Church" meant the bishops and the clergy, and the ordinary people "belonged" to the Church, it was now made clear that the Church was the community of all the faithful and that the work of the laity was just as important as that of the clergy. Furthermore, the new Constitution on the Church implied that the Church was more correctly seen as the people of God served by the hierarchy rather than the hierarchy served by the people of God. "This idea permeates the whole Constitution," said the editors of a commentary on the Vatican decree.[2]

The justification for an active role for lay men and women was clear and unmistakable. It was further developed in the Decree on the Apostolate of the Laity. Joseph Cardijn, now a monsignor, was a consultant to the preparatory commission discussing the decree. He sent many memos to the commission underscoring his belief that an authentic apostolate of the laity was grounded in ordinary life. In 1963 he had finally compiled his thoughts about the laity into a book with the English title *Laymen Into Action* that was widely circulated among the bishops at the council. He wanted to make clear the case for the laity. If the bishops didn't make a clear, strong pronouncement and dare to examine the lay apostolate in depth, Cardijn felt the Church would be signing its death sentence and would move even further in the strong, clerical current which slowly but surely over the last three hundred years had been bringing about paralysis.[3]

Then a remarkable thing happened. Due to his advancing age, Cardijn wrote to Paul VI in 1965 asking to be relieved as general chaplain of the Young Christian Workers. The Holy Father responded by naming him a cardinal. So, at the age of eighty-three, Cardijn was given the red biretta at a ceremony in St. Peter's basilica. No longer did he have to sit in the gallery—which he called the pigeon loft—with the other consultants. He took his place in the deliberations of Vatican II as a full member. At the end of the council he rejoiced in the promulgation of the Decree on the Apostolate of the Laity, in the preparation of which he had directly shared and which spells out the mission of lay people in the Church.

Lay people have their own role in the Church's mission. Therefore their apostolic formation takes on a distinctive quality from the specific and peculiar character of lay life and the spirituality proper to it. Apostolic formation presupposes an integrated human formation in keeping with the talents and situation of each person. For the lay person should thoroughly understand the modern secular world. He ought to be involved in his own society and capable of adjusting himself to its specific character and culture. . . .

Apostolic formation cannot be limited to purely theoretical instruction. Slowly indeed, and carefully, from the very beginning of his formation, the lay person must learn to look at reality with the eyes of faith, make judgments about it, and act on them. By active involvement he forms and perfects himself in the company of others, and thus embarks on active service to the Church. . . .

With such a formation the lay person can involve himself vigorously in the reality of the secular order and effectively undertake his role in its affairs. At the same time he is a living member and witness of the Church and makes her actively present to the secular order.[4]

Francis Wendell, O.P., commenting on that statement, said, "The See, Judge, and Act method, conceived by Thomas Aquinas, activated by Cardinal Cardijn, and canonized by Pope John XXIII is indeed a continuing process and a discovery that is invaluable to the layman. It keeps the lay person with his feet in the order of reality and his head and heart in the realm of faith."[5]

Keegan at the Council

Pat Keegan, by then president of the Christian Worker Movement, an organization of former Jocists, was invited to address the council in St. Peter's during the discussions on the lay apostolate—the first layman in 1,500 years to address a council of bishops.

This scheme [on the Lay Apostolate] marks for us a point of fulfillment in the historical development of the lay apostolate. We sincerely hope that it marks also the beginning of a whole new state of development. The scheme is the natural outcome of the Church's new awareness of herself. It is also the result of the progressive discovery by men and women of their responsibility and role within the total apostolate of the Church. The very existence of the document is proof that the lay apostolate is no luxury, nor passing fashion.

No document could have provided a codification of all that is being done. Nor would one have wished that it should. This scheme leaves the field open for further developments and, at the same time, points to the common ground in apostolic endeavor. Because circumstances and needs will differ, precise forms and structures cannot be imposed. It is clear that an apostolic lay action must be rooted in the actual situation and needs of the world.[6]

During the council, Pat spent many hours in eating places around the Vatican, exchanging ideas with the bishops and their consultants. An interesting story has been told about Pat during those days. One of the bishops with whom he became good friends was Karol Wojtyla of Poland. At one bull session, Pat was vehemently expounding on his belief that the pope was a virtual prisoner in the Vatican and so unable to keep in close touch with the outside world. "How can he go out when they even make him wear those silly red slippers?"

Some time after Wojtyla had become Pope John Paul II, he spoke with a visiting Englishman. Lifting up his white cassock, he said, "If you see Pat Keegan, tell him I'm still wearing my own shoes." And he pointed to his shoe-clad feet. It is possible his many travels throughout the world were partly in response to Pat's prodding. Pat was on a first-name basis with many officials in the Vatican and he was not reluctant to voice his views.[7]

Mike Woodruff, president-elect of the American movement, was part of a delegation from the States that went to Rome to observe the council sessions. There he met with many council advisors and discussed with church notables the importance and necessity of lay leadership. He felt that if the council statements were to be implemented there must be initiative and action on the part of laymen themselves. There is the danger, he noted, of not having the decrees carried out because the everyday American Catholic would not discuss and understand their importance and take concrete action to put these ideas into effect.[8]

On his return to the national office, Mike outlined the direction he thought the movement should take. He felt the acceptance of the lay apostolate at the council presented an opportunity for members of the movement to speak to their bishops, offer their services, and report on their work. Furthermore, he said, the national office should stress to its membership a working knowledge of the four decrees related to laymen: The Constitution on the Church, the Decrees on the Laity, The Church in the Modern World, and Ecumenism. They should be the subject of study days throughout the country.

"The opportunity is here, now. The challenge is ours. It is for us to take the action to make these decrees a reality. We of the YCM must take the lead, the lead for which we have been trained and formed."[9]

The pronouncements that came out of Vatican II seemed to open great possibilities for the future. The pioneering efforts of the specialized movements—giving young workers a sense of their dignity and their mission in the world, striving for human rights, working for social justice in the work place, forming lay Christians committed to social action in all areas of life—these were now recognized as legitimate concerns of the Church in the modern world.

When Marie Powers left the vice-presidency of what was now called YCM in 1965, she was upbeat about the future.

> Many people say the young generation is "going to the dogs," but I don't agree. The young people that I have met respond to the request of the late Holy Father to become involved in the world. . . . Each week all over the U.S., young people are saying yes to involvement. They are taking a new interest in civil rights, politics, the migrant worker problem. They are becoming vibrant members of the Mystical Body, active, thinking Christians committed to the Church. Proof of this is that young people upon leaving the YCM are going into certain professions for a religious motive rather than to make a lot of money.
>
> Our apostolate is all things. Our work is as wide as the world; as far-reaching as each human person. It is the work of a lifetime. It means committing ourselves in a profound and enlightened way of doing Christ's work in the world.[10]

In spite of such optimism, membership continued to decline. Because they didn't see a need for the kind of education that the YCM offered nor the kind of apostolic commitment that it demanded, many who joined didn't stay long. Some who joined after 1965 did so to meet other young people and, perhaps, find "a good Catholic spouse." To them, it was "merely a social club."[11]

Changes in Church Thinking

Further complicating the recruitment of new young workers into an apostolic organization were the changes developing within the Church itself. Pronouncements coming out of the Vatican Council were altering the image of the Church built on a rock, solid and unchangeable. Catholics of all ages were questioning what it meant to be a Catholic. Devotional practices were discouraged; new emphasis was placed on Scripture; the Mass was updated and translated into the vernacular. This was no problem for Young Christian Workers. If anything, it was what they had been looking forward to for many years, even when it was considered radical by others.

A far different shift involved the understanding of sin. A new sense of morality was developing, based less on a system of Church laws and more on personal conscience. The council had proclaimed the right of the individual conscience to "immunity from coercion in matters religious." This particularly affected the area of sexual morality and the issue of birth control. Sexual practices were becoming more permissive as a result of the development of oral contraceptives and, to some extent, the early stirrings of feminism. Individual priests and lay persons, especially the young, began to question the traditional teachings of the Church regarding marriage and procreation. Young men and women often concluded that anything was permissible as long as you didn't hurt anyone.

The idea of ecumenism advocated in the Vatican Council was another major change. Where at one time the apostolic thrust had been to bring outsiders into the fold of the "one, holy, catholic, and apostolic Church," now it was recommended that Catholics get to know and share with those outside the Church. The inquiries on parish life that used to center on the local church were now titled "Parish and Community." A 1966 inquiry entitled "Communication between Parish and Neighborhood" quoted Jim Cunningham's book, *The Resurgent Neighborhood*, 1965: "Today the Church can be part of the neighborhood in many ways. . . . Churches can train groups of their lay people in many ways for the skills needed for responsible neighborhood renewal work, just as it has trained lay people for charitable work and fund-raising." A judgment question followed: How can parish involvement in the community increase understanding and unity among all faiths?

The following week's inquiry discussed a passage from the Decree on Ecumenism from the Second Vatican Council Report and suggested as a follow-up action that the group visit a local Christian church "in order to break down some of the barriers between men of different faiths that for so long have made cooperation difficult."

Meanwhile, another issue took center stage in the lives of many young adults—opposition to the Vietnam War. Related to this was rebellion of youth in all areas during the mid-to-late sixties. Young Christian Students in the college movement became involved with Students for a Democratic Society which increasingly argued that the only way to bring about needed social change was through revolution.

Some members of the YCM national team were also being influenced by the rebellious spirit that was becoming so prevalent among young people. Jack McCartney, director of the training course for YCM leaders, was approached on many occasions, particularly by the college YCS leaders, to put radical speakers on the agenda. Jack to this day feels that the YCM lost its sense of identity in the sixties. The pioneering spirit of the movement was being outstripped by the rapid changes in society.

The decline in YCW membership in the early years of the sixties had been largely a result of complacency, but as the decade wore on, disenchantment with the Church became the dominant factor. Loss of membership was most pronounced in the Midwest. Many of the remaining active sections were in Hispanic neighborhoods on the East and West coasts.

In New York welfare and community problems were becoming more crucial than the labor union focus of ten years earlier. Puerto Ricans were very politically and community conscious. The chaplains worked with young people who were growing up in a very confused situation. When they got together in the YCM, they began to get interested in politics and helped local leaders develop a considerable power base in the city. Rene Martin, an organizer in Spanish Harlem, said many years later, "We should have continued to work in the Spanish communities, the black communities, with the low-income whites. Instead, we ended up being involved with middle-class whites whose problems were inside, the kind you talk to a shrink about. The problem with some of the guys was meeting girls, relating to girls at a meeting, should they go to college or not go to college."[12]

Young priests who worked in minority parishes, however, were interested in Scripture, dialogue, current ideas on sociology, and community organizations rather than the social doctrine of the papal encyclicals. These activist priests could only be sold on the value of the YCM if it broke away from its theoretical emphasis and returned to its earlier focus on "formation through action."

Unfortunately, the leaders on the national staff insisted on following the pattern that had been successful in previous years. Nancy Diley Delaney, national secretary in 1964, has said that the YCW/YCM did not develop critical thinking which would have allowed for more understanding of the changes that were occurring in the sixties. Leaders in those days played a strong role in the evolution of the civil rights movement, and many of them went into community action programs when they left the movement. However, as leaders of the movement, they did not have the resources for new, creative thinking. Until 1967 they were locked into the programs based on the seven areas of life and the papal encyclicals. Msgr. Hillenbrand's unlimited faith in the old ways was reinforced by the encouraging words of John XXIII and the decrees of the Vatican Council. He did not seem to realize that a rapidly changing world might need new solutions. And he continued to be the guru of the movement's leadership.

The Need for Strong Lay Leaders

When Sheila Smith from Ramsey, New Jersey, was asked to become the national secretary in the fall of 1965, her first inclination was to say no. Though she was a committed and active leader and had started numerous sections in Maplewood and Newark, she had just moved to a new apartment and had a new job. Mike Woodruff, then an organizer in New York, came to see her about the Chicago job, but she turned him down. Then, after a week of soul searching, discussion with her local chaplain, and a phone call from Joan Ziolkowski, the retiring secretary, she decided to give it a try. This is her story.

Before I came out to Chicago, we had had the East Coast Convention. We had so much spirit. The Washington people, the New Jersey people, the New York people, Rhode Island. It was wonderful. My God, I don't want to leave it here. It seemed silly to take the leaders out of the strong areas because then you can become weak. I was really very torn. I did come and I found it extremely challenging, partly because we really didn't train national members. We were called a team, but there was no team development.

The person before you would show you what your job was and you'd sit in on meetings and pick up on what was going on. . . . We had people from different walks of life, with very different standards for personal living and for other things—how you related to people, how you communicated with other people, your respect for other people. Some of the fellows were, well, what I would call cowboys. They had an attitude that was hard to deal with, and I didn't especially want to. There were times when the guys were very hard to get along with. . . .

There was also a trap that some national people fell into because your life was unreal. The national would come across as "You must do this, and you're going to do that." I saw people that forgot to stay involved. I think that when you are trying to work with grass roots people, you never can be too far away. You cannot only be talking about these great worldwide issues, because the members you are trying to have an impact on are living in the real world with its challenges, like trying to find a job that will pay them enough, whatever.

I love people. When I came here, my circle was too narrow. It wasn't that the team members weren't nice. It was just that I felt hemmed in. Very quickly I joined a section and got involved in the Austin Community Organization at St. Lucy's parish.

Going on the road helped a lot. Getting back with the grass roots and feeling the spirit and the energy was as good as a day of recollection. . . .

Trying to live with twelve people at the girls' house was hard. I grew a lot, but it was hard. When Mary Benson came from Arizona to join the staff, she was twenty and brand new. She worked in the office putting out *Impetus* [the newsletter for YCM members], and she worked from three to ten at the phone company. I was twenty-five when I joined so I was older. We had some high school leaders living with us. We were young, but they were younger. I became the housemother. You had to cook for a week, but you may never have cooked before. You had to do this, besides running a program.

Everyone on the national team worked hard. One girl came from Phoenix and worked in a factory and lived at the house and gave us her money.

One thing that proves the YCW was not as aggressive as I thought it was regards the role of women. I can remember accepting the role of vice-president for a year and Linda Mann, the previous v.p., telling me I was too outgoing and might overshadow Mike's leadership. I thought you were brought in because you had capabilities, that you ought to be able to use those capabilities. Then, and to this day, it was beyond my comprehension why we had to be subservient to the male leadership. I think that was a big factor in our movement's decline. We had all the guys either going to Vietnam or going to college to stay out of Vietnam, or becoming COs. The guys really weren't there. Maybe the women could have done it (been the leaders), they're really not too bad. Maybe they can make a contribution. . . . they've been hiding behind the guys for so long. That to me was very wrong. I felt that some of the males in the YCM were male chauvinists, very, very much so. I felt that some of the women allowed that, so we all have some responsibility.

I have thought about people in the sixties. I was a woman. I was here not because I was a women or a man, but I was a Young Christian Worker, and I was here to work. I wasn't here to bitch and moan. A concern that we could become a girls' movement? Would you rather have a girls' movement or no movement? . . . There was a need for those shattered young men coming back from Vietnam, and we had nothing for them. We were gone. If we could have maintained it, if we could have acknowledged the capabilities of women, we could probably have come back together. The guys in the seventies and eighties would have been more open to women. They have them as bosses now. It's possible that could have happened, but hindsight is 20/20. So, we built on a weak foundation. We wound up with our male leaders being taken away by the army or by college. We didn't have strong men.

They were good people, I will always believe that, the people who worked on the national team. But they did not always have the skills it took to do the job that needed to be done. It wasn't their fault; it was the circumstances. It was the changing mores, the times, especially for young people that brought about the end of the YCM. When I think about that, I feel sad, but then reality sets in and I think back on how hard it was. But the movement is not dead. It is living in all of us. I don't think you would find anyone that gave time and energy to the YCW who's not still giving time and energy to others.[13]

As numbers in the movement had declined, the pool of trained leaders available for national leadership had also declined. The results are vividly described by Sheila Smith. Going on the full-time team in Chicago required a sacrificial commitment that some potential leaders did not want to make, especially those who joined in the years when apostolic zeal was diminishing in the sections. There are many letters in the archives from members who declined the invitation to take a national office. The search for male leaders was especially difficult because so many had to go into service. One of the strongest sections in the sixties was in Phoenix which had good male leaders because many of them lived on a nearby air force base.

The quality of leadership on the national team was always a concern because of the demands made on rather young people, even those who came on with the best of intentions. It was not always easy to prejudge the capabilities of persons asked to assume national responsibility, and occasionally it did not work out. Health problems and psychological problems sometimes developed because of the physical and mental strain on the leaders. Getting along with differ-

ent personalities, making appropriate decisions, meeting deadlines—
these could all be areas of stress. The problem was more pronounced
from the mid-sixties on because national leaders tended to be younger
and less experienced. The counsel of older and more experienced lay
persons would have been helpful, but it was not always available.
Experienced leaders were expected to leave when they married. Russ
Tershy who was married when he ran the YCW training school in the
fifties was an exception.

Former members have told us about other problems which
affected morale in the national office. One of these was the problem
of sexuality. This was a period when the reality of sexual orientation
was little understood and never talked about. When very capable
leaders came on the national team who were gay, a few male leaders
found it difficult to deal with. Other male leaders adopted a very
macho style toward the girls to assert their authority and treated them
in a derogatory way. Some of this behavior may have been fairly normal
in the maturing process of young adults, but it was harder to accept
in a supposedly idealistic, Christian community.

The Developing Chaplain Problem

The presence of the chaplain as a resource person and counselor
was important in all local YCW sections, but it was even more critical
in the development of the national team. Msgr. Hillenbrand did what
he could, but his poor health and parish commitments limited the
time he could spend at the national office. In the sixties, he was no
longer able to spend a day a week there. On occasion, the national
leaders would confer with him at his north suburban parish in
Hubbard Woods. He went to the national study weeks and the council
meetings and gave inspiring talks, but he became more and more out
of touch with day-to-day issues.

As early as 1958 a group of prominent, experienced Chicago
chaplains had gone to see Msgr. Hillenbrand to ask him to step down
from the national chaplaincy because of his health and because they
thought it would be better policy to have a change in the chaplain
position on a regular basis. Monsignor did not even listen to their
rationale. Instead, like the old professor talking to his students, he
pointed out their own shortcomings and dismissed them.[14] Five years

later a group of chaplains from outside Chicago planned a meeting on the same subject, but nothing came of it. When some of the national leaders got wind of the meeting, they were furious. The revered monsignor had given them a vision of their important role in God's plan for the world; he gave their lives a spiritual dimension that was a continuing source of strength. In spite of his irascibility and stubbornness at times, they loved him.

In 1960 John Hill was appointed by Cardinal Meyer to assist the monsignor, but he was in a parish and could give only a day or two a week to the leaders. He worked with individuals, but his impact on policy decisions was limited; the monsignor still had the final word. In 1963 Fr. James Halpine from Oklahoma replaced Hill as assistant national chaplain, but he was called back to his diocese in 1966. He worked with the leaders of all the national movements, college and high school YCS and CFM as well as YCW. He remembers the YCW leaders as mature people who were more down to earth than the college YCS leaders, watched finances well, and planned carefully.[15] Helene Mrokowski Evans, on the national team in 1964, recalls that Halpine gave most of his time to the students, and YCW leaders worked largely on their own.[16]

Near the end of Fr. Halpine's term in Chicago, priests were beginning to leave the priesthood. The new thinking about ministry in the Church was very unsettling to many of them and they had a real identity crisis. Some had expected great new opportunities and freedom of action after the council decrees. When some bishops reacted by retrenching and tightening their control over the clergy, many priests became frustrated and left. Others who had long found celibate life difficult also began to leave. In the four years after the end of the Vatican Council, over three thousand priests left the active ministry in the United States, and many more followed in later years. Some of them had been YCW chaplains. This increased the pressure of work on those who remained. The interest in training lay leaders waned. The results took too long in coming, and sometimes the effort seemed fruitless. Priests interested in social action opted for personal involvement in the civil rights movement and action on other urban problems.

To revive interest in the movement, experienced chaplains began to hold regular meetings again. They also discussed the need for a full-time assistant national chaplain exclusively for the YCM. The lay leaders wrote to Bishop McGucken, chairman of the Commission on Lay Organizations, and asked his help in getting a full-time priest. With the growing shortage of priests, however, no bishop was willing to release anyone for the job.

When Mike Woodruff from Portland became the national president in August 1966, there was no regular chaplain on hand, though individual priests came in from time to time to celebrate the liturgy. Though now located in better quarters—they had moved into a remodeled factory building across the street from the old rooming house on Jackson Boulevard in 1962—conditions continued to deteriorate. Dues were not coming in, the car used by the organizers was sold, and from time to time the treasurer had to ask local Chicago leaders for money to help pay the grocery bills.

At the council meeting of January 10, 1967, the leaders looked for new ideas to boost the spirit and strength of the movement. One idea was a new program design and the other was the suggestion for structural changes in the organization.

A New Look at the Social Inquiries

It was agreed that the members were no longer looking at the social inquiry in terms of their everyday lives and that the "seven areas of life" did not have any appeal. Furthermore, the inquiry outlines tended to stifle ingenuity and creative approaches to real issues. The leaders decided to make drastic changes.

In the new introductory booklet published in 1967, *A Time to Begin*, the Observe, Judge, Act method was described as follows:

> *Observe:* The object of observing is to take a genuine interest in others, to be sensitive to their needs and aspirations, and to look closely at situations which affect their lives. The idea is to understand the importance of each person living a truly human Christian life and develop a genuine concern that the young people around us achieve their goals. The technique for observing is based on friendship and open exchange.
>
> *Judge:* Discover causes and effects of problems noted in the facts. It is not strictly a matter of determining the morality of situations, rightness or wrongness, sinfulness

or not sinfulness. Rather it is the member's opportunity to decide whether the situations they have observed are contributing to, or taking away from people's worth and value as human beings. Do these situations help or hinder people in becoming complete human and Christian persons as Christ would analyze them? What does Christ think of the situation? How would He want it to be?

Act: Decide on a definite personal action or group action and report the following week.[17]

This people-centered focus was a far cry from the inquiries on broad, global issues of previous programs, important though they might be. The perception that this was a new approach to the inquiry shows how far the previous program had moved from a concern for people and become more like a discussion club outline.

When the inquiry program was prepared for 1967-68, it had an entirely different look. "Tell It Like It Is" was composed of separate, movable booklets slipped into a small folder. One part on politics was similar to previous programs. Another section was on young adult life and included inquiries on friends, sex and the single life, sexual identity, drinking, your job and your future, your vocation, finances, and family. A booklet on international life was also included.

The "Review of Influence and Facts" was presented as a challenge to the member to respond to the situations "in which Christ has placed you and where you can exercise a human and Christian influence."

Scripture readings were in a separate booklet and were in miscellaneous order, except for a few that related to the seasons of Christmas, Easter, and Pentecost. Each Scripture selection had a related reading from a modern author like Dietrich Von Hildebrand, Karl Rahner, Carl Rogers, Michael Quoist, or Paul VI. The idea was to show the relevance of Christ's teachings to the modern world.

The other segment in the folder was a leaflet called "Crisis." It contained inquiries on topical issues that might come up and need attention, such as free love, the draft, war and peace, drugs, racism, riots, youth revolt—issues which did not fall into any theoretical framework.[18]

The 1968–69 program was concerned with issues such as black power, world hunger, civil disobedience, poverty in the United States (Appalachia, migrant workers, black ghettos), marriage, and community. It was recognized that new problems might arise that could not be foreseen, such as unemployment if the Vietnam War ended, so allowance was made to fit them in if the need arose. Those who wrote the inquiries focused on obvious problems and concerns in the lives of young workingmen and women, a sharp contrast to some programs in the previous decade. Programs were no longer submitted to Msgr. Hillenbrand for his imprimatur. This freed the program writers from his blue pencil and editorial changes.

The presentation of the program in separate sections was meant to indicate that local leaders could take whatever series of inquiries best met their needs and in any order that made sense to them. From all reports, the new design was well-received, but some sections still had difficulty with the "Review of Influence." Many members were not geared to looking for situations outside the inquiry topic that required immediate judgment and action.

The other idea for improvement involved structural change. It had long been apparent that the country was just too big and too diverse to have the uniformity envisioned by the national office. A plan was presented that would split the national organization into three separate and autonomous regions with a very loose superstructure. An executive committee would meet at intervals to coordinate the three regions. It was felt this would eliminate the need for a national office. The plan had many obstacles, not the least of which was the commitment the national YCW had to the other movements sharing the Chicago office, YCS and CFM. It was also felt that the national office provided the movement with a public identity. It was finally decided to simply reduce the size of the national team. Serious consideration was given to the need for better trained organizers, however, who would still travel to different parts of the country. That idea proved to be unworkable because there were no resources and personnel for an in-depth training program. Poorly trained organizers, however well intentioned, could not do the job.

A Struggle for Survival

When Claire Grenier was asked to join the national staff in 1968 after three years on the local level in Rhode Island, she felt honored.

Unfortunately, YCW staff life wasn't what she had expected. Problems were growing; membership continued to dwindle.

Claire recalls those days:

> It seemed as time went on that even though I and the other staff members were enthusiastic and committed, we didn't have the expertise and resources needed to solve the immense problems facing the YCM. The old ways weren't working, i.e., the program book, working with parish priests, finding members in the Church; yet the new ideas we tried to implement weren't working either.[19]

In August 1968 Rene Martin from Pawtucket, Rhode Island, was elected national president. No girl was available for the vice-presidency. Rene was a carpenter when he joined the movement and had spent two years as an organizer in Phoenix, St. Louis, and Washington, D.C. When he arrived in Chicago, he was dismayed by the religious apathy and cynicism on the national staff. Some of the male leaders were not even going to Mass regularly. The movement was approaching its final days.

In his remarks at the opening of the August 1968 council meeting, Rene said:

> We must face the fact that the movement has been declining. Some of the causes for this are:
>
> 1. Increase in affluence in the life of the young adult which gives a freedom to structure their lives in a direction of what they consider happiness. This happiness is centered around material goods and a desire to do the "in" thing, thus leaving little time for involvement in YCM.
>
> 2. Decline in the Church. Young adults no longer feel any strong ties with the structured Church. Questions we must ask ourselves are: How do we weave Christianity into the movement? Due to a decreasing number of available priests, is it possible to develop lay moderators?
>
> 3. The Vietnam War is drawing away many of the potential YCMers. An additional problem is being placed on the national office. One of our most experienced orga-

nizers must leave the staff because he has received his induction orders.[20]

Fr. Pat O'Connor from Greensburg, Pennsylvania, agreed to come in later that year to assist Msgr. Hillenbrand because, in his words, "there was no one else." He had been a YCW member in Detroit in the fifties before entering the priesthood and had a long association with the movement. He would travel to the national office periodically for day-long sessions with the staff. He remembers them as dedicated people, but there were not many repeaters at the national conventions. Unfortunately, he was not allowed to move to Chicago as a full-time chaplain, so the young leaders were mostly on their own. He saw his role as a stop-gap measure, not knowing how long the movement would last.[21]

Rene Martin, the YCM president in those last days, describes his experience:

> I really didn't know where my life was at, at the time, but I was very much into the Catholic faith and I thought that was my calling and what God wanted me to do, so I quit my job and went to the national office. I was about as ready to be a national leader as Jimmy Carter was ready to be president. But there I was.
>
> While I was in Washington, D.C., I think I was very successful in organizing people. I enjoyed it. But, when I went into Chicago, I thought what the hell's going on here. Everyone was walking around with beards and long hair and I was straight out of Pawtucket, Rhode Island. I felt like I had moved into some place I knew nothing about. I was in favor of the Vietnam War, I was nonpolitical. I hadn't done any reading.
>
> The majority of the people who were really affected by the movement were the people who joined the national staff, the people who made a full commitment. It had a tremendous impact on them. But on the local level, by the time I came along, I don't think it made much of an impact on individuals in the sections.
>
> Within the structure, you tried to train leaders who would affect the community they were working in. Whether

that worked earlier, I don't know, but it wasn't working when I came in. All the theories were there. What would happen was we would send people out and they didn't know what to do, how to get groups together, how to contact pastors. Oftentimes, even though they may have been talented people in the neighborhoods or the groups we brought them in from, they didn't have a lot of training. So, we had training courses over Christmas in '68 and '69, two-week training courses.

We had young girls coming on the staff who were being influenced by the sixties. Some were getting involved with guys. All of a sudden, you take a small town girl out of East Poughkeepsie into the big city and in six months, she becomes thoroughly radicalized. They go home and see their parents and they're strangers. People who lacked formation could really be thrust into situations that totally confused their minds.

Have you seen the movie *Platoon* where the young man goes into Vietnam and he's immersed in an insane situation? As a result, all his sense of morality, what he has been taught about right and wrong, is challenged. He has to figure out who he is.

The situations that we would send people out into, the cities and towns that we would send organizers out into, certainly weren't Vietnam, but they were challenging everything. This was something that was going on with youth. It had a tremendous impact on the people who were coming in from the towns to work on the national staff. It was affecting them. We were all being radicalized.

One side of the coin was that good things were happening in the country. I think there was a renewal process taking place, a dynamic that was working to affect people's way of thinking about the way things had been done in the past. Msgr. Hillenbrand referred to it as the pendulum of a clock, that the world was split between the conservatives and liberals and this happened to be the liberal end of the swing.

The dynamics of change were taking place. And this is what you had. They [earlier leaders] had built this incredible structure. I do think we had some very powerful people, a guy like Msgr. Hillenbrand who had been a very dynamic fellow. I didn't know him when he was, but from what I have seen, I knew that he had been. The guy had tremendous impact on the lay apostolate. They did create this whole system ... but the system just wasn't working. It was not training leaders. The whole structure was on paper, but it didn't exist in reality.

We tried pulling all the groups into it, trying to make it a more Christian movement, more ecumenical, which had come out of the Vatican Council, but we never had much success. They had their own groups.

We were great at filling up paper saying absolutely nothing. It was like we were explaining air. If I read today some of the stuff we put out, I'd say, "Where is the substance? What is it saying?"

Each week in our program on a subject, we'd have readings on the first page. We would use poets and the like along with the Gospel, to show the relevance. The concepts were the same, but we'd give it a secular shot in the arm to make the whole thing more relevant to the times.

All you have to do is read Vatican II on religious freedom and you can do anything you want. In the end we have to be ourselves and how we perceive our relationship with God. We worked hard at this stuff. We did our best to hold together what had been created, which nobody understood. We tried so hard, we wanted to, but we just didn't know how.

The early leaders were the builders. The whole social consciousness really mushroomed in this country. Everybody was socially conscious. It was like the reemergence of real values. It was a nation of change. There was a lot of anti-structure attitude, so we were trying to say, let's be relevant. Let's become relevant to the young people. We were trying to remold what to us was an archaic structure.

We weren't getting any support at all. My concern was, I felt responsible for the people on the staff. I could see the disruption taking place in their lives, taking place in my life. One of the reasons I came back to Rhode Island was that

I knew all this stuff about revolution was wrong, in the fiber of my thinking. After about a year of being national president, I was pushing to close the national office.

I think some of the priests had dreams about what they envisioned, but they were not putting them to work. I think some of them were resentful that we closed the national office. I still think it was the right thing to do. It had to happen.[22]

There were no sections in Chicago after 1968. St. Paul and Milwaukee were down to a handful of sections. Most of the active sections on the West Coast and in the east were in Hispanic parishes. A few sections continued in the small towns of the Midwest, but some were little more than social clubs. Only twelve cities sent representatives to the National Council Meeting in January 1969, and some of them were brand new.

At the council meeting in August 1969, Rene Martin announced that he was returning home to Rhode Island where he would continue to work with young adults locally. He suggested that the others do the same. He felt the national office was like a head without a body to support it. When he suggested that members should continue to be active in their local areas, he did not intend that the movement should be dissolved altogether, but that was the effect. The decision not to go along with the regional plan presented two years earlier was based on the belief that the movement needed a central office to give it identity. That belief proved to be well-founded.

YCW sections continued for several years in some cities (San Diego had short-lived sections on and off until 1978), but without the national leadership and its program, its failures and mistakes notwithstanding, the movement died. Fr. Edward Hogan, who was appointed Brooklyn diocesan chaplain in 1969, tried to revive the renamed YCW there for a few years in the early seventies, but he was moving against the tide. Most of the chaplains of the old days had long since gone on to other things. So had the young working people.

Msgr. Hillenbrand felt that the organization should continue in some way and he asked Claire Grenier to stay on for a while to take care of the mail and keep in touch with the few remaining groups. In the months that followed, the files of the national office were packed and sent to the archives at the University of Notre Dame. YCS had already folded. Only CFM was left on Jackson Boulevard when Claire closed the door of the YCM office in early 1971, and they too were having problems trying to fit their movement to the new thinking of the post-Vatican Council world.

Judgment from Hindsight

Middle-class affluence, increased social and occupational mobility among young people, the lack of positive support from the hierarchy, the changes in societal values, the youth rebellion against authority—all these contributed to the demise of the Young Christian Workers as an organized movement in the United States. Internal problems related to the quality of leadership in the last decade and the lack of a full-time chaplain were the other factors that weakened the movement. In the end its apostolic view of "A new youth for a new world" became irrelevant. Fast-moving changes in the world had outstripped its progressive goals. It no longer fit the times.

A movement, any movement, reflects the times and the culture in which it is born. It represents a collective effort to bring about social change and establish a new order of social thought and action. Sociologists identify movements as widespread efforts by groups in society which "begin during periods of unrest and dissatisfaction with society and which are motivated by the hope that society can be changed."[23]

Because the times and the culture changed drastically in the sixties, the kind of moral and social reform which motivated the Young Christian Workers in earlier decades no longer seemed to meet the needs of the younger generation. It was supplanted by single issue movements concerned with civil rights, ecology, women's rights, peace, and so on. The Young Christian Workers had anticipated many of the new movements in their action programs, especially the civil rights movement.

The changes in the Church precipitated by the Second Vatican Council also played a role in the demise of the apostolic movements throughout the world. Pluralism as affirmed in John XXIII's encyclical *Pacem in Terris* allowed for widely varying opinions as to the way the presence of the Church should be manifested. The creative responsibility of the lay person in the modern world, as developed in *Gaudium et Spes*, seemed clear enough, but rapid and complex changes in society made specific directions uncertain. No longer did the Church claim to have all the answers for society. Evangelism and ecumenism seemed a contradiction.

Marcel Uylenbroeck, who had replaced Cardijn as international YCW chaplain, addressed the problem faced by the YCW in a 1973 speech to the General Assembly of the Council of the Laity in Rome. He spoke of the crisis he had observed in all parts of the world, in spite of the differences between continents. "In this period of transition, of deep transformation . . . it appears mainly as a sort of insecurity; people no longer see clearly, it is a period of seeking, seeking for identity—man's identity within the Church. It seems to me that this seeking is significant of the cultural crisis in which we live."

He then went on to describe his own experience in the YCW which he felt was probably the same for many.

> Scarcely ten years ago, in the midst of the Council when the lay apostolate was being discussed, there was a strong, firm, overall vision. The warm and clear ideas of Cardinal Cardijn created unity in St. Peter's Basilica. We had a vision of the world; we spoke of God's plan for the world and for the Church and of our mission within this plan; we were led by this enthusiastic, dynamic vision which was really a call for us, we were ready to sacrifice ourselves and everything we had to respond to this call. We did not have any day-to-day policies. We were animated by something great and prophetic. The speeches of Pius XI and Pius XII could give the Church's reply to all the problems of the world, were received as such, and could view those problems with a prophetic vision.[24]

It was Uylenbroeck's conviction that the Pastoral Council of the Church should collaborate with the laity to discover the role of the Church in the post-Vatican II world. This did not happen. Instead, the pastoral concern of the Church seemed to turn in on itself. The certainty of vision which characterized the pre-Vatican Church was gone, but there was nothing to replace it. The outward-looking, apostolic movements of the Church were supplanted by intrachurch ministries which opened to the laity after the Vatican Council. The

Tony Zivalich and Msgr. Hillenbrand at Notre Dame, 1976.

connection between the Church and the everyday world was neglected.

In 1976 a large group of former YCW leaders gathered at the University of Notre Dame to honor Msgr. Hillenbrand, the great priest who had played such an important role in the development of the specialized movements. The dissolution of the Young Christian Workers had been a great disappointment to him. Until the end, he'd had undiminished faith that Christ wanted lay people to continue to spread the apostolate of the Church in the world. In the ebbing days of his life, he too wondered what had gone wrong.

I remember sitting with the monsignor in a parlor at Notre Dame that weekend. There was such a sad look in his eyes as he questioned me about a former leader who had opted to leave the Church that he loved so dearly. He wondered if he had been responsible. Had he done something wrong? Yes, some had apparently lost the faith, I said. Those things happen. But it was not his fault, I assured him. He'd had an immeasurable impact on all of us who knew him. He had opened our eyes to great visions of what we could do and we were grateful.

Followers of the Lord must live with change. That is the way of the world. I squeezed his hand.

That was the last time I spoke to Hillenbrand. He died in 1979. Msgr. Daniel Cantwell, speaking at his funeral, echoed the sentiments of all who knew him. "Reynold Hillenbrand lives. He lives in glory. He touched us profoundly; we can never be the same. I make only one boast. I am a Hillenbrand man."[25]

The Young Christian Worker movement in the days before Vatican II had a sureness of purpose and a Christian vision for the world. Its method and organizational style brought the social teachings of the Church into the lives of ordinary people. Its realistic method—Observe, Judge, Act—deeply ingrained its members with a Christian social conscience and a habit of service that has remained with them. Its organizational style, based on the small group, gave support to the individual man or woman trying to bring Christian values to the world. Moreover, its stress on a lay spirituality, based on the Gospels and active participation in Eucharistic worship, made God and religion more meaningful to thousands of young men and women. Its leadership training motivated those who chose it to become more than they might otherwise have dreamed of.

There is still a need for idealistic young people who will accept the challenge of Christian leadership in today's world. Human dignity is still being abused; there are serious problems that must be solved. In 1989 Avery Dulles, S.J., bemoaned the loss of the apostolic movements and spoke out for the need "to reanimate the Catholic presence in secular and public life."[26] The world still needs Christ's message of love and social justice. In the words of Reynold Hillenbrand, "It is God's work and it depends on you. If you do not do it, it will not be done."[27] Who will answer?

A Note of Hope Twenty Years After Cardijn

In July 1987, on the twentieth anniversary of the death of Joseph Cardinal Cardijn, 150 former Young Christian Workers from coast to coast gathered at St. Mary of the Lake Seminary in Mundelein, Illinois, to look back on their YCW experience. They reflected on the vision of the YCW/YCM and what it had meant in their lives. They had gone through the traumatic days of adjusting to a Church vastly different

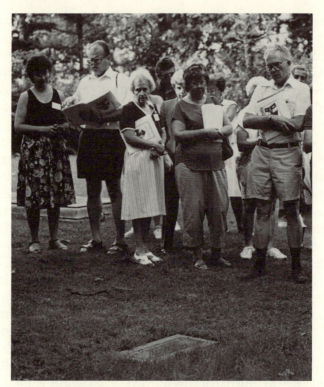

*Former YCWs at Msgr. Hillenbrand's grave at
Mundelein Seminary, Mundelein, Illinois.*

from the one in which they had grown up before Vatican II and they
had survived. They expressed a renewed hope in Jesus Christ. They
represented the many thousands of Young Christian Workers who
grew in their faith in spite of the convergence of changing times and
the new understandings of the Church as it opened its windows to the
world.

They gathered in the cemetery at Mundelein at the grave of Msgr.
Reynold Hillenbrand to thank God for this devoted priest who had
touched them in an indelible way. With tears in their eyes, they vowed
that they would continue to Observe, Judge, and Act as Christians.
They prayed for their children, and they prayed with the hope that
somehow the Holy Spirit would inspire a new generation as they had
been inspired.

The international YCW also went through trying times, adjusting its apostolic vision to the new sense of church which followed Vatican II. Though its membership declined, it has survived in Europe and in many countries throughout the world. The movement in the English-speaking countries had the greatest loss in the late sixties and early seventies. In Australia, where it was reduced to a handful of groups, it has had a resurgence in recent years and now numbers many sections throughout the country trying to deal with the serious moral and social problems of today that face young adults. In fact, a team of Australian YCW organizers recently visited the West Coast of the United States in hopes of finding young Americans who could be interested in developing as Christian leaders for the twenty-first century in an updated version of the Young Christian Workers. *Deja vu*? The spirit of Paul McGuire lives on.

Notes

[1] *Lumen Gentium*, Section 31, "The Lay Vocation," translation published by America Press, 1966.

[2] Peter Foote, et al., "Editors' Preface," *CHURCH, Vatican II's Dogmatic Constitution on the Church: Text and Commentary* (New York: Holt Rinehart and Winston, 1969), p. 3.

[3] Marguerite Fievez, *Cardijn* (Bruxelles: Editions Vie Ouvriere, 1978), p. 210.

[4] "The Principles of Formation for Lay People," Section 29, English translation of the Decree on the Apostolate of the Laity by John Mulholland, 1965, National Council of Catholic Men.

[5] Francis Wendell, O.P., *Laymen, Vatican II's Decree on the Apostolate of the Laity: Text and Commentary* (Chicago: Catholic Action Federations, 1966), p. 61.

[6] "The Historic Council Speech," *Briefing* 90, The Bishops' Conference of Great Britain, March 23, 1990, p. 110.

[7] Fr. John Fitzsimons, to author, April 19, 1990.

[8] Rory Ellinger, "Report on Vatican II—Mike Woodruff," *Impetus*, January–February, 1966, p. 1.

[9] Mike Woodruff, quoted by Rory Ellinger, *ibid.*, p. 2.

[10] Marie Powers, speech at YCM council meeting, July 1965. Transcript in Zotti papers.

[11] Twenty-two point nine percent of former members responding to a survey on their YCW experience said they saw the movement as primarily "social" though with an important educational and religious aspect. These were persons who joined in areas where there was a strong emphasis on social activities, like dances, to draw in new members. Some who joined in the sixties said it was "only a social club."

[12] Rene Martin, recorded conversation with author, March 12, 1987.

[13] Sheila Smith Hebein, in recorded conversation with author, June 29, 1989.

[14] Weber, Egan, et. al., in separate conversations in 1985.

[15] Rev. James Halpine, letter to author, January 1988.

[16] Helen Mrokowski in taped discussion with author, September 16, 1989, Zotti papers.

[17] *A Time to Begin*, YCW, Chicago, 1967. UND archives.

[18] *Tell It Like It Is*, YCW, Chicago, 1967. UND archives.

[19] Claire Grenier Deane, recorded conversation with author, January 1988.

[20] Minutes of National Council Meeting, August 1968. UND archives.

[21] Rev. Patrick O'Connor, letter to author, January 13, 1988.

[22] Rene Martin, conversation with author, *op. cit.*

[23] J. Ross Eschleman and Barbara Cashion, *Sociology* (Boston: Little Brown, 1983), p. 497.

[24] Marcel Uylenbroeck, "Reflections on the Situation of the Laity in the World" (Extracts from a report given at the General Assembly XII of the Council of the Laity, October 12, 1973), *Young Christian Workers Monthly Donors Bulletin*, Brooklyn, New York, December 1973.

[25] Msgr. Daniel Cantwell, "Reiny: Funeral Homily for a Priest," *The Chicago Catholic*, June 22, 1979, p.2. Cantwell was chaplain for many years to the Catholic Labor Alliance, an organization of laymen concerned with social justice. He was also chaplain for the Chicago Catholic Interracial Council and Friendship House, a Catholic interracial center. He attended St. Mary of the Lake Seminary when Reynold Hillenbrand was the rector.

[26] Avery Dulles, "Talk to the Catholic League," *Origins*, December 29, 1988.

[27] Words of Reynold Hillenbrand quoted by former members on many occasions since.

14

Whatever Happened to the Young Christian Workers?

Where are the men and women today who devoted so much time and energy in their youth to the goal of Christianizing the world? Did the YCW movement fulfill its goal of forming leaders who would be Christian witnesses throughout their lives? Did it develop mature adults who would continue to fight social injustice wherever they encountered it? To find out the answer to those questions, I decided to seek out former members and ask them.

I sent a simple questionnaire to as many former members as I could find. Admittedly, it was not scientific. I am neither a sociologist nor a statistician. I just wanted those who responded to tell me about themselves and what the YCW experience meant in their lives. (See a copy of the questionnaire in appendix.)

It is estimated that at least twenty thousand persons joined a YCW section over the course of the movement's thirty-year existence in this country. Accurate membership rolls were not always kept, especially in the early days. Some membership lists we did find were based on dues-paying members, and we soon discovered that many sections were lax in sending in dues. Addresses in the existing records were old, and women who married had different names. Because so many years had elapsed, we knew it would be impossible to find them all. We hoped that those we did find would help us find others. Many of them did just that. We found over 1,000 members of whom 610 responded.

Who Were They?

Based on the statistics I accumulated and tallied with the help of William J. McCready, a professional research analyst, the typical young person was a white-collar worker who joined the YCW at the age of twenty-one and stayed an average of 4.2 years in the movement.

Almost two-thirds (63.5 percent) were high school graduates when they joined. Some (4.7 percent) had not finished high school. Though 31.8 percent had some schooling after high school, only 13.5 percent were college graduates. (The number of those who attended college or graduated was higher among those who joined after 1955.)

A high proportion of them came from immigrant families in the lower socioeconomic level of society. Fifty-one percent of their fathers had no education beyond elementary school, and two-thirds of them worked in what could be classified as working-class jobs—unskilled labor, semi-skilled labor, skilled tradespersons, farmers, and service workers. Eleven and one-half percent spent a year or two in high school, but only 21.3 percent graduated; 16.9 percent had some education beyond high school.

Almost half of their mothers left school after eighth grade, and one-third attended some high school, although only 21 percent graduated. Only 13.7 percent had some schooling beyond high school. Almost three-fourths did not work outside the home. Most of those who did were widows who worked in unskilled jobs, offices, and retail sales.

YCW members were white-collar workers, mostly in clerical

Table 1

Occupation of members when they joined the YCW:	
Clerical	46.5%
Skilled trades, semi-skilled, and unskilled	9.4
Service, including waitresses, telephone operators, and transportation workers	4.1
Sales, retail, and other	3.9
Teachers and nurses	13.1
Students with part-time jobs	12.7
Managers and semi-professional	10.0
Unemployed	.3

positions (see Table 1). Fewer than 10 percent were in traditional blue-collar jobs.

Why Did They Join?

The respondents had several reasons for joining. About three-fourths were attracted by the friendliness of the people in the YCW. Over half were also attracted by what they saw going on and the kind of action being done.

Two-thirds of them were also attracted by the religious values of the movement. This suggests that many of them were "good kids" who liked the idea of being a functioning Christian. Judging from their written comments, they soon saw that YCW was different from other religious organizations in its apostolic thrust. Many said their understanding of religion in school was vastly different from what they acquired in the movement. Religion was no longer limited to their personal life but was to be acted upon in their relations with others. A large number of respondents stated that the YCW experience totally changed their value system.

Table 2

What Did They See as YCW's Purpose?	
Social action	54.7%
Apostolic action	51.7%
Christian service	33.9%
Personal religious growth	33.0%
Social club with educational aspect	22.9%
Education/leadership training	17.9%

The above percentages add up to several times 100 percent because most respondents indicated that the movement had several purposes. Their answers are listed according to their frequency on the form.

Apostolic action and social action were clearly the most often cited by former members. Those in the early years saw the movement as primarily apostolic, reaching to bring the Christian message to others. In the fifties, the primacy of social action increased. Personal religious growth was cited in each of the decades of its existence, but education and leadership training were cited more often by members from the sixties. The inquiry program discussed in previous chapters as largely educational in the later years is reflected in the answers of these members. Apostolic action as well as social action involvement continued through the years, but in the sixties they were more often cited as the purpose by those who had been Young Christian Workers for more than three years (see Table 2).

The purpose of the YCW as a social club was cited by many of those who joined the movement in places where there was an emphasis on dances and boy-meets-girl kinds of activity. Many who saw this as a primary purpose also stated that it had a "religious" or "educational" aspect that was very important. A few, however, said that to them "YCW was only a social club." Most of the latter were in the group that belonged a year or less. This group felt that they did not get much out of the movement other than, in some cases, a good Catholic spouse.

Did the YCW Make a Difference?

What influence did the YCW experience have in later life? We asked for its effects in seven categories: career choice, family life, community, church and parish, politics, and work, as well as the tendency to take a stand on issues. We also asked if they had taken leadership initiative in any of these areas. The following table illustrates their response, in percentages:

Table 3

Effects of YCW Involvement			
	Strong effect	Some effect	No effect
Church or parish	55.2	18.1	26.7
Family Life	40.8	20.7	38.5
Community	41.6	17.6	40.8
Social Issues	37.4	20.5	42.1
Work*	35.8	14.0	50.2
Politics	40.0	17.1	42.9
Career Choice	28.2	12.4	59.4
Leadership	38.8	11.4	49.8

These figures are based on totals which exclude full-time mothers.

As can be seen, involvement in church and parish life was the strongest effect. Many persons have taught CCD or participated in Renew programs, parish councils, parish school activities, and parish organizations. Some took full-time employment in their local diocese, usually in departments related to lay ministry, parish councils, religious education, and social justice issues. Examples include Marlies Rogers, co-director of the Office for Parish Councils in Milwaukee, and Mary Helen DeLaune Grabbe and her husband Gene, directors of religious education and of family ministries, respectively, in the diocese of Memphis, Tennessee. Dolores Grier is a vice-chancellor in the New York archdiocese, responsible for community relations.

About 24 percent were in the Christian Family Movement for at least several years, but a few, like Regina Bess Finney in Oakland and Mary Mannix Zeit in New York, were active and functioned with their husbands as CFM leaders for many years. Others were involved in ecumenical affairs, Cursillo, and Marriage Encounter. In recent years many have been involved in Bible study and prayer groups. Don Servatius and Robert O'Keefe of Chicago became deacons; Bernadine Wambold Skeldon of Toledo and Jeanne Skepnek Bell of Chicago are the wives of deacons.

Family life was the next principal area of YCW influence. Many married another YCW member. Others sought a spouse who was a good Catholic or who shared their ideas about apostolic action and the need for social action involvement. Although some have had marital problems and divorced, others comment on the successful marriages they and other YCW members have enjoyed. Many raised large families and trained their children to be committed Christians. Some were successful and their children have become active, Catholic young adults, but others report that some of their children no longer attend church regularly, if at all. Regardless of religious practice, many feel that their children have developed a sound social conscience. Most wish their children could have had the experience of YCW formation.

A major family organization for young mothers resulted when former YCWs Edwina Hearn Froehlich and Viola Brennan Lennon realized that modern medical technology was depriving young mothers of their God-given right to bear and feed their babies naturally. Together with a small group of mothers, some of whom had been in the Christian Family Movement, and two supportive doctors, they founded La Leche League, which over the years has encouraged natural childbirth and become a major force in restoring the practice of breast-feeding in the United States.

Former leaders have been active in community affairs, ranging from leadership in sports and recreational activities when their children were young to school boards, community action organizations, civic organizations, block clubs and neighborhood renewal, open housing, refugee assistance, and interracial councils, as well as organizations for the seniors and the handicapped.

Table 4

Anti-war (Vietnam), anti-nuclear, and peace	44.8%
Poverty and hunger	39.9
Pro-life (some preferred to call it anti-abortion)	39.5
Minority issues and open housing	36.9
Education	36.2
The environment	29.1
Women's issues	29.0
Handgun control	17.1

Well over half take a public stand on social issues, and most included three or four. We have ranked the issues they feel most strongly about. (See Table 4.)

Other issues of concern cited with less frequency were drug and substance abuse, the sanctuary movement, Central American issues, legislative issues (local and national), and prison reform.

Over one-third have been actively involved in such issues, participating in demonstrations and organizing or working with groups dealing with specific issues, while another 32 percent contribute money to support the issues they favor. This indicates that a total of 67.8 percent have a strong position on major social issues.

The concern with issues got some into politics. John Czarnecki became an alderman in Milwaukee, and Joseph Ferris was an assemblyman in the New York State legislature, because they saw politics as an opportunity to affect social problems. Many did not seek elective office but worked in political campaigns for candidates they felt were concerned with human issues. One respondent said she attaches "a religious imperative to supporting candidates and programs that tend to reflect the Church's social teachings." Others have made it a general practice to take voting seriously, look at candidates carefully, and encourage others to vote intelligently.

Action Related to Work Life

Three hundred twenty-four persons were full-time workers over their entire adult life. Two hundred eighty-six women (70 percent of the women who responded) were full-time mothers for many years. Of those persons, men and women, who remained in the work force, roughly half were active in unions or other work-related organizations. Twenty-eight persons became full-time union employees, usually as organizers. Eighty-seven (27 percent) helped to initiate unions in their place of work or took positions of responsibility in their local unions.

Many women who remained in the home and raised families said they deliberately chose to do so because they felt it was the most Christian service they could do. Most of them found time to be heavily involved in volunteer work as their children grew up. As of today, only seventy-six (18.5 percent) of the women respondents are not employed. Some of these still have children in school, and some are retired. In 1984, 62 percent of American women between sixteen and sixty-four were in the labor force. All of our women are over age forty-five, which may account for the fact that their numbers in the labor force are higher.

Many women took jobs when their children reached college age and the cost of raising a family escalated. Others, reflecting the widening role of women in society, were no longer content to stay home. They had learned to think and act in society as Young Christian Workers, and they saw there were opportunities for them in the working world. Many of them went back to school to become teachers, social workers, and nurses, but some returned to office jobs.

Seventy-four percent of the young men and women in the movement went to college after they left the YCW. Fifty-one persons even received graduate degrees, including a few Ph.Ds. The proportion of the school returnees is considerably higher than is true of the general population. Many individuals stated emphatically that the YCW experience broadened their horizons—they recognized that they had underdeveloped talents and wanted to learn and do more. Many were attracted to careers of service such as education, social work, and health service that required additional education. In the first years after they left the YCW, thirty-four persons worked in the field of human services that includes teaching, counseling, and social work. In later years one hundred seventy-three persons (28.3 percent) switched into these fields. Twenty-six others are now in religious life, either as priests or sisters. Another twenty-one went into health-related fields like nursing.

The return of many men to school in their thirties and beyond is not uncommon in today's society. However, many of their contemporaries who acquire advanced education do so because of the chance to make more money and acquire social prestige. A significant number of Young Christian Workers who returned to school to qualify for teaching and service-oriented fields say they now work for less money than they could earn in business.

Lists of former members in the archives indicate that many of both sexes worked in the Peace Corps, VISTA, PAVLA, the Poverty Program, lay missionary work in South America, and so on, before settling down as social workers, teachers, or community organizers on their return. Those who answered our survey confirm this. Many of our respondees work for human service agencies in local government, such as juvenile probation counseling, jail ministry, unemployment counseling, drug enforcement, service to the aging, youth work, and other social services. Others are staff workers involved in social service, such as Catholic Charities, Catholic Relief Service, the Urban League, Bread for the World. Many of those who stayed in the business world tell us they sought out jobs in businesses whose philosophy and product were compatible with their personal standards of morality.

Some of the interesting employment cited include doing sociological research in women's issues, working with handicapped children, teaching labor relations at a university, developing and running a small religious publishing company, and researching technology in the health care field "to help in finding a better, more healthy life-style for people." Positions of note include deputy labor commissioner in California, labor consultant to the mayor of Atlanta, director of a community service institute among Hispanics, founder of an archdiocesan program for Hispanics, and a labor lawyer who serves both as the director of a county program providing advocacy for the aging and as a representative on the San Diego Economic Conversion Council.

To recite the stories that so many sent us would be unwieldy. Jim Clifford's story is fairly typical.

> After leaving YCW, I started graduate school in labor and industrial relations. In 1971 I was hired by the city of Grand Rapids to work with their manpower department. I was responsible for establishing the first Urban/Rural Concentrated Employment and Training Program in the country. In 1978 I was the director of a human resources department which included the funding of local agencies with a quarter of a million dollars in funding plus staff through CETA. I am now Director of employee development for the city. None of this would have occurred had I not developed a very definite set of values in the YCW which have served me well.[1]

It is unreasonable to expect former YCWs to have been influenced to act in all of the categories listed on the questionnaire, but some found the time and energy to be heavily involved. On average the 610 persons who responded were influenced by their YCW formation in four of the seven areas listed, though some also gave credit to their parents and their early Catholic education. A few were also inspired by contact with other action-oriented groups like Friendship House and the Catholic Worker.

The high number of persons who went into careers in human service, served regularly as volunteers in parish and community organizations, and took active stands on public issues related to Christian social values seems to be markedly greater than would be expected in a randomly chosen group of 600 average Catholics in the general population.

Apart from the personal testimony of former leaders who credit their formation as active Christian witnesses to the YCW movement, it is evident that the high degree of responsible concern and service reflected in the answers of our respondents suggests something more than an accidental pattern. This is further confirmed when we compare our responses to Catholics in several other recent studies.

The Notre Dame Study of Catholic Parish Life is a recent study which looks at the relation of parish participation and civic participation. Its results indicate that 27.1 percent of persons active in parish affairs are also active in civic organizations, whereas over 50 percent "belong" to nothing outside their parish, and over one-third participate in neither. Those involved in leadership roles in the parish are more likely to be involved in service organizations.

David C. Leege, author of the *Notre Dame Report on Catholics and the Civil Order*, says education is "the best overall predictor of both parish participation and civic participation.... Education raises sights and raises the sense of responsibility. Education develops skills and the most important attribute of leadership—self-confidence."[2] Although the author is referring to formal school education, his comments about the effects of education certainly could be applied to the formation engendered by the YCW experience. The YCW formation was cited by many as "better than a college education." Others have said it "opened their minds" and made them aware of their potential. It also encouraged many of them (74 percent) to return to formal school when they left the movement.

The figures suggest that former YCW members are far more active in many fields, parish and civic, than is true of the average Catholic. The Notre Dame Study found that 14 percent of Catholic parishioners are active in three or more parish organizations and three or more civic organizations. My study shows that 50.2 percent are engaged in three or more parish organizations and over 40 percent are heavily engaged in civic affairs. In Table 3, the figures in the column entitled "Strong effect" give the percentages for those involved in three or more organizations in the categories listed. In addition, my study indicates that 50.2 percent of former YCWs have taken leadership roles in both kinds of organizations as a result of YCW formation. These figures are based on the personal testimony of the respondents.

Sally O'Kane Dolan, a former Young Christian Worker, recently completed a doctoral dissertation on the personality characteristics of Roman Catholic women as a function of their current life-style and education. One of the purposes of the study was to assess how Catholic women, both religious and lay, had responded to the challenges of Vatican II. Because she wanted subjects from areas outside New York where she lives, she asked if I could give her the names of women who would be willing to fill out her questionnaire. I agreed to help her if she would make a subdivision in her study which would compare YCW women with other Catholic women. I wrote to a random list of 100 former YCW women asking them to cooperate in Sally's study. The results were significant.

Women Religious were significantly more involved in social justice issues than were the Catholic laywomen. However, when the data on Catholic laywomen were analyzed, a significant finding became apparent. Of the thirty-four Catholic women who were involved in social justice work, thirty-one were former members of the Young Christian Worker Movement.

The results did not indicate that an early Catholic education significantly influenced the later involvement of these women in social justice issues. All of the women involved in social justice issues credited the early influence of their YCW training with their later involvement. Their commitments today include involvement in peace movements, labor unions, parish councils, shelters for the homeless, human rights coalitions, soup kitchens, pro-life groups, and a women's world banking group.

When the subgroup of YCW women was compared to the Catholic women religious and other Catholic laywomen on such personality variables as dominance, assertiveness, aggressiveness, self-sufficiency, and conformity, there was no significant difference among the groups.[3]

Did the Movement Train Leaders?

A stated goal of the specialized lay movement was to form committed Christian leaders who would bring about necessary social change. More than 50 percent of our respondents said they took leadership roles in the areas where they were involved, though only a few reached high positions of leadership in the public domain. Many of them started organizations, projects, activities that they saw to be needed in parishes, communities, and at work. An even greater number held office in such organizations. "Observe, Judge, Act" was cited over and over again as the way many have made decisions and gotten involved in personal and social action.

On a recent visit to London I spoke to present and former leaders of the English YCW, asking this same question. In a country where the numbers of Young Christian Workers in relation to the general population was far greater than here, it would seem that the chances of leaders reaching positions of public leadership would be greater. I was told that many leaders did reach leadership levels in government and civic life, but it was mostly on the local level. The "old-boy" syndrome still controls who reaches top positions. Maurice Foley who was in the YCW from 1947 to 1951 did become a Member of Parliament representing the city of Birmingham. He later became a junior Minister of Defence for the Navy. When Britain entered the Common Market, the Prime Minister invited him to take a position in Brussels. There he became the Deputy Commissioner of the European Economic Commission (EEC) on the commission concerned with third world development. One of his accomplishments in Parliament was his involvement in the Lormé Agreement which secured funds for non-governmental organizations including the YCW. I had the good fortune to meet Mr. Foley, and he told me that the reason he was able to go higher in government than most of the former leaders involved in civic affairs was because he had the backing of the transportation workers union with which he had been affiliated.

In other European countries, particularly France, the Netherlands, and Belgium, former Jocists have held positions of leadership in the trade unions as well as government and international affairs. Over the last fifty years, numerous ministries in the national government have come from the ranks of the Young Christian Workers. The minister of Labor and the Minister for Home Affairs in Belgium are recent examples. Others have been active in various levels in the EEC.[4]

The many thousands of former European Young Christian Workers (men and women alike) who took responsibility and became leaders in civic and working life over the years are testimony to the formation and commitment to service and social reform that resulted from their participation in the YCW movement.

What Are They Doing Today?

Former Young Christian Workers in the United States over the years have led active lives since leaving the movement. Some are disappointed that they have not seen as much positive change in the world as they hoped for. Others are disillusioned by some of the things that have happened in the world and in the Church. After many years of action, some are simply burned out as activists and "tired of causes."

The following table is a picture of where they are in terms of their religious faith today:

Table 5

Practicing Catholics	83.6%
Charismatics	9.1%
Lay ministers	22.0%
Occasional churchgoers, those who have been disillusioned or have some doubts, but still consider themselves nominal Catholics	7.7%
No longer attend church, but consider themselves Christian	5.3%
Belong to other denominations (including some "born-again Christians")	1.8%
Nonbelievers	.7%
Missing responses	.9%

The number of members who remain practicing Catholics appears to be higher than the findings of other statisticians, notably Andrew Greeley[5] whose research shows that although 85 percent of born Catholics still identified themselves as such, only 50 percent of them attended church regularly in 1975. We did not ask the 7.8 percent of our respondents who no longer identify themselves as Catholics their reasons, but it is interesting to note that many of that group state that they continue to act with a social conscience based on the teachings of the Gospels. A few call themselves "secular humanists." Among them are those who take issue with the Church teachings on sex and abortion.

Mathew Ahmann, a long-time professional Catholic social activist, discussing the impact of the Jocist movement transplanted to the United States in the forties, said, "No other movements" (and he included Young Christian Students and the Christian Family Movement along with the Young Christian Workers) "have so energized Catholic laity and done so in consonance with the evolving tradition of social action and social teaching in the Church. Indeed, I would wager that these movements had a very substantial impact on the shape of the present hierarchy and the configuration of socio-political

Catholic behavior in the country. Finally, the inspiration in these movements came both from a social philosophy and a biblically based theology. I found it interesting that one of the pleas of Pope John XXIII was to base the formation of Christian conscience on the methodology of these movements."[6]

What about Personal Christian Service?

As our former members have aged, many of them have stopped being active in groups concerned with major social problems, though they still give moral support and financial aid to causes they believe in. They now tend to be more involved in personal service. Some, 39.4 percent, are actively involved and give many hours as volunteers in self-help support groups, food pantries, helping the sick and handicapped, and other kinds of personal service. Others, 44.3 percent, give money and are occasionally involved. Now that their children are raised, they have more time for such activities. Moreover, their witness as Christians giving service to those who need help is more real to them than the big institutional changes and global concerns. They continue to read the newspapers and hope things will get better, but they don't have as much energy for the big fights. Instead, they serve those in need and do what they personally can to reach out and bring the Christian message to those close at hand.

Former Members Have Their Say

"We invite you to share with us your personal story and your feelings about the YCW, positive or negative." This was the last line of the questionnaire. There followed about two inches of space. Some added several more pages to tell their story. We have quoted from these comments throughout these pages. Lest it would seem that we picked out only the most positive, we think it only fair to include some negative comments.

I never felt comfortable with my involvement in the YCW. I hated the damned, idealistic meetings and the ridiculous actions they expected us to do. However, I loved most of the people in the movement that I was directly involved with. I participated out of respect for them. I also had a "give it a chance" approach. But I never did settle in. I feel I have been a better than average Catholic. . . . I would have done the same without ever having been involved with YCW.

I believe that the YCW and other lay apostolic movements have been critical to sustaining the Roman Catholic Church in the United States and elsewhere. This is true though many former members of Catholic Action despair of the behavior of the hierarchy. The hierarchy continues to falter in its support and even its recognition of the role of lay persons in either the world or the Church. The movements are needed today as much as ever, but the wisdom, commitment, and charisma demanded to organize today is more than in the fifties and the sixties.

The YCW led us into some very unrealistic directions, taking vulnerable Catholic youth, without any understanding of their own humanism (as a result of celibate, unknowing clergy dictating to laity), and inspiring them to the monumental task of Christianizing the world, instead of Christianizing themselves. But, as in all projects, there was a lot of good and we learned many skills.

It is hard to say if I have a sense of awareness from being in YCW or if I was in YCW because I was concerned. My husband and I feel strongly about social justice and unions. He is an economist with the federal government.

My years in YCW were hard work but enjoyable. Some things seemed far out. I did not get involved if I considered they were too far out. I was able to begin some lasting friendships, some of which continue to grow after thirty years. YCW gave me a good base to build my life on.

My feeling about the YCW and my experience in it are generally positive. I did feel the thinking was too narrow at times and the inability to rethink positions or approaches to social action in the turbulent sixties led to its general demise. However, up until that time many members "needed" to belong to a group with strong guidelines. YCW gave an opportunity to develop and to share social concerns when it was not yet a popular idea in the Catholic Church.

Since we do not want to end on a negative note, we include this last comment which speaks for the 80 percent of respondents who expressed very positive feelings, some of whom we have quoted throughout the book (13 percent did not make any comment).

The YCW has had a profound influence on my life and how I view the world. It has left me with an abiding knowledge that not only can we make a difference but we have an obligation to continue trying.

Looking back at the YCW experience, the great majority have positive feelings about the movement which impacted on their values and their behavior so strongly. Only thirty-eight persons (6.2 percent) had negative comments, and they were concerned with areas where they felt the movement missed the boat—things like the attitude toward the role of women and, in some cases, the tendency to be on the side of issues they now consider to be excessively liberal. A few of those with negative comments felt that local groups did not live up to their high-minded goals or had what they now describe as excessive idealism and unrealistic goals.

If the 610 persons who responded truly represent the thousands who were involved, it is safe to conclude that the YCW did form a majority of its members to be Christian witnesses throughout their lives. They are still concerned with human dignity and the need to achieve social justice and peace in the world. They also believe that Christian service to those in need is paramount. They have accepted the reality that they are the people of God and must be about His work in the world.

The Young Christian Workers did not change the world, as its early leaders dreamed, but Observe, Judge, and Act continues to have a profound effect on their decision-making. Most now say that though they didn't change the world, *they* were changed.

Phil Ripp, a YCW organizer who has spent his adult life in the education and service of others, argues to the contrary: "You *do* change the world when you change people. How else? The rippling effect of individuals in action over the years is still being felt."[7]

Notes

1. James P. Clifford, YCW survey response, November 28, 1987. Zotti papers.
2. David C. Leege, "Catholics and the Civic Order: Parish Participation, Politics, and Civic Participation," Report No. 11, October 1987, *Notre Dame Study of Catholic Parish Life*, Notre Dame, Indiana.
3. Sally O'Kane Dolan, Report of findings from a study by Dolan, Meier, Dill, and Campbell on *Personality Characteristics as a Function of Their Current Lifestyles and Early Religious Education*, doctoral dissertation submitted to Hofstra University, New York, 1990.
4. Marguerite Fievez, letter to the author, August 23, 1990.
5. Andrew Greeley, *American Catholics Since the Council: An Unauthorized Report* (Chicago: Thomas More Press, 1985), pp. 50 and 55.
6. Mathew Ahmann, "Views of a Social Activist," *U.S. Catholic Historian*, Vol. 5, No. 2, 1986, pp. 325–326.
7. Phil Ripp, in recorded conversation, San Jose, California, October 1, 1985.

Appendix

In making our survey, we found addresses for some twelve hundred former members who were either YCW or YCM, but many of our questionnaires came back marked, "Moved, no forwarding address," or "Deceased." We ended up with 610, a response rate of over 50 percent (sample questionnaire follows).

On a final follow-up, another eighty-nine said that the movement had a positive effect on their lives, but they had no time to answer the questionnaire. Seventy-six said their YCW days were too long ago to remember. A few said the YCW to them was just a social club and they saw no point in answering. Six said they didn't believe in answering questionnaires. We never heard from 276 persons on our list.

Is Our Sample Valid?

Our evaluation of the effect of the YCW on its members is based on 610 responses. Of these, 67.6 percent were female, a proportion somewhat higher than the presumed male-female ratio in the movement. Part of this may be due to the fact that more men than women on our mailing list were deceased. The number of young women in the movement was probably about 60 percent overall, due especially to the absence of young men in the war years.

We had good response from most of the cities where federations existed: Brooklyn, New York, Baltimore, Chicago, South Bend, Cleveland, Toledo, Milwaukee, Detroit, St. Cloud, New Ulm, St. Paul, Manchester and Portsmouth in New Hampshire, Omaha, New Orleans, Portland, Los Angeles, and San Francisco, as well as cities where there were just one or a few sections.

We heard from 227 persons who joined the movement from 1938 through the forties, 288 from the fifties, and 95 from the sixties. Twenty percent of those we heard from had been in the cell movement of the forties, before the national YCW began, though many continued through the later forties as Young Christian Workers or as married persons in the Christian Family Movement. The latest year in which members said they joined was 1967. In fact, the number of our respondents who joined after 1962 total only 4.4 percent of the total. This was the period when the movement was rapidly losing membership and turnover was very high. The peak years when our respondents joined were 1956, 1957, and 1958, the years when the movement was at its national membership peak.

Overall, the ratio of our respondents in time and place seem to reflect the total membership reasonably well, considering our sampling was not done scientifically, but rather "catch as catch can." This, plus the high percentage of responses from those we were able to track down suggest that our evaluation of the effects of the movement on its members based on this sample is reasonably valid.

Another factor which lends credibility to the survey is the number of years the 610 respondents were in the movement. The assumption was made by the leaders of the movement that individuals must be members for at least three years to get a solid Christian formation as a worker-apostle. In our sample, 77.7 percent were Young Christian Workers for three or more years. Another 15.8 percent were members for two years. Only 6.5 percent of our sample were in one year or less. Therefore, we can judge that our sample does indeed represent those who should have benefited from the leadership formation of the movement.

Survey of Former Young Christian Workers

Name _____ Age _____ Date _____
Address _____ Phone _____

Year you joined YCW (CA)___ No. of years in YCW _____ City _____
In High School YCS years: College YCS _____ Years; CFM _____ Years

Father's occupation _____ and level of education _____
Mother's occupation _____ and level of education _____

Your occupation when you joined YCW_____
Employment since YCW: (Include full-time mothering where applicable.) _____
_____
_____

If you were a full timer for the movement, list years involved, what you did and where you did it:
_____

Education before YCW: High school: Public_____ Catholic _____ No. of years. ___
                College: No. of years _____ Where? _____

1. What most attracted you to the YCW? The people in it _____
The things they were doing _____ The idea of being involved in something
important _____ Its religious/spiritual values _____ Nothing better to do _____
Other (explain) _____

2. What did you see as the purpose of YCW when you were in it? _____
_____

3., Check actions taken by you, your group or the federation in your city.

Individual Actions

_____ Acts of Service

_____ Helping persons with problems

_____ Influencing others regarding:

   dating and marriage _____

   work _____ unions _____church

   attendance _____ honesty_____

   interracial attitudes _____

   other _____

Public Actions

_____ Picketing or demonstrations

_____ Union involvement

_____ Representing young workers

   (explain) _____

Group Service and Education

_____ Marriage preparation courses

_____ Other educational programs

_____ Vacation activities, such as

   cottage _____outings _____

_____ Christmas card sales

_____ Group homes for workers

_____ Publications (What kind?)

   _____

_____ Dances and social affairs

_____ Centers and meeting places

_____ Anything else you can think of?

   _____

   _____

(Continued on other side)

4. What action have you taken since YCW, as a probable result of your YCW experience? Please be specific.

Choice of career? _____

Choice of spouse? Family life? _____

Community involvement? _____

Church or parish involvement? _____

Political involvement? _____

Taking a stand on issues? _____

Involvement in union or other work-related organizations? _____

Leadership in any of the above? _____

5. Circle phrases which describe you today (several may apply).
Religion: Charismatic, lay minister, practicing Catholic, occasional churchgoer, disillusioned but still a believer, some doubts, non-churchgoing Christian, nonbeliever, joined a non-Catholic church.

Peace, Justice and assorted social issues: (example: anti-nuclear action, handgun control, interracial concerns, Pro-life, woman issues, hunger, education issues, environmental issues.)

Actively involved, give financial support, tacit intellectual approval, tired of "causes", opposed to aims of such groups.

List issues you feel strongly about and state pro or con.

_____

_____

Personal Service: (Self-help support groups, food pantries, service to the handicapped, the sick, senior citizens, etc.)

Actively involved, occasionally involved, regular monetary support, give money when asked, no time, do not participate.

Special Interests: (Please specify) Hobbies? The arts? Intellectual activities? Other?

6. We invite you to share with us your personal story, and your feelings about the YCW, positive or negative. Use additional paper, if necessary.

United States Distribution of the YCW, 1962

■ = Federation: Four or more sections affiliated in a Diocesan Organization.

● = Unfederated Area: One or more sections organized. No federation.

▲ = New Group: Organized recently; in contact with national headquarters.

Bibliography

Books

Cardijn, Canon Joseph. *Challenge to Action*. Chicago: Fides, 1955.
——. *The Church and the Young Worker*. London: Young Worker Publications, 1948.
——. *Laymen Into Action*. London: Chapman, 1964.
Cogley, John. *Catholic America*. New York: Dial Press, 1943.
De la Boyodere, Michael. *The Cardijn Story*. London: Longmans Green, 1958
Dolan, Jay P. *The American Catholic Experience*. New York: Doubleday, 1985.
Ellis, John Tracy. *American Catholicism*. Chicago: University of Chicago Press, 1969.
Eshleman, J. Ross and Barbara Cashion. *Sociology: An Introduction*. Boston: Little, Brown, 1983.
Ferman, Louis et al. *Poverty in America*. Ann Arbor: University of Michigan, 1965.
Fievez, Marguerite and Jacques Meert. *Cardijn*. Bruxelles: Editions Vie Ouvriere, 1978.
Fitzsimons, John and Paul McGuire. *Restoring All Things: A Guide to Catholic Action*. New York: Sheed and Ward, 1938.
Flynn, George P. *American Catholics and the Roosevelt Presidency*. Lexington, Ky.: University of Kentucky Press, 1968.
Fogarty, Michael P. *History of Democracy in Western Europe*. Notre Dame, Ind.: University of Notre Dame Press, 1968.
Foote, Peter et al. *Church: Vatican II Dogmatic Constitution on the Church*. New York: Holt Rinehart & Winston, 1969.

——. *Laymen: Vatican II's Decree on the Apostolate of the Laity.* Chicago: Catholic Action Federations, 1966.

——. *Men and Nations: Vatican II's Pastoral Constitution on the Church in the Modern World, Part II.* Chicago: Catholic Action Federations, 1968.

——. *World: Vatican II's Constitution on the Church in the Modern World, Part I.* Chicago: Catholic Action Federations, 1967.

Geaney, O.S.A., Dennis. *You Are Not Your Own.* Chicago: Fides, 1954.

Geise, Vincent J. *You Got It All: A Personal Account of a White Priest in a Chicago Ghetto.* Huntington, Ind.: Our Sunday Visitor, 1980.

——. *Training for Leadership.* South Bend: Fides, 1953.

Geissler, Eugene S. *The Training of Lay Leaders: An Introduction to Catholic Action.* South Bend, Ind.: Catholic Action Students, 1941.

Greeley, Andrew. *American Catholics Since the Council: An Unauthorized Report.* Chicago: Thomas More Press, 1985.

——. *The Catholic Experience.* New York: Macmillan, 1967.

Halsey, William. *The Survival of American Innocence.* Notre Dame, Ind.: University of Notre Dame Press, 1980.

Hennessy, S.J., James. *American Catholics.* New York: Oxford University Press, 1981.

Jackson, Kenneth T. *Ku Klux Klan in the City.* New York: Oxford University Press, 1967.

Leckie, Robert. *American and Catholic.* Garden City, N.Y.: Doubleday, 1970.

Liu, William and Nathaniel Pallone. *Catholics/USA: Perspectives on Social Change.* New York: Wiley & Sons, 1970.

O'Malley, Joseph M. *Canon Joseph Cardijn: The Workers' Apostle.* Montreal: Editions Ouvriere, 1947.

Parker, Richard. *The Myth of the Middle Class.* New York: Liveright, 1972.

Putz, C.S.C., Louis. *The Modern Apostle.* Chicago: Fides, 1957.

——. *Theology of the Lay Apostolate.* Notre Dame, Ind.: University of Notre Dame Press, 1958.

Tiburghien, Pierre, adapted by Louis J. Putz, C.S.C. *Apostles of the Front Lines.* South Bend, Ind.: Apostolate Press, 1943.

Van Der Meersch, Maxence. *Fishers of Men.* London: Geoffrey Chapman, 1957.

Wendell, O.P., Francis N. *The Formation of the Lay Apostle.* New York: Third Order of St. Dominic, 1954.

Articles

Ahmann, Mathew. "Views of a Social Activist." *U.S. Catholic Historian,*
Vol. 5, No. 2, 1986, pp. 225–27.
Austin, Leonard. "Miracles in Manchester." *The Torch,* March 1944.
Cardijn, Joseph. "The Young Worker Faces Life, Part II." *YCW Bulletin
for Priests,* April 1950, pp. 11–13.
———. "Thoughts About the United States YCW." *Apostolate,* Fall 1963,
pp. 8–13.
Dohan, Dorothy. "Portrait of a Young Worker: Dolores Kozlowski."
The Torch, March 1954.
Ellinger, Rory. "Report on Vatican II—Mike Woodruff." *Impetus,*
January-February 1966, pp. 1–2.
Fitzsimons, John. "New Spirituality for Lay Apostles." *YCW Bulletin for
Priests,* December 1951, p. 12.
Foote, Peter. "New Light on the Young Adult Movement." *Apostolate,*
Fall 1963, pp. 14–30.
Gannon, B.V.M., Ann Ida. "Perspectives on Women in Business."
Chicago Studies, April 1989, pp. 47–63.
Geaney, Dennis. "YCW Roundup." *YCW Bulletin for Priests,* October
1952, pp. 23–27.
Hillenbrand, Reynold. "The Priesthood and the Worker." *YCW Bul-
letin for Priests,* March 1952, p. 3.
Hoffman, C.SS.R., James. "Meet the Young Christian Workers." *The
Liguorian,* February 1960.
Joseph, Rita and Robert L. Reynolds. "Catholics and U.S. Labor."
Jubilee, 1954.
Kenney, Philip. "Thoughts on the YCW Chaplain's Job." *Apostolate,*
Spring 1956, pp. 16–19.
Kitzmiller, James. "Some Encouragement." *The Cells,* n.d.
Langdale, Eugene. "The Spirituality of Worker Leaders." *YCW Bulletin
for Priests,* September 1950, pp. 1–6.
Marx, O.S.B., Paul. "Spiritual Formation and the Social Action
Apostolate." *Apostolate,* Fall 1959, pp. 1–23.
McGuire, Paul. "Apostolate of the Workers." *Columbia,* January 1938,
pp. 23–24.

——. "New Youth for a New World." *Columbia*, June 1938, pp. 6, 18.

——. "Approach to the Christian Commonwealth." *Columbia*, November 1938, pp. 3, 17.

——. "March of Catholic Action." *Columbia*, October 1939, p. 10.

——. "Doing It the Hard Way." *Columbia*, March 1940, pp. 7, 22.

——. "Preparation for Catholic Action." *The Sign*, Vol. 18, October 1938, pp. 140–143.

——. "The Pope of Catholic Action." *The Sign*, Vol. 18, April 1939, pp. 548–550.

——. "The Group in Catholic Action." *The Sign*, Vol. 20, September 1940, pp. 93–95.

Stern, Sol. "NSA and the CIA." *Ramparts*, March 1967, pp. 29–38.

Supreme Knight's Report. "Crusade for Christian Justice." *Columbia*, October 1939, p. 4.

——. "Paul McGuire Dies." *The Advertiser*, Adelaide, South Australia, June 17, 1978.

Uylenbroeck, Marcel. "Reflections on the Situation of the Laity in the World." *Young Christian Workers Monthly Bulletin*, Brooklyn, N.Y., December 1973, p. 10.

Van Houche, Louis. "Catholic Action Through Jocism." *The Catholic Mind*, Vol. XXXV, July 8, 1937, pp. 281–288.

Unpublished Works

Curtis, Jerome P. "Commentary on the YCW in the 60's." May 16, 1989. Report prepared for author.

Dolan, Meier, Dill, and Campbell. "Personality and Characteristics as a Function of the Current Life-styles and Early Religious Education." Ph. D. diss., Hofstra University, New York, 1990.

Fitzgerald, Margaret K. "American Jocism, July 1938 to September 1943." A report prepared for Msgr. Francis Donnelly, 1965.

Leege, David C. "Catholics and the Civic Order: Parish Participation, Politics, and Civic Participation." Report No. 11, October 1987. *Notre Dame Study of Catholic Parish Life*, University of Notre Dame, Notre Dame, Ind.

Meinecke, Paul. "Summary of Programs & Progress of St. Boniface

Section, YCW." Report to the archbishop, San Francisco, 1946.
Robb, Dennis. "Specialized Catholic Action in the United States, 1936–1949." Ph. D. diss., University of Minnesota, 1972.
Soderburg, Margaret Ann. "The Politics of Catholic Youth: A Comparative Study of the YCW." Ph. D. diss., Washington University, St. Louis, Mo., 1963.

Pamphlets & Leaflets

Geissler, Eugene. *Training of Lay Leaders: An Introduction to Catholic Action*. South Bend: Catholic Action Students, 1941.
Hillenbrand, Reynold. *5 Point Social Program*. Chicago: YCW, n.d.
Mitchinson, Edward. *Doctrine of Work*. Chicago: YCW, n.d.
O'Toole, James J. *What is Catholic Action?* New York: Paulist Press, 1940.
Roy, O.M.I., Henri. *The JOCist Movement*. Manchester, N.H.: JOC, 1944.
Sanders, C.R., Dennis. *To Build Together: The Role of the Priest in the Lay Apostolate*. St. Louis, Mo.: Resurrection Fathers, n.d.
Senser, Robert. *Specialized Apostolate in Action*. Chicago: Young Christian Workers, 1959.

YCW Publications

A Challenge to the Girls in YCW. Chicago: YCW, n.d.
A Time to Begin, Introducing YCM. Chicago: YCM, 1967.
Fundamentals. Chicago: YCW, n.d.
How to Start a Section. Young Christian Workers, 1947.
How to Start a YCW Girls' Section. YCW Girls' Headquarters, 1949.
Introducing YCW: A Program for Beginning Groups in the Young Christian Workers Movement. Chicago: YCW, 1960.
Manifesto of the International YCW. Brussels: International YCW, 1958.
Platform of the United States Young Christian Workers. Chicago: YCW, n.d. For private circulation.
This is the Young Christian Workers: A Manual. Chicago: YCW, n.d.
Want to Start Something: How to Start a YCW Section, A Handbook for Beginners. Chicago YCW, 1951.
The YCW Chaplain. Chicago: YCW, 1960.
YCM Manual, An Overview. Chicago: YCM, mimeograph, n.d.

Sets of YCW Publications

Apostolate. Chicago.
Cells of Restoration. San Antonio, Texas.
The Cells. Toledo, Ohio.
Catholic Action Priests' Bulletin. Chicago.
Impact: The Magazine for the Working Girl. Chicago.
Impetus. YCW, Chicago (national).
La Jeunesse Ouvriere: Journal Jociste. Manchester, N.H.
Leaders' Bulletin, Business Girls' Federation. Chicago.
Leaders' Bulletin, YCW Girls. Chicago (national).
YCW Leaders' Bulletin. Chicago (national).
YCW Priests' Bulletin.
Voice of the YCW. San Francisco.
Assorted local bulletins. Chicago, St. Paul, and other cities.

Manuscript Collections

Hillenbrand, Reynold. Papers. University of Notre Dame Archives, Notre Dame, Ind.
Runkle, Donald M. Papers. Zotti papers.
Survey of former YCWs (610 questionnaires filled out).
Young Christian Movement. Papers. University of Notre Dame Archives, Notre Dame, Ind.
Young Christian Worker. Papers. University of Notre Dame Archives, Notre Dame, Ind.
Zotti, Mary Caplice. Papers, including materials from Toledo, Omaha, Los Angeles, Manchester, N.H., and materials donated by former members soon to be deposited in University of Notre Dame Archives.

Interviews on Tape

Ardito, Frank, Jack and Connie McCartney, and group, Chicago, February 27, 1987.
Berkery, Rev. John, Msgr. John Kean, and Msgr. John Mahoney, Brooklyn. March 9, 1987.
Braun, John and Marie Powers. Minneapolis, October 17, 1986.

Brislen, Loretta Fenton. Chicago, August 17, 1985.

Burke, James. Chicago, January 3, 1988.

Conrad, Nancy Lee. Baltimore, March 3, 1988.

Cooper, Mary Ann and Karen Twitchell. Portsmouth, N.H., March 17, 1987.

Cosby, Bill and Jo. Chicago YCW, in Framingham, Mass., March 13, 1987.

Crowley, Patricia. Chicago, Spring 1988.

Deane, Sam and Claire. Chicago, January 1988.

Donnelly, Muriel, Kay Weber Murphy, and Rose Terebessy. New York City, March 8, 1986.

Dunne, Ann. St. Paul, Minn., in Washington, D.C., March 12, 1986.

Egan, Msgr. John J. Chicago, September 6, 1985.

Evans, Helene Mrokowski and group. Detroit, September 16, 1989.

Farrell, Rev. Martin. DesPlaines, Ill., June 26, 1986.

Fitzgerald, Margaret K.. Brooklyn, March 8, 1987.

Fitzsimons, Rev. John. Liverpool, England, in Chicago, October 23, 1986.

Foote, Peter. Chicago, December 6, 1987.

Froehlich, Edwina Hearn. Chicago, August 26, 1985, and October 1985.

Good, Bill and Trudie Lucey. New York City, March 8, 1986.

Grier, Dolores. New York City, March 10, 1986.

Hebein, Sheila Smith. Ramsey, N.J,. and Chicago, June l989.

Hogan, Rev. Edward. Brooklyn, in Oak Park, Ill., August 14, 1986.

Howe, Dorothy Lynch. Chicago, September 9, 1985.

Hughes, Millard, Lloyd St. James, and group. Chicago, November 1987.

Kampa, Dennis. Osseo, Minn., October 20, 1986.

Kanaly, Msgr. Donald and Msgr. William Quinn. Chicago, November 30, 1985.

Kenney, Msgr. Philip. Manchester, N.H., March 17, 1987.

Kibblehouse, Barbara and Wilmington, Del., group. March 12, 1986.

Kilgallon, Rev. James. San Diego, October 7, 1985.

Lucker, Most Rev. Raymond. New Ulm, Minn., October 21, 1986.

Martin, Rene. Providence, R.I.,.March 12, 1987.

McCartney, Jack. San Francisco and Chicago, July 1989.

McLaughlin, Jim and Barney Ritter. San Mateo, Calif., October 2, 1985.

Neville, Winifred and group. New York City, March 8, 1986.

Neville, Winifred. Baltimore, March 11, 1986.

Neville, Winifred and New York City and Brooklyn groups. New York City, March 5, 1987.

O'Shea, David and Rita Joseph. Agoura, Calif., October 6, 1985.

Palo, Debbie and Joan Thomas. Brooklyn, March 10, 1987.

Pezzullo, Caroline. New York City, March 9, 1986, and March 11, 1987.

Provencher, Lorraine Noel and JOC group. Manchester, N.H., March 16, 1987.

Putz, Louis, C.S.C. South Bend, Ind., September 23, 1985.

Reese, Msgr. Thomas. Washington, D.C., March 11, 1986.

Ripp, Phil and Peggy. San Jose, Calif., October 1, 1985.

Runkle, Donald B. Chicago, October 24, 1985.

Salerno, Al and Rosalie. New York City, March 5, 1987.

Scanlon, Simon, O.F.M. San Francisco, October 4, 1985.

Schackmuth, Rev. William. Chicago, January 15, 1988.

Smith, Rosemary and group. Cleveland, Ohio, Spring 1986.

Sullivan, Jeannine. Providence, R.I., March 12, 1987.

Tershy, Russell and San Jose YCM group. San Jose, Calif., September 30, 1985.

Tershy, Russell. Los Gatos, Calif., September 30, 1985.

Tyacke, Jean Pew. Los Angeles, and Johannesburg, South Africa in Chicago, December 31, 1986.

Weber, Rev. Gerard. Los Angeles, October 5, 1985.

Zabinski, Loretta Borkowski. South Bend, Ind., in Minneapolis, October 18, 1986.

Zobel, Marylu Langan. New York City, in Chicago, Spring 1989.

Index

Cursillo, 295
Curtin, Dorothy, 64, 135
Curtis, Jerry, 158–59, 229, 238, 248, 250, 254
Cushing, Archbishop, 89

D

Dagenais, Margaret, 6, 23
Dalidchik, Stephanie, 132
Dansart, Ed, 102, 103, 107, 121
Darby, Ruth, 22
Davis, David, 207
Davis, Leo, 197
Day, Dorothy, 5, 6, 29, 31, 32, 34, 63, 198
Dearden, Cardinal, 249
Decree on Apostolate of Laity, 262
Decrees on the Laity, 265
de Hemptinne, Christine, 77–79, 81, 84
Delaney, Dick, 155, 218, 240, 241, 243
Delaney, Nancy Diley, 151, 268
Detroit Committee for Fair Housing Practices, 253
Detroit Young Christian Workers, achievements and problems of, as typical, 245–58
Devaux, Louis, 76
Deverall, Richard L. G., 52
Divini Redemptoris (encyclical), 19, 30, 95
Doctrine of Working, 132
Doddridge Farm, 62
Doherty, Sally, 214
Dolan, Sally O'Kane, 300–1
Doniat, Johanna, 58
Donnelly, Francis, 17, 58, 63, 111, 192
Doyle, Tom, 136
DuFresne, Oliver, 192
Dulles, Avery, 285
Dunne, Jack, 135, 153, 207

E

Eckstein, Billy, 57
Economic and Social Council of United Nations (ECOSOC), 206
Ecumenism, 265, 266–67

Education
 versus action, 229–33
 as American priority, 13–32
 in movement, 184–85
Egan, John, 60, 74, 82, 94, 104, 105, 106, 111
Eisenmenger, Al, 238
Enoch, Betty, 14
Evaluation questionnaire on membership, 291–307, 311–12
 action related to work life, 297–301
 individual reflections of members, 304–7
 influence on later life, 294–97
 leadership development, 301–2
 life since leaving, 302–4
 on personal Christian service, 304
 profile of members, 292–93
 reasons for joining, 293–94
 sample validity, 309–10
Evans, Helene Mrokowski, 255, 273

F

Fair Employment Practices Commission, 186, 187
Fair Labor Standards Act (1938), 87
Farrell, Martin, 29, 41
Fell, Mrs. George, 30
Fenton, Loretta, 53–54, 74, 107, 109, 170
Ferrari, Vince, 37
Fievez, Marguerite, 79, 207, 232
Filles de Marie, 78
Finney, Regina Bess, 295
Fitzgerald, Gerald, 14
Fitzsimons, John, 22, 171–72
Foley, Maurice, 302
Foote, Peter, 178, 235–36
Formation through Action, 159
Forum, 93
Foundation for Youth and Student Affairs, 217
Fraser, Jerome, 249, 250
Fredericks, Carol Jean, 214
Friendship House, 299
Froehlich, Edwina Hearn. *See* Hearn, Edwina
Fulton Sheen Guild Preparing for Catholic Action, 22